Luther as Heretic

Luther as Heretic

Ten Catholic Responses to Martin Luther, 1518–1541

Translations from the Richard C. Kessler Reformation Collection
Pitts Theology Library, Candler School of Theology, Emory University

Edited by
M. PATRICK GRAHAM
and
DAVID BAGCHI

PICKWICK *Publications* · Eugene, Oregon

LUTHER AS HERETIC
Ten Catholic Responses to Martin Luther, 1518–1541

Pickwick Publications
An Imprint of Wipf and Stock Publishers
199 W. 8th Ave., Suite 3
Eugene, OR 97401
www.wipfandstock.com

PAPERBACK ISBN: 978-1-5326-7364-1
HARDCOVER ISBN: 978-1-5326-7365-8
EBOOK ISBN: 978-1-5326-7366-5

Cataloging-in-Publication data:

Names: Graham, M. Patrick, editor. | Bagchi, David V. N., editor.

Title: Luther as heretic : ten Catholic responses to Martin Luther, 1518–1541 / edited by M. Patrick Graham and David Bagchi.

Description: Eugene, OR: Pickwick Publications, 2019. | Translations from the Richard C. Kessler Reformation, Collection Pitts Theology Library, Candler School of Theology, Emory University. | Includes bibliographical references and index.

Identifiers: ISBN: 978-1-5326-7364-1 (paperback). | ISBN: 978-1-5326-7365-8 (hardcover). | ISBN: 978-1-5326-7366-5 (ebook).

Subjects: LCSH: Luther, Martin, 1483–1546—Adversaries. | Reformation—Germany.

Classification: BR329 L95 2019 (print). | BR329 (ebook).

Manufactured in the U.S.A.   07/25/19

Contents

Contributors | vii
Preface | ix
Abbreviations | xi
Timeline of Key Dates | xiii

1 Introduction | 1
        —DAVID BAGCHI

2 Johann Tetzel: *Rebuttal Made by Brother Johann Tetzel* | 18
        —DEWEY WEISS KRAMER

3 Johann Eck: *Response on Behalf of Hieronymus Emser* | 47
        —DAVID BAGCHI

4 Hieronymus Emser: *To the Bull in Wittenberg* | 74
        —ARMIN SIEDLECKI

5 Augustin Alveldt: *A Sermon in which Brother Augustin of Alveldt Expresses His Complaint* | 82
        —KURT K. HENDEL

6 Wolfgang Wulffer: *Against the Unholy Rebellion of Martin Luder* | 102
        —MARTIN LOHRMANN

7 Augustin Alveldt: *Against the Wittenberg Idol Martin Luther* | 116
        —GEOFFREY DIPPLE

8 Johannes Cochlaeus: *The Seven-Headed Luther* | 141
        —RALPH KEEN

9 Konrad Wimpina and Others: *Against Martin Luther's Confession* | 169
        —DEWEY WEISS KRAMER

10 Paul Bachmann: *Response to Luther's Open Letter
to Albert of Mainz* | 186
—WILLIAM R. RUSSELL

11 Johann Eck: *Address at Regensburg* | 200
—DAVID RYAN STEVENSON

Index of Topics | 215
Index of Modern Authors | 219
Index of Names | 221
Scripture Index | 225

Contributors

David V. N. Bagchi is Senior Lecturer in Early Modern & Ecclesiastical History and Co-Director of the Andrew Marvell Centre for Medieval and Early Modern Studies at the University of Hull.

Geoffrey Dipple is a Professor of History and the Chair of the Social Science Department in the Augustana Faculty of the University of Alberta.

M. Patrick Graham is Librarian and Margaret A. Pitts Professor Emeritus of Theological Bibliography, Candler School of Theology, Emory University.

Kurt K. Hendel is the Bernard, Fischer, Westberg Distinguished Ministry Professor Emeritus of Reformation History, Lutheran School of Theology at Chicago.

Ralph Keen is the Schmitt Chair of Catholic Studies, Professor of History, and Dean of the Honors College at the University of Illinois at Chicago.

Dewey Weiss Kramer is Professor Emerita of German and Humanities of Georgia Perimeter College/Georgia State University.

Martin J. Lohrmann is Assistant Professor of Lutheran Confessions and Heritage at Wartburg Theological Seminary in Dubuque, Iowa.

William R. Russell is Pastor of Augustana Lutheran Church (a Congregation of the Evangelical Lutheran Church in America), Minneapolis, Minnesota.

Armin Siedlecki is Head of Cataloging and Rare Book Cataloger at the Pitts Theology Library, Candler School of Theology, Emory University.

David Ryan Stevenson is a Latin teacher and independent scholar.

Preface

THE CATHOLIC RESPONSES TO Martin Luther project began in the shadow of Germany's Decade of Luther and the advance toward 2017 and the commemoration of the 500th anniversary of Luther's Ninety-Five Theses. Since 1987 the Pitts Theology Library (Candler School of Theology, Emory University) had been building the Richard C. Kessler Reformation Collection through the acquisition of original materials from the great reformer, his friends, and his opponents. As the collection neared 4,000 items—more than a thousand of which were by Luther himself—the Pitts Library was fully engaged in exhibits and other programs to mark the anniversary of Luther's emergence on the stage of world history. However, it had become increasingly clear that while the publications of Luther and other great reformers were readily available in English translation, the same could not be said for their Catholic opponents (with the notable exception of Erasmus). Therefore, in the interest of ensuring that both sides of the religious debates of Luther's day were accessible to contemporary English-speaking audiences, the current project was developed as a contribution that the Kessler Collection could make to teaching and scholarship.

Therefore, in 2015 with the assistance of Mathew Pinson, Associate Dean of Advancement and Alumni Engagement for the Candler School of Theology, and with the encouragement of Candler's Dean Jan Love and Richard Kessler, a proposal was developed to translate into English several Catholic pamphlets from the Kessler Collection. These had been issued in Latin or German, and most had never before been translated into English. The Halle Foundation (Atlanta) saw merit in the proposal and graciously agreed to fund it. Without the foundation's support and commitment to the project, it would not have moved forward, and so we are deeply grateful to W. Marshall Sanders (executive director), Eike Jordan (chair of the board of trustees) and members of the Halle Foundation board of trustees for their confidence in the Pitts Theology Library and commitment to this initiative to help contemporary audiences better appreciate the complexity of sixteenth-century German debates sparked by Luther's reforms.

The editors are also grateful to the staff of the Pitts Theology Library—particularly to the director, Dr. Bo Adams, and to the curator of archives and manuscripts, Dr. Brandon Wason—for their ongoing encouragement and support in many details, ranging from budgetary matters to the scanning of pamphlets and mounting early drafts of the translations on the library's web site.

As for the course of the project, translators were invited to review a list of Catholic pamphlets from the Kessler Collection and proceed with a relatively free hand to develop their translations, providing each text with a brief introduction. In some cases the translators worked from a critical edition of the text, but in others the translators worked from a scan of the Pitts pamphlet. We are profoundly grateful to each of the translators for their careful and conscientious work with these difficult texts, for their collaborative spirit, and for their responsiveness to editorial inquiries.

The introductions and translations were edited and made publicly accessible on the Pitts website. Further editorial work on these texts was done in preparation for the current volume, and a general introduction to the collection has been added, along with indexes created with the assistance of Roy T. Wise, an energetic and generous supporter of the Kessler Collection since its founding. We are deeply grateful to Wipf and Stock and to its editorial staff for including this volume under its Pickwick Publications imprint and for their assistance in bringing the work to publication.

Our hope is that this collection of translations will prove useful for teaching and research and foster a deeper understanding of the sixteenth-century debates by allowing readers today to hear the voices that have been largely silent for the English speaking world for centuries. If such is the case, then the vision of Richard Kessler and his initial Emory partner, Prof. Channing Jeschke, director of the Pitts Theology Library, will be further vindicated and affirmed.

The Editors

Abbreviations

ADB	*Allgemeine Deutsche Biographie*. Leipzig: Duncker & Humblot, 1898
ARG	*Archiv für Reformationsgeschichte / Archive for Reformation History*
BHR	Bibliotheca Humanistica et Reformatorica
CCath	Corpus catholicorum
CSEL	Corpus scriptorum ecclesiasticorum Latinorum
EVV	English versions
LW	*Luther's Works*. Edited by Jaroslav Pelikan and Helmut T. Lehman. St. Louis: Concordia; Philadelphia: Fortress, 1955–1986
NDB	*Neue Deutsche Biographie*. Berlin: Duncker & Humblot, 1953
NCE	*New Catholic Encyclopedia*. 2nd ed. Detroit: Thomson/Gale; Washington, DC: Catholic University of America, 2003
OER	*The Oxford Encyclopedia of the Reformation*. Edited by Hans J. Hillerbrand. Oxford: Oxford University Press, 1996
PL	*Patrologiae cursus completus . . . Series Latina*. Edited by J.-P. Migne. Paris: Garnier Fratres, 1844–1891
RGST	Reformationsgeschichtliche Studien und Texte
SCJ	*Sixteenth Century Journal*
SASRH	St. Andrews Studies in Reformation History
SCH	Studies in Church History
SMRT	Studies in Medieval and Reformation Traditions
TP	*Theologie und Philosophie*
WA	*D. Martin Luthers Werke: Kritische Gesamtausgabe*. Weimar: H. Böhlau, 1883–present
ZKG	*Zeitschriften für Kirchengeschichte*

Timeline of Key Dates

ca. 1465   Konrad Koch ('Wimpina') born in Bad Wimpfen, Swabia

1465   Johann Tetzel born in Pirna, Saxony

1466   Paul Bachmann ('Amnicola') born in Chemnitz, Saxony

1478   Hieronymus Emser born in Ulm, Swabia

1479   Johann Dobneck ('Cochlaeus') born near Nuremberg, Bavaria

1480   Augustin Alveldt born in Alfeld, near Hildesheim, NW Germany

1486   Johann Maier ('Eckius') born in Eck (now Egg) in Swabia

1509   Emser appointed chaplain to Duke George of Saxony's court at Dresden

1517   Tetzel promoted plenary indulgences for the rebuilding of St. Peter's Basilica in Rome. His sub-commissioners active in Brandenburg (neighboring Electoral Saxony) and other places
Luther's Ninety-Five Theses on the power of indulgences

1518   Wimpina and Tetzel publish 106 Theses against Luther's theses
Luther's *Sermon on Indulgences and Grace*
Tetzel's *Rebuttal . . . against a Presumptuous Sermon*

1519   The Leipzig Disputation between Luther, his colleague Andreas Bodenstein von Karlstadt, and Eck. A pamphlet war ensues, including Eck's *Response of Behalf of Hieronymus Emser* (1519) and Emser's *To the Bull at Wittenberg* (1520)
Wulffer appointed to Duke George of Saxony's chapel at Leipzig

1520   Alveldt appointed lector in Holy Scripture at the Franciscan house in Leipzig

1522 Luther's *A Sincere Admonition to All Christians to Guard against Insurrection and Rebellion*
Wulffer's *Against the Unholy Rebellion of Martin Luder*

1523 Alveldt appointed guardian of the Franciscan house at Halle

1524 Duke George of Saxony's campaign for the canonization of the eleventh-century Saxon bishop Benno results in the solemn translation of his relics to the cathedral at Meissen. Luther attacks the event in his *Against the New Idol and Old Devil to be Translated in Meissen.* Alveldt responds with *Against the Wittenberg Idol Martin Luther.*

1529 Alveldt elected head of the Saxon province of the Franciscans

1530 The Diet of Augsburg. The Lutheran *Confession* is presented and is countered by the *Confutation* composed by the Emperor's theologians.
Bachmann's *Response to Luther's Open Letter to Albert of Mainz*

1541 Colloquy of Catholic and Protestant theologians meets at the Diet of Regensburg. Eck's *Address to the Imperial Court.*

1

Introduction

—DAVID BAGCHI

READING THE "OTHER SIDE" OF THE REFORMATION

> Our knowledge of the Reformation suffers from a one-sided-
> ness, a degree of uncertainty, while we are incomparably better
> acquainted with the reformers and their colleagues than with
> their opponents.[1]

THESE WORDS WERE WRITTEN in 1889 by a German Protestant historian, wel-
coming the appearance of a 500-page biography of one of Luther's Catholic
opponents. One hundred and thirty years later, it can safely be said that this
proviso no longer applies.[2] A succession of studies has both broadened and
deepened our appreciation of the so-called "Catholic controversialists," the
collective name given to theologians who wrote against Luther and the other reformers. It is now widely acknowledged that their role was not purely

---

1. Wilhelm Walther in his review of Hermann Wedewer, *Johannes Dietenberger,
1475–1537: Sein Leben und Wirken* in *Historische Zeitschrift* 63 (1889) 311.

2. An indication that studies of Luther's Catholic opponents are no longer considered marginal to the study of Luther himself can be seen from the inclusion of the late
Heribert Smolinsky's essay, "Luther's Roman Catholic Critics," in *The Oxford Handbook
of Martin Luther's Theology*, edited by Robert Kolb, et al. (Oxford: Oxford University
Press, 2014), 502–10; and also from the inclusion of Jared Wicks's essay, "Martin Luther
in the Eyes of His Roman Catholic Opponents," in *The Oxford Encyclopedia of Martin
Luther*, edited by Derek R. Nelson and Paul R. Hinlicky (Oxford: Oxford University
Press, 2017).

a reactive one of negating the claims of Luther and other reformers with
polemic, but that it embraced more positive strategies as well. For instance,
it is clear that some Catholic writers used the printing press to reach and to
teach the public, in order both to buttress their faith and to provide them
with ready-made arguments against the blandishments of whatever wolf in
sheep's clothing they might encounter.[3] Others tried to show that Luther's
teachings could be disproved on his own terms, on the basis of scripture
alone, and did not merely confront him with reams of canon law and scholastic theology.[4] In addition, we are now much more knowledgeable than
before of the differences within the ranks of the Catholic controversialists,
who did not present a unified or uniform front against their opponent in
their understanding of the papacy, for example.[5]

In short, the Catholic controversialists can no longer be dismissed as
knee-jerk reactionaries and supporters of the *status quo*, or as undifferenti-
ated representatives of a moribund late-medieval scholasticism. Rather, they
appear to us now as writers who were as thoughtful and committed as their
Protestant counterparts. Of course, they do sometimes seem deficient both
in reasoning and in reasonableness, to say nothing of Christian charity; but
their pig-headedness in this respect is no worse than their opponents.' Each

3. Augustin von Alveldt made this intention very clear in his German-language
*Eyn gar fruchtbar und nutzbarlich buchleyn von dem Babstlichen stul [A Very Fruitful
and Useful Little Book Concerning the Papal See]* (Leipzig: Melchior Lotter the Elder,
1520). From its pastorally-minded preface one might not easily recognize this as an
anti-Lutheran work at all. He wrote, "But so that everyone might follow safely the way
to God, I have made a small booklet (*ein kleines buchlen*) for all people, which is no less
fruitful than it is useful, concerning the right flock, which [alone] possesses the right
way, means, and method to reach God, and by which it will undoubtedly reach him"
(sig. Aiv).

4. This was especially true of Dietenberger and Schatzgeyer. See Ulrich Horst, "Das
Verhältnis von Schrift und Kirche nach Johannes Dietenberger," *TP* 46 (1971) 223–47.

5. For example, Alveldt, Thomas Murner, Thomas Illyricus, and Schatzgeyer all
expressed in their defences of papal primacy against Luther a more or less muted conciliarism. They were all Franciscans, and Franciscans at this time were still wary of
attributing too much power to the papacy. Schatzgeyer in particular expressly subordi-
nated papal power to that of the church as embodied in a council. See *Ainn wahrhafftige
Erklerung wie sich Sathanas Inn diesen hernach geschriben vieren materyenn vergwentet
unnd erzaygt unnder der gestalt eynes Enngels des Liechts* (Munich: n.p., 1526), sig. Giv.
The humanists Sir Thomas More and Desiderius Erasmus held to an understanding of
ecclesiastical consensus that tended towards a species of conciliarism. See Eduard H. L.
Baumann, *Thomas More und der Konsens. Eine theologiegeschichtliche Analyse der 'Responsio ad Lutherum' von 1523* (Paderborn: Schöningh, 1993), 46; Michael Becht, *Pium
consensum tueri. Studien zum Begriff consensus im Werk von Erasmus von Rotterdam,
Philipp Melanchthon und Johannes Calvin*, RGST 144 (Münster: Aschendorff, 2000).

saw in the other a threat to Christ's church equal to or greater than the threat posed by the Ottoman Empire. No wonder they fought dirty.

There is of course much work still to be done to understand the Catholic controversialists fully, both as individuals and as a cohort. But at least they are now understood in their own terms and judged by their own criteria, as an important part of the full picture of the Reformation. The time when they were valued by Protestant historians merely as foils to enable Luther's theological brilliance to shine more brightly, or by Roman Catholic historians for the degree of their loyalty to Tridentine orthodoxy, is long gone.

There is one respect, however, in which Walther's words of 130 years ago still hold good, at least for monolingual anglophones. While the writings of sixteenth-century Protestants are readily available in English, in print and online, it is still difficult for those who lack a working knowledge of sixteenth-century Latin and German to access the writings of the Catholic controversialists, despite the availability of some superb translations.[6] The present volume, using examples of Catholic controversial writing from the extensive Kessler Reformation Collection, therefore, meets a pressing need. Each translation, by an experienced translator, is prefaced by a detailed introduction, which sets both the writer and the writing in context. The purpose of this general introduction is to provide a wider perspective designed to contextualize and to characterize both the personalities involved and the nature of their literary response to Luther.

THE AUTHORS

In contrast with the evangelical pamphleteering of the day, publishing against the Reformation was no free-for-all, and Catholic writers generally did not take up the pen unless commanded to do so by their secular or ecclesiastical superiors. Evangelical propagandists saw in the need to challenge abuses and in their duty as baptized Christians to proclaim the

---

6. Erika Rummel, ed., *Scheming Papists and Lutheran Fools: Five Reformation Satires* (New York: Fordham University Press, 1993) includes selections from Murner's brilliant verse satire, *The Great Lutheran Fool*. Elizabeth Vandiver, Ralph Keen, and Thomas D. Frazel, eds., *Luther's Lives: Two Contemporary Accounts of Martin Luther* (Manchester: Manchester University Press, 2002) offers a translation of Cochlaeus's life of Luther. Particular mention should also be made of Johann Tetzel's *Rebuttal against Luther's Sermon on Indulgences and Grace*, translated with an introduction by Dewey Weiss Kramer (Atlanta: Pitts Theology Library, 2012), which makes a contemporaneous Catholic response to Luther's critique of indulgence available for the first time and is included in the present volume.

gospel in season and out, sufficient reasons to publish a pamphlet or even a series of them. The only constraint was finding a printer prepared to handle the work. A famous example is that of Argula von Grumbach, who in her pamphlets called the authorities of the University of Ingolstadt out on the grounds that no one else was doing so. The requirement to defend God's word and the demands of natural justice (the authorities had imprisoned and kept incommunicado a Lutheran student), she explained, overrode even the biblical injunction on women to keep silent.[7]

On the other hand, with few exceptions, Catholics published only if they had direct authorization to do so. Even the indulgence preacher Johann Tetzel, who had the most personal score of all to settle with Luther, wrote his *Rebuttal* not in a private capacity but as "inquisitor of heretical depravity" for Saxony and ultimately as part of the legal process against Luther.[8] Duke George of Albertine Saxony used his authority as a prince, entrusted by God with the care of the souls of his duchy, to mobilize his bishops, his household, and the printing shops of Dresden and Leipzig to ban Luther's works and to publish refutations of them. The success of his scheme can be seen from the fact that the presses in his lands were responsible for nearly half of all vernacular Catholic controversial theology in German-speaking lands between 1518 and 1555, a still more impressive statistic when one considers that the campaign ended in 1539, with George's death.[9] Many of the writings represented in this selection (by Alveldt, Bachmann, Cochlaeus, Emser, and Wulffer) were commissioned by Duke George, either directly or through his bishop, Adolf II (of Merseberg). While George was the most determined of the German princes to oppose the Reformation, he was not alone. The agency of Joachim, Margrave of Brandenburg, in commissioning

---

7. Peter Matheson points out that this was von Grumbach's initial position. She developed a more positive justification for women speaking out against false teaching in her later works. See Peter Matheson, ed., *Argula von Grumbach: A Woman's Voice in the Reformation* (Edinburgh: T. & T. Clark, 1995), 43.

8. See Kramer, *Johann Tetzel's Rebuttal.*

9. Mark U. Edwards, Jr., *Printing, Propaganda and Martin Luther* (Berkeley: University of California Press, 1994), 36. Duke George's propaganda campaign is discussed in Mark U. Edwards, Jr., "Catholic Controversial Literature, 1518–1555: Some Statistics," *ARG* 79 (1988) 189–204; Christoph Volkmar, *Die Heiligenerhebung Bennos von Meissen (1523–1524)*, RGST 146 (Münster: Aschendorff, 2002); Volkmar, *Catholic Reform in the Age of Luther: Duke George of Saxony and the Church, 1488–1525*, SMRT 209 (Leiden: Brill, 2018); David V. N. Bagchi, *Luther's Earliest Opponents: Catholic Controversialists, 1518–1525*, 2nd ed. (Minneapolis: Fortress, 2009), 230–36. For Duke George's own literary activity, see Hans Becker, "Herzog Georg von Sachsen als kirchlicher und theologischer Schriftsteller," *ARG* 24 (1927) 161–269; Mark U. Edwards, Jr., *Luther's Last Battles: Politics and Polemics, 1531–46* (Leiden: Brill, for Cornell University Press, 1983), 20–67.

Konrad Wimpina's controversial works is made clear in the introduction to the document *Against Martin Luther's Confession at Augsburg*, which is included in this collection.

There were important exceptions to this rule. Johann Eck first entered the lists against Luther in a private capacity when he circulated a manuscript of annotations on the *Ninety-Five Theses* among friends. Johannes Cochlaeus, who was to become a more prolific opponent of Luther than even Eck, and a far more influential one in the long term,[10] wrote his early works independently. But both these exceptions serve to establish the rule: on the strength of his performance against Luther at the Leipzig Disputation, Eck was conscripted as an expert adviser to Pope Leo X over the official condemnation and was instrumental in first drafting and then promulgating the bull *Exsurge Domine*;[11] Cochlaeus, having established a reputation as an energetic and effective freelance controversialist, was eventually appointed as Duke George's court-chaplain in order to concentrate on his writing and so contribute more effectively to the duke's campaign.[12]

This constraint goes some way to explaining who became controversialists and why. Those entrusted by the authorities with the responsible task of defending the church's faith and practice had to be theologically competent and able to communicate effectively in writing. It is, therefore, not surprising that their backgrounds were predominantly clerical and/or monastic. The so-called "pamphlet war" in Germany, which ran from 1518 to 1525, involved over fifty writers on the Catholic side. Of those whose status can be determined, almost half (48 percent) were secular clergy. Of these, about two-thirds were lower clergy and included men such as Emser, Cochlaeus, and Wulffer who held court chaplaincies, and those, like Eck whose principal employment was as an academic. The rest were of episcopal rank or above, and these tended to be non-German. 41 percent of these writers were members of religious orders, and by far most of these were Dominicans (like Wimpina and Tetzel) or Franciscans (like Alveldt). The eleven Dominican friars outnumbered the five Franciscans active during the pamphlet war, but the Franciscans managed to publish more anti-Luther titles than the Dominicans. Only three writers can be assigned with confidence to other orders, among them the Cistercian Bachmann.

What is more surprising is the involvement in this campaign of Catholic laymen, who accounted for nearly 11 percent of identifiable writers

---

10. See below in Ralph Keen's introduction to the *Seven Heads of Martin Luther*.

11. See Scott H. Hendrix, *Luther and the Papacy: Stages in a Reformation Conflict* (Philadelphia: Fortress, 1981), 107.

12. See Edwards, *Printing, Propaganda, and Martin Luther*, 36.

between 1518 and 1525, and of women, both religious and in the world. At first sight this might seem to undermine the point we have already made about the need for authorization, as neither group was generally accorded any competence to discuss theological matters. But those laymen who entered the lists were either themselves personages of considerable authority whose role entailed the defence of the church (King Henry VIII of England and Duke George of Saxony, for example), or, as in the case of Sir Thomas More and Desiderius Erasmus, they were acting at the behest of such personages. In contrast, lay people who wrote in support of the Reformation "represented the full spectrum of sixteenth-century urban society."[13]

Assessing the volume of literary activity by Catholic women against the Reformation is more complicated. In 1523, a pamphlet was published consisting of the letters of the sibling-nuns Katharina and Veronika Rem to their brother, Bernhard, defending their decision to remain in their cloister in Augsburg.[14] This contribution to the traditionalist cause was, however, an unconscious one: Bernhard had had the sisters' letters printed without their knowledge.[15] A more famous supporter of convent life in the midst of a Lutheran city was Caritas Pirckheimer, abbess of the Poor Clares in Nuremberg.[16] In 1523 she wrote a letter of support to Hieronymus Emser, which was intercepted and published, with barbed comments, by unfriendly hands.[17] But since this was done against her knowledge, in the service of the evangelical cause, it can hardly be considered part of the Catholic campaign in print. Only two women can be positively identified as Catholic polemicists. The first, Anna Bijns, was a Dutch poet who published scathing verses against Luther and the reformers, beginning in 1528. Because she also inveighed against married life, she is normally assumed to have been a nun or to have led a quasi-monastic life, though there is no other evidence for this assumption.[18] Although Bijns was clearly a woman not overly concerned

---

13. Miriam Usher Chrisman, "Lay Response to the Protestant Reformation in Germany, 1520–1528," in *Reformation Principle and Practice. Essays in Honour of A. G. Dickens*, edited by Peter Newman Brooks (London: Scolar, 1980), 51.

14. *Antwurt Zwayer Closter frauwen im Kathariner Closter zu Augspurg an Bernhart Rem* (Augsburg: Ulhart, 1523).

15. See Merry Wiesner-Hanks, ed., *Convents Confront the Reformation: Catholic and Protestant Nuns in Germany* (Milwaukee: Marquette University Press, 1996).

16. See P. S. D. Barker, "Caritas Pirckheimer: A Female Humanist Confronts the Reformation," *SCJ* 26 (1995) 259–72; Charlotte Woodford, *Nuns as Historians in Early Modern Germany* (Oxford: Oxford University Press, 2002), 78–105.

17. *Eyn missive oder sendbrieff so die Ebtissin von Nüremberg an den hochberümbten Bock Empser geschriben hat, fast künstlich und geistlich auch güt Nünnisch getichtet* (Nuremberg: Höltzel, 1523).

18. See Hermann Pleij, *Anna Bijns, van Antwerpen* (Amsterdam: Prometheus,

about offending conventional opinion, it is perhaps significant that her verses avoided the detailed discussion of theological matters, which she was not authorized to tackle. Instead, they addressed the baleful moral consequences of Lutheranism, in particular the slaughter of the Peasants' War. The other author was Elizabeth Gottgabs, abbess of a convent in Oberwesel, who published a polemical tract late on in the campaign, in 1550.[19] As an abbess, Gottgabs would fall into our category of "higher clergy," of episcopal rank or above, and like others in that category would have assumed that her status gave her authority enough to publish.

THE WRITINGS

The selection contained in this volume gives the reader new to the study of the Catholic controversialists a good idea of the range of literary styles and genres adopted by them. Almost half their publications in the period to 1525 were written in the form of scholarly treatises or disputations.[20] This was a natural choice for the academics in their ranks, as the disputation was a routine means of both teaching and research at universities. Most famously, it was the form that Luther used to promulgate and then to defend his *Ninety-Five Theses*, and many of the contributions to the indulgence debate followed Luther's lead. (We see examples of the genre here in Tetzel's *Rebuttal* and in *Against Martin Luther's Confession* by Wimpina et al., in which the Schwabach Articles are refuted in turn.) The disadvantages of the point-by-point approach were that the resulting refutations were often lengthy and repetitive (they had to be at least as long again as the original and often vastly exceeded this ratio) and that the debate inevitably remained within a framework set by one's opponent. But for the controversialists, these disadvantages were outweighed by the importance of ensuring that every statement made by one's opponent could be refuted in detail, and here the disputation genre had no equal.

The next commonest literary form adopted by the controversialists during the pamphlet war, though far behind the disputation, was the open letter, ostensibly addressed to an individual but meant of course to be read as widely as possible.[21] The form is represented in this collection by Eck's

---

2011).

19. *Ein christlicher Bericht, Christum Jesum im Geyst zuerkennen, all altgleubigen und catholischen Christen zu nutz, trost unnd wolfart verfast* (Mainz: F. Behem, 1550).

20. See Bagchi, *Luther's Earliest Opponents*, 195.

21. There is evidence that, over the longer term, after 1525, the open letter overtook the disputation as the literary genre most favored by Catholic controversial writers.

Response on Behalf of Hieronymus Emser, and by Bachmann's *Response to Luther's Open Letter Addressed to the Cardinal Archbishop of Mainz.* This was among the most flexible and adaptable of genres. It allowed a writer to address the issues raised by an opponent without being confined to a framework set by the foe and without the need for *ad hominem* attacks. In practice, however, personal vituperation in the second person remained a feature of these open letters.

Only 7 percent of Catholic controversial publications during the pamphlet war took the form of printed sermons. One reason for this was that not all these writers had parish responsibilities: Cochlaeus, who held a series of chaplaincies and canonries, could declare at the age of sixty-two that he had never preached in his life.[22] The idea of adopting the sermon genre was, therefore, not one that sprang readily to all members of the cohort. But for some it was a vital weapon in their armory. Alveldt, who as a Franciscan friar belonged to a preaching order, published several sermons besides the one in this anthology. The sermon allowed the preacher/writer to address the reader directly, often appealing to the emotions as well as to reason, and to stress the importance of right belief, not as an abstract good but as an urgent matter of salvation. Printed sermons also lent themselves readily to being read aloud in the hearing of others. After the pamphlet war, prompted by the success of Luther's postil collections, Catholic controversialists such as Eck began to publish their sermons in collections keyed to the liturgical year. These became important resources for parish priests and others looking for an arsenal of arguments with which to protect their flock from the influence of Protestantism and, as John Frymire has pointed out, they give us the clearest indication we have of the sort of ideas that would have been disseminated from Catholic pulpits in this period.[23]

Other literary genres were used by the Catholic controversialists, but not in large numbers. The dialogue, in which two or more fictitious figures present their worldviews, often in a semi-dramatized form, was used by a handful of Catholic polemicists before the Peasants' War. Johann Dietenberger and Sebastian Felbaum were notable for writing dialogues in

---

See Thomas Brockmann, *Die Konzilsfrage in den Flug- und Streitschriften des deutschen Sprachraumes, 1518–1563* (Göttingen: Vandenhoeck & Ruprecht, 1998), 690.

22. Gotthelf Wiedermann, "Cochlaeus as a Polemicist" in *Seven-Headed Luther: Essays in Commemoration of a Quincentenary, 1483–1983,* edited by Peter Newman Brooks, 196–205 (Oxford: Clarendon, 1983), 200.

23. John M. Frymire, *The Primacy of the Postils. Catholics, Protestants and the Dissemination of Ideas in Early Modern Germany,* SMRT 147 (Leiden: Brill, 2010). Despite the title, Frymire's emphasis is on the role of Catholic preaching.

German.[24] An inventive development of the dialogue was Johannes Coch-laeus's series of books issued under the brand "Seven-Headed Luther," in which Luther was made to conduct a dialogue with himself, based on con-tradictions drawn from his writings. Finally, the "oration" was a short-lived form used by a number of Italian writers. Such *orationes* consisted of formal addresses to the Emperor Charles V and were designed to counter Luther's own address *To the Christian Nobility of the German Nation*. (Johann Eck's *Oratio* at Regensburg, included in this collection, was not an oration of this sort but a sermon addressed to the Imperial court.)

The choice of literary genre in many cases determined the language in which a controversialist chose to write. Disputation-style writings and letters were far more likely to be written in Latin, while sermons were more likely to be in German.[25] As the debate developed, Catholic writers in the Holy Roman Empire adopted the vernacular in increasing numbers. None-theless, as Mark U. Edwards, Jr. points out, between 1518 and 1544 fewer than half the Catholic anti-Reformation works published in the empire were in German, compared with more than 80 percent of Luther's own writings over the same period.[26]

This imbalance might help to explain why Catholic controversial writ-ings sold more poorly than those of their opponents. Of the ten titles trans-lated in this collection, six were never printed again and two were reprinted only once. Only Wimpina's *Against Martin Luther's Confession*, with four reprints, and Eck's *Address*, with three (two in Antwerp, one in Paris), can be considered popular. This contrasts with Luther's works, each of which was reprinted four or five times on average.[27] The number of reprintings is a key indicator of demand because of the nature of sixteenth-century printing. Print runs were low by modern standards (most scholars guess that a handpress could make about 800–1,000 impressions before the soft metal type and/or any engraved woodblocks would begin to deteriorate beyond acceptable limits). Because the presses would run again only if an initial print run sold out, the number of reprints gives us a fair notion of the number of sales. The exception to this rule was where a publisher expected strong demand in other regions and so might commission an initial print run there: it was often cheaper to print locally than to haul such heavy items

24. See Ulman Weiß, "Sich 'der zeit vnd dem marckt vergleichen': altgläubige Dia-loge der frühen Reformation," in *Flugschriften der Reformationszeit: Colloquium im Er-furter Augustinerkloster 1999*, edited by Ulman Weiß (Tübingen: Bibliotheca academica Verlag, 2001), 97–124.

25. Bagchi, *Luther's Earliest Opponents*, 195.

26. Edwards, *Printing, Propaganda, and Martin Luther*, 40.

27. Edwards, *Printing, Propaganda, and Martin Luther*, 18.

as books many miles. This might explain why Eck's work was reprinted in Antwerp and Paris.

It is possible of course that our impression that Catholic controversial writings sold poorly is due to the accidents of survival. Sixteenth-century pamphlets, which were sold unbound, were ephemeral publications not designed to last. Those that have, and so can be found in major libraries and research collections today, have been acquired and preserved. Past book collectors may well have had a bias in favor of collecting books by well-known authors, which might explain why the works of Luther and his lieutenants survive in large numbers, while those of Bachmann or Wulffer do not. This is a possibility, but even contemporaries were aware of the fact that writings critical of the church sold, while those which defended it did not. Catholic writers often had to subsidize the printing of their works: Cochlaeus could not afford to publish until the relatively late date of 1522 for this reason, and Alveldt's *Against the Wittenberg Idol* seems to have seen the light of day only because it was published by his fellow controversialist Emser. Even those Catholic printers who handled these publications out of conviction were obliged to print Evangelical works as well to make ends meet and suffered financially, when they were prevented from doing so.[28] Pope Adrian VI assumed that printers refused to handle Catholic authors, because they had been bribed not to, but the real reason was their poor sales.[29]

Several explanations have been offered to explain why Catholic controversial writings, on average, enjoyed lower sales than their Reformation rivals. We are aware from our own media culture that challenges to the establishment—be they satire or conspiracy theories—always make a bigger splash than defences of the *status quo*, no matter how reasonable or compelling. This phenomenon was recognized by the Catholic controversialists and their supporters and indeed had been noted long before. The highest-ranking of the early clerical literary opponents of the Reformation, Johann Fabri, the vicar-general of Constance, recalled biblical and patristic warnings that the people's ears will always itch after novelties and that the simple folk are always easily misled.[30] Another alleged factor is anticlericalism, a rather imprecise phenomenon that has been held to include anti-monasticism and anti-curialism. Although a consensus on the nature or degree of anticlerical sentiment in the early years of the Reformation is lacking, there is sufficient evidence to suggest that catalogues of clerical failings were

28. Bagchi, *Luther's Earliest Opponents*, 200, 231.

29. Bagchi, *Luther's Earliest Opponents*, 22.

30. Johann Fabri, *Opus adversus nova quaedam et a christiana religione prorsus aliena dogmata Martini Lutheri* (Rome: Silber, 1522), sig. Vivr.

more popular than defences of the priestly order.[31] A further factor working against the sale of Catholic propaganda in the Holy Roman Empire was that while the Edict of Worms was zealously enforced in Catholic areas, inhibiting heterodox and orthodox publications alike, it was only selectively applied by Evangelical authorities, to the detriment of Catholic books.[32]

THE STRATEGY OF LUTHER'S CATHOLIC OPPONENTS

It might seem surprising to attribute a "strategy" to the Catholic controversialists, whose very name suggests that their effort was predominantly reactive rather than pro-active. But the term helps us to characterize the response and the three distinct approaches it adopted before the death of Luther and the convoking of the Council of Trent.

Polemics (1518–c. 1530)

The earliest phase began with the initial, desultory reactions to Luther's *Ninety-Five Theses* in 1518 and came to an end with the submission of the *Confutatio* of the Ausgburg Confession to the emperor in 1530.[33] This was both a summary and a summation of Catholic controversial activity to that point and represented the first and last occasion on which the controversialists cooperated on a common project. The intervening years witnessed the height of the pamphlet war and the aftermath of the Peasants' War. The subject matter of this phase was largely determined by Luther himself: first, of course, the question of indulgences; then the question of papal primacy; and then issues debated at Leipzig in 1519. These exchanges were followed

31. See Peter Dykema and Heiko Oberman, eds., *Anticlericalism in Late Medieval and Early Modern Europe*, SMRT 51 (Leiden: Brill, 1993); Geoffrey Dipple, *Antifraternalism and Anticlericalism in the German Reformation: Johann Eberlin von Günzburg and the Campaign against the Friars*, SASRH (Aldershot, UK: Scolar, 1996). There have also been important discussions of the Catholic controversialists' defences of the clerical estate. See David Bagchi, "'Eyn mercklich underscheyd': Catholic Reactions to Luther's Doctrine of the Priesthood of All Believers, 1520–25," in *The Ministry: Clerical and Lay*, edited by W. J. Sheils and Diana Wood, SCH 26 (Oxford: Blackwell, 1989), 155–65; Geoffrey L. Dipple, "Luther, Emser, and the Development of Reformation Anticlericalism," ARG 87 (1996) 39–56; Benedikt Peter, *Der Streit um das kirchliche Amt: die theologischen Positionen der Gegner Martin Luthers* (Mainz: Von Zabern, 1997).

32. John L. Flood, "Le livre dans le monde germanique à l'époque de la Réforme," in *La Réforme et le livre. L'Europe de l'imprimé (1517–v.1570)*, edited by Jean-François Gilmont (Paris: Cerf, 1990), 100.

33. See Herbert Immenkötter, ed., *Die Confutatio der Confessio Augustana vom 3. August 1530*, CCath 33, 2nd ed. (Münster: Aschendorff, 1981).

by those prompted by Luther's great treatises of 1520, especially the *Address to the Christian Nobility*, with its demand that the new emperor Charles V undertake the thorough reform of the church, and the *Babylonian Captivity of the Church*, with its radical attack on the sacramental system and especially on the sacrifice of the mass.

It would, however, be a mistake to portray the Catholic side during this phase as entirely reactive. At crucial moments, they took the initiative. For instance, they were able to force Luther to address the question of papal power in the course of the indulgences debate, and therefore to shift the controversy from an area that had been only vaguely defined hitherto to one that was far more secure dogmatically from their point of view.[34] Similarly, they took full advantage of the bloodshed of the Peasants' War to attribute the armed rebellion to the influence of Luther's seditious doctrines. A series of Catholic pamphlets from the pens of Cochlaeus, Emser, Fabri, Sylvius, and others drove home essentially the same message: "we warned that this would happen."[35]

Politics (c. 1530–1541)

The Diets of Augsburg in 1530 and of Nuremberg in 1532 marked a new phase in Catholic-Lutheran relations in the Holy Roman Empire and entailed a new—or at least a considerably modified—role for the Catholic controversialists. They had to accept the fact that at least for the time being a significant proportion of their compatriots lived under a heretical government. This did not at all lessen the need for polemic, but it set that polemic in a new context of *Realpolitik*. Old-fashioned, controversial polemic remained part of their armory, but at the same time their writings take on a more overtly "political" flavor than before, with the recognition that only the secular authorities could restore the *status quo*.

An instructive example is provided by the prolific controversialist Johannes Cochlaeus. His literary output over this period hardly flagged: according to the standard catalogue of his writings, Cochlaeus was responsible

---

34. Johann Eck latched on to Luther's passing comment, in his *Explanations* of the *Ninety-Five Theses* of 1518, that the Roman Church had not always been superior to the Greek Church and turned it into a thesis to be debated with Karlstadt and Luther at the Leipzig Disputation in 1519. Luther naturally responded with a counter-thesis, which asserted that papal primacy was unknown either to scripture or to the early church councils. See Scott H. Hendrix, *Luther and the Papacy. Stages in a Reformation Conflict* (Philadelphia: Fortress, 1981), 78–85.

35. See Edwards, *Printing, Propaganda, and Martin Luther*, 149–62.

for over seventy publications between the years 1530 and 1541.[36] Some of these are simply forewords to the works of others, while others are humanistic editions of earlier authors, and others still are simply Latin renderings of his own German works or vice versa. But most are substantial writings that amply repaid Duke George of Saxony's decision to employ him as a propagandist. About half of his output during this time can be described as "routine" theological refutations of doctrinal error: these include treatises on the priesthood, the sacrifice of the mass, and the invocation of the saints. The remainder can be described as having some political dimension.

One must of course be careful about using such a term anachronistically: Catholic controversial writings had been strongly "political" from the outset, inasmuch as they portrayed Luther's teachings as tending to sedition. I mean that these works of Cochlaeus were either addressed to crowned heads with the express intention of affecting policy, or else that they were designed to support a specific initiative by a secular leader. A cluster of works in the earlier part of this phase focuses on the Diet of Augsburg and its ramifications, defending the emperor from Evangelical attacks. They were followed by reactions to Luther's 1531 *A Warning to his Dear German People*, in which the Wittenberger promoted for the first time the right of resistance against the emperor. Cochlaeus was conscripted into this debate by his employer, Duke George. In a series of writings Cochlaeus developed the duke's contention that Luther was a dangerous rabble-rouser, whose influence could be seen not least in relation to the beliefs of the Anabaptists of Münster. This task preoccupied Cochlaeus until about 1534, a date that coincided with the first of his "Philippics" against Melanchthon (1534–1549), all of which emphasized the competence and the responsibility of the secular rulers to suppress heresy.[37] Of a piece with this belief were Cochlaeus's overtures to rulers outside the empire. Despite Henry VIII of England's early promise as an anti-Lutheran campaigner, he had proved to be a broken reed, especially after the executions of Cochlaeus's friends Sir Thomas More and Bishop John Fisher. From 1535, therefore, Cochlaeus looked to the north, to the kingdom of Scotland. Cochlaeus's attention in the late 1530s, as that of many controversialists, was drawn to the promised general council "in German lands" for which the emperor had been agitating. Cochlaeus supported the idea of a council but was determined to disabuse anyone of the notion that it might lead to the toleration, still less the vindication, of the Protestant cause. In booklets published in 1537 and 1538, he cited the

36. Martin Spahn, *Johannes Cochläus: Ein Lebensbild aus der Zeit der Kirchenspaltung* (1898. Reprint, Nieuwkoop: De Graaf, 1964), 352–62.

37. Ralph Keen, ed., *Johannes Cochlaeus: Philippicae I–VII*, BHR 54, 2 vols. (Nieuwkoop: De Graaf, 1995).

example of Jan Hus, who had been justly condemned by a German council, that of Constance, with the full support of a German emperor. As the new decade dawned, Cochlaeus's attention turned to another imperial initiative, the religious colloquies, which as much as anything underlined the fact that heresy was now politically recognized in the Holy Roman Empire.

Cochlaeus's literary activity gives us a flavor of the heavily political output of the Catholic controversialists during this phase of operations. While his prolificity made him atypical, he himself nonetheless sat comfortably in the middle vis-à-vis the other literary supporters of Rome. He could not be counted a hardliner in the mould of an Eck or a Pighius, as he was too ready to make concessions when circumstances required them. But he was certainly not a moderate, like Witzel or Gropper, either. To that extent, he and his literary output at this time can be taken to typify this phase.

Propaganda (1541–1545)

When the colloquy of Regensburg ended in failure in 1541, thanks not least to the recalcitrance of hardliners like Eck, the search for accommodation between the Catholic and Protestant territories within the empire came to an end. At about the same time, policy at Rome began to shift from one of reform and reconciliation to one of confrontation and repression. In these circumstances, little could be achieved either by polemic hurled at the other side or by appeals to secular authorities to extirpate heresy, and so we see a turning inwards of the Catholic literary response, which became geared to the demands of propaganda. This involved teaching the faithful the basics of their faith, portraying alternatives in the worst possible light, and equipping teachers with basic counter-arguments. Attention largely but not entirely turned away from the production of intricate refutations of the latest heterodox publication towards the need for catechisms for the laity and postils for the clergy.

Again, Cochlaeus's publications during his later years can be used to illustrate this shift. He continued to engage in detailed rebuttals of reformers' writings, though his attention now turned from Luther to other names both large and small: Melanchthon, Calvin, Bucer, Bullinger, Osiander, Wolfgang Musculus, and Ambrose Moibanus. But in other respects it is clear that the readership he intends is not so much his religious opponents as those on his own side. To this later period belonged the eventual publication of his infamous *Commentary on the Deeds and Writings of Martin Luther* (1549). Just as significant for our purposes, however, was his role in the publication of a series of eight legal treatises by the jurist Konrad Braun (or Conradus

Brunus) between 1548 and 1550. These were mostly substantial folio volumes, which set out the legal basis, among other things, for detecting and prosecuting heresy and sedition. Cochlaeus's motive was unmistakable: the refutation of heresy by theologians such as he was essential for preserving the true faith; but it had to go hand-in-glove with the legal prosecution of heresy by those with the appropriate authority.

THE ACHIEVEMENT OF LUTHER'S CATHOLIC OPPONENTS

Each of the authors we have mentioned in this survey was committed to stopping Luther's Reformation in its tracks. By that criterion, they failed. But this did not mean that their efforts were all in vain. The experience and expertise they built up by their generally careful refutations of Luther and other reformers qualified them to contribute to the church's official actions. Johann Eck's detailed knowledge of Luther's writings up to 1520 helped determine the shape and tenor of *Exsurge Domine*, the bull that set out the grounds for the Wittenberger's excommunication.[38] Eck and others also contributed to the official imperial rebuttal of the Augsburg Confession and represented the emperor's side at the various colloquies of the 1530s and 1540s.[39] Controversialists' writings were even consulted during the proceedings at Trent—though for obvious reasons the substantial theological treatises of the likes of John Fisher were of more value to the council than the brief pamphlets represented in this edition.[40]

Undoubtedly, both the Holy Roman Emperor and the pope could have done more to support their work, ideally by facilitating a central office of communication, through which intelligence could have been shared and a co-ordinated response essayed. We can see something like this—a virtual, epistolary network of controversialists—beginning to take shape at the behest of Pope Adrian VI in 1523, but his death the same year brought this initiative to a close.[41] At a lower level of commitment, the papacy might have provided sinecures to enable the controversialists to pursue their writing single-mindedly, or at least have subsidized the higher cost of publishing Catholic works commercially. The Vatican archives contain numerous

38. Volker Reinhardt, *Luther der Ketzer. Rom und die Reformation*, 3rd ed. (Munich: Beck, 2017), 118.

39. See Immenkötter, ed., *Die Confutatio der Confessio Augustana*.

40. For the reception of Fisher's work by the fathers at Trent, see Richard Rex, *The Theology of John Fisher* (Cambridge: Cambridge University Press, 1991).

41. Bagchi, *Luther's Earliest Opponents*, 222–27.

heartfelt appeals for support of this kind, made by the likes of Cochlaeus to high-ranking curial officials. They generally went unheeded. Rome's unsympathetic attitude towards her literary champions was summed up by Cardinal Aleander, who declared that "explanations [rationes] and disputations achieve nothing." He went further, blaming the success of the Reformation on the Catholic theologians themselves: without their disputing, which gave publicity to the very heresies they meant to suppress, Luther would never have received the support he did.[42]

The Catholic controversialists received much stouter support from some lay Catholics of high standing. Especially noteworthy were the efforts of Duke George of Albertine Saxony, who turned decisively against Luther and all he stood for after hearing him defend aspects of Hussitism in Leipzig in 1519. Duke George then launched a concerted campaign of Catholic, anti-Lutheran propaganda from his twin capitals of Leipzig and Dresden, conscripting churchmen under his influence to take up the pen and offering chaplaincies to established writers, as we have seen. Also, as we have seen, he forced the print shops, on pain of closure, to publish only Catholic books. Duke George's efforts were mirrored on the other side of the North Sea by those of King Henry VIII of England. Henry personally headed an impressive team of theologians who between them refuted almost all Luther's Latin publications in the early 1520s. It included, in addition to Bishop John Fisher, the Lord Chancellor Sir Thomas More, the court preacher Edward Powell, and Catherine of Aragon's confessor Alfonso de Villa Sancta.[43] The fact that three of these writers ended their lives at the hands of a fourth illustrates both the strengths and the weaknesses of royal patronage: it could be very effective while it lasted, but a change of mind (as in King Henry's case) or a change of regime (as in Ducal Saxony) could bring it to an immediate end.

It can safely be said that the achievements of the Catholic controversialists were hard-won. The life and work of a controversialist without the benefit of patronage, or of some other support network such as a religious community, could be difficult, and it says much for their personal commitment to the cause that they battled on. Perhaps the most outstanding example in this respect was Georg Witzel, who had defected to the Lutheran side early on but had become disillusioned on discovering that the lives of Lutherans were no better than those of Catholics. He therefore returned to

42. See the letter of Aleander to Cochlaeus, Oct. 1521, in W. Friedensburg, "Beiträge zum Briefwechsel der katholischen Gelehrten Deutschlands im Reformationszeitalter (aus italienischen Archiven und Bibliotheken)," ZKG 18 (1898) 129.

43. Richard Rex, "The English Campaign against Luther in the 1520s," Transactions of the Royal Historical Society 5.39 (1989) 85–106.

the Catholic fold, on the grounds of its antiquity, and was able to write informed critiques of evangelicalism, while urging the church to reform itself and so diminish the appeal of its critics.[44] But he—and the family he had acquired as a Lutheran pastor and had never abandoned—was hounded by the likes of Eck who always suspected him of being a fifth columnist.

An example like Witzel's inspires respect even today, but we owe it to Luther's Catholic opponents to avoid hagiography and censure alike. Only by learning more about them can we hope to arrive at a deeper understanding of them and their place in Reformation history. This collection is offered as a means to make the controversialists better known and to inspire further investigation.

---

44. See Barbara Henze, *Aus Liebe zur Kirche Reform: die Bemühungen Georg Witzels (1501–1573) um die Kircheinheit*, RGST 133 (Münster: Aschendorff, 1995).

2

Johann Tetzel

Rebuttal Made by Brother Johann Tetzel[1]

—Dewey Weiss Kramer

INTRODUCTION

THE THEOLOGICAL DEBATES SPARKED by Martin Luther's publication of his *Ninety-Five Theses* in 1517 picked up new strength in 1518, as Luther published his *Sermon on Indulgence and Grace*,[2] which was enthusiastically received and saw twenty-two printings by 1520. Luther's opponent, Dr. Johann Tetzel, Order of Preachers, inquisitor of heretics, sub-commissioner for the preaching of the St. Peter's indulgence in the dioceses of Mainz and Magdeburg, responded just a month later with the publication of his

1. I would like to thank the following for their contributions to this translation effort: Dr. M. Patrick Graham, formerly Director of the Pitts Theology Library, for the opportunity to work on this project; the support of the Institute for Ecumenical and Cultural Research of St. John's University (Collegeville, Minnesota) for my 2003–2004 tenure as Guest Scholar there; Dr. Manfred Hoffmann, formerly Professor Emeritus of the Candler School of Theology at Emory; Dr. Kurt K. Hendel, Bernard, Fischer, Westberg Distinguished Ministry Professor of Reformation History at the Lutheran School of Theology at Chicago, for his valuable advice and suggestions; and as with all my endeavors, academic and personal, my husband, Dr. Victor A. Kramer. This introduction (though shortened here) and translation largely reproduce what appears in *Johann Tetzel's Rebuttal against Luther's Sermon on Indulgences and Grace*, translated with an introduction by Dewey Weiss Kramer (Atlanta: Pitts Theology Library, 2012).

2. Commonly cited with the German title, *Ein Sermon von Ablaß und Gnade*, the first edition was issued, *Eynn Sermon von dem Ablasz vnnd gnade . . .* (Wittenberg: Rhau-Grunenberg, 1518). WA 1:240ff.

Rebuttal.[3] This work was far less popular, and although it was reprinted in a few sixteenth-century editions of Luther's collected works, it has remained little noticed, not easily accessible, and never translated into either modern German or English. Only three extant copies are known today, two in German libraries (Staatsbibliothek, Munich and Universitätsbibliothek, Würzburg) and one in the Kessler Reformation Collection of Pitts Theology Library, Candler School of Theology, Emory University.

Language and Format

While both Luther's *Ninety-Five Theses* and Tetzel's response to them (*106 Theses*) were composed in Latin, following the established practice for theological and academic exchange, Luther wrote his response to Tetzel's *106 Theses* (*Eyn Sermon vom Ablass und Gnade*) in vernacular German. When Tetzel responded to Luther, he also resorted to the vernacular, answering Luther's twenty "articles" or theses by first quoting each of them *verbatim*.

Translation of the title of Tetzel's pamphlet proved problematic. While *Vorlegung* in contemporary New High German (NHG) denotes "presentation," in Early NHG it could denote "contradiction" (*widerlegen* = to contradict). Tetzel's usage of this word contains elements of both meanings, and this translation will use "rebuttal" as a more appropriate expression of the tenor of the piece and of the attitudes of the author.

Historical-Chronological Account

The genesis of this small work extends over just a few months of the earliest days of the Reformation, as the following chronology demonstrates.[4]

March 31, 1515: Pope Leo X issues a bull granting plenary indulgences for those contributing to the rebuilding of St. Peter's in Rome. Prince-Elector Albrecht of Brandenburg, archbishop of Magdeburg, Mainz, and Halberstadt is granted authority to promote it throughout his dioceses, and by early 1517 the sale of this indulgence is being led by Johann Tetzel, the

3. Johann Tetzel, *Vorlegung gemacht von Bruder Johan Tetzel Prediger Orde[n]s Ketzermeister: wyder eynen vormessen Sermon von tzwentzig irrige[n] Artickeln Bebstlichen ablas vn[d] gnade belange[n]de allen cristglaubige[n] mensche[n] tzuwissen von notten* (Leipzig: Melchior Lotter, 1518). See n. 10 below.

4. Scott H. Hendrix's *Luther and the Papacy: Stages in a Reformation Conflict* (Philadelphia: Fortress, 1981) is the definitive study of Luther's developing attitude toward Rome. Pages 34–38 cover specifically Luther's interaction with Tetzel from 1517 to 1519, but the whole of chs. 2 and 3 chronicles the events from October 1517 to December 1518 and so is germane to Tetzel's interaction with Luther.

Dominicans' inquisitor of heretics, and the sub-commissioner for the promotion of the St. Peter's indulgence.

October 31, 1517: Alarmed at the extravagant and spiritually destructive claims of the indulgence preachers in his region, Martin Luther issues his *Ninety-Five Theses*.

January 20, 1518: At their regional chapter meeting in Frankfurt an der Oder, three hundred Dominicans gather to debate in Latin the *Ninety-Five Theses*. Tetzel presents the *106 Frankfurt Theses*—composed by fellow Dominican, Konrad Wimpina—to refute Luther.[5]

January–March, 1518: In response to Tetzel's presentation at Frankfurt an der Oder, Luther produces his *Resolutiones* (in Latin), which was not published until early summer 1518.[6] He is also increasingly aware of a popular, Dominican campaign against him as a heretic.[7]

Lent 1518: Responding to these academic and popular campaigns against him, Luther publishes *A Sermon on Indulgence and Grace*,[8] which presents the ideas of his *Ninety-Five Theses* for popular consumption and in non-academic language.

March or April 1518: Tetzel responds with his *Vorlegung*[9] and later with the more comprehensive and in Latin, *50 Theses*—this time without Wimpina's assistance.[10]

End of April/Beginning of May 1518: Luther issues a second printed response to Tetzel in his *Eine Freiheit des Sermons päpstlichen Ablass und Gnade belangend*,[11] which takes some notice of Tetzel's *50 Theses*.[12] Afterwards, Luther essentially goes his own way, and Tetzel is never again heard from in print, dying one year later, on July 4, 1519.

---

5. See Jared Wicks, *Luther's Reform: Studies on Conversion and the Church* (Mainz: Von Zabern, 1992), 151; Peter Fabisch and Erwin Iserloh, eds., *Dokumente zur Causa Lutheri, (1517–1521) 1. Teil: Das Gutachten de Prierias und weitere Schriften gegen Luthers Ablassthesen (1517–1518)*, CCath 41 (Münster: Aschendorff, 1988), 314. (Cited hereafter as *Dokumente zur Causa Lutheri*.) The *106 Frankfurt Theses* are reprinted in *Dokumente zur Causa Lutheri* (Text 10), 321–37.

6. *Resolutiones disputationum de Indulge[n]tiarum virtute* (Wittenberg: Johann Rhau-Grunenberg, 1518). WA 1:523.

7. Cf. Wicks, *Luther's Reform*, 151. Chapter 7, "Roman Reactions to Luther: the First Year, 1518," 149–88, discusses the Luther-Tetzel exchange.

8. See n. 2 above.

9. See n. 3 above.

10. Tetzel's *50 Theses* reprinted in *Dokumente zur Causa Lutheri* (Text 12), 369–75.

11. *Eyn Freyheyt desz Sermons Bebstlichen ablasz vnd gnad belangend . . . wider die Vorlegung, ßo tzur schmach seyn, vnd desselben Sermon ertichtett* (Wittenberg: Johann Rhau-Grunenberg, 1518). WA 1:380–81.

12. *Dokumente zur Causa Lutheri*, 364.

Toward a Modest Re-evaluation of Johann Tetzel

With this translation of his *Rebuttal,* Tetzel is granted a new hearing, and instead of the caricatured money-grubber, one hears a genuine concern for the salvation of souls, praise of God's inestimable mercy, and a concern for the whole of Christendom. In his impassioned outcry of rebuttal twenty, Tetzel foresees what tragic consequences will follow upon Luther's ideas— the splintering of Christianity. In addition, rather than the caricature of Tetzel as stupid, ignorant of Latin, and unable to write his own theses, the *Rebuttal* is: well-structured; exhibits a credible understanding of scripture, Catholic doctrines, and the major Christian theologians; and shows him fully as proficient as his opponent in Latin and the ability to use scripture to support his arguments.

A Few Notes on Translation Format

In order to conform to modern English usage, paragraphs have been introduced where warranted, and the long, multiple relative clause-laden sentences characteristic of sixteenth-century German have been broken into shorter units where feasible. Words or phrases in [brackets] denote the translator's addition for reasons of clarity. While the German original uses the singular/plural form of "indulgence" variously—no article, the definite article, or the indefinite article, usually without expressing a specific nuance—the English plural expresses the German singular as well or better, without change of meaning. Thus I often use the plural form, "indulgences," where Tetzel and Luther use the singular. This translation prefers inclusive language where Tetzel's and Luther's use of the nouns and pronouns denoting human beings implies "all persons" in general. Notes have been kept to a minimum, and so no attempt has been made to cite the voluminous literature on the Luther-Tetzel conflict.

TRANSLATION

This is a rebuttal made by Brother Johann Tetzel, the Order of Preachers' inquisitor for heretics, necessary for all faithful believers in Christ to know, against a presumptuous sermon of twenty erroneous articles concerning papal indulgences and grace.[13]

13. Tetzel's pamphlet was published in March or April of 1518. In addition to the copy owned by the Pitts Theology Library, two others are extant and held at the Staatsbibliothek, Munich and at the Universitätsbibliothek, Würzburg.

So that Christians not be unduly upset and misled by a sermon of twenty erroneous articles, presumptuously attacking aspects of the sacrament of penance and the truth of indulgences, which was printed and distributed during Lent, the title of which reads, *A Sermon on Indulgences and Grace, etc.*, and after the title continues, "You should know first of all that certain modern teachers such as the Master of the Sentences" and ends in the twentieth article, "But may God give them and us right understanding,"[14] I, Brother Johann Tetzel, of the Order of Preachers, inquisitor of heretics, have had that same sermon of twenty erroneous articles printed, together with its title, opening, and conclusion. And I refute each article of the said sermon with constant reference to holy scripture, as everyone will judge from the following pages.

I do this in spite of the fact that in the nineteenth article of the said sermon is written, "And let the scholastic doctors[15] be scholastics. The whole lot of them with their opinions are not able to substantiate a single sermon." These words should upset no good Christian person. Because if the sermon of twenty erroneous articles hopes to convince anyone, then its author would first have to sweep away the "scholastic doctors," who all harmoniously oppose these articles in their writings. St. Augustine writes,

Tetzel's pamphlet was reprinted in J. E. Kapp, *Sammlung einiger zum Päbstlichen Ablass überhaupt, Sonderlich aber zu der im Anfang der Reformation zwischen D. Martin Luther und Johann Tetzel hiervon geführten Streitigkeit gehörigen Schriften* (Leipzig: Martini, 1721), 317–56; V. E. Loescher, ed., *Vollständige Reformations-Acta und -Documenta* (Leipzig: Gross, 1720), 1:484–503; Walther Köhler, ed., *Dokumente zum Ablassstreit von 1517* (Tübingen/Leipzig: Mohr, 1902; 2nd ed., 1934) (rebuttal 20 incomplete); Walther Köhler, *Luthers 95 Thesen samt seinen Resolutionen sowie den Gegenschriften von Wimpina-Tetzel, Eck und Prierias und den Antworten Luthers darauf* (Leipzig: Hinrichs, 1903).

The best critical edition is that of Fabisch and Iserloh, eds., *Dokumente zur Causa Lutheri* (for full bibliographic citation, see n. 5 above), which was intended to correct and expand upon Köhler's 1903 work, *Luthers 95 Thesen* and makes readily accessible—some for the first time—Roman Catholic writings of the earliest stage of the Reformation. Its emphasis lies on the historically crucial texts concerning the preaching of the St. Peter's Indulgence in the dioceses of Mainz and Magdeburg, as well as the earliest Roman reactions to Luther's *95 Theses*, from 1517 to 1519. The editors provide extensive historical background and bibliographical details for each document.

14. Martin Luther, "Ein Sermon von Ablass und Gnade, 1517" (WA 1:239–46).

15. This quotation appears in Luther's sermon (article nineteen) and in Tetzel's *Rebuttal*. Tetzel's Latin term *doctores* and the German *Doctorn* refer to the most influential teachers of Christendom both ancient and modern. Much of both Luther's and Tetzel's arguments are concerned with the authority of the "modern" doctors (e.g., Thomas Aquinas, Peter Lombard)—questioning or affirming it, as well as the reliability of the professors of theology at contemporary universities. Hence the term refers equally to teachers who hold the doctoral degree and to theologians in general. This translation uses both terms interchangeably.

"When one wants to dispute with the heretics, then one must do so above all on the basis of the authorities," that is, holy scripture and the discourse of reliable theologians uniformly. Just so, "When one wants to instruct Christian believers, it occurs properly by using solid, supporting *rationes*,"[16] that is, through rational evidence and teaching. The heretics know this, and so whenever they want to promote a heretical falsehood among the people, they first reject and scorn all the scholars who have written openly against this particular error, just as Wycliffe and Jan Hus did.

This same Jan Hus not only considered satisfaction for sin unnecessary, but also sacramental confession itself, and persuaded the people accordingly. For this reason the holy ecumenical Council of Constance[17] condemned him to the stake. Such ways are also being pursued in this erroneous sermon of twenty articles. For the Master of Hoenszyn,[18] along with many thousand doctors (of whom many are numbered in the ranks of the revered saints),[19] are scorned in the erroneous sermon, in spite of the fact

16. St. Augustine of Hippo (354–430), church father whose theological and philosophical works have exercised tremendous influence on the development of Christian doctrine for both Eastern and Western Churches. Luther was a monk of the Augustinian Order, which followed the *Rule of St. Augustine*. For this citation, see *PL* 32:1377–84.

17. John Wycliffe (c. 1329–1384), Oxford theologian, translator of the Bible into English, critic of the temporal authority of the church. He rejected transubstantiation, purgatory, and indulgences. Though condemned as heretic, he died of natural causes, but his works were formally condemned by the Council of Constance (1414), and his remains were exhumed and burned.

Jan Hus (or Johannes Huss; 1374–1415), Czech priest, theologian, preacher, and rector of the University of Prague. Influenced by Wycliffe's ideas on church reform, he led the reform movement in Bohemia. He rejected transubstantiation and demanded communion in both kinds. Summoned to the Council of Constance (1414) under imperial guarantee of safe conduct, he was condemned as a heretic and burned at the stake on July 6, 1415.

18. Peter Lombard (1100–1160), French theologian, known as the Master of the *Sentences*, as noted in Luther's opening lines. The *Sentences* (1157–1158) are a four-volume presentation of the essentials of Christian doctrine. From the early thirteenth to the mid-seventeenth centuries, students of theology were required to comment on all or part of this text. As focus of theological study, this work was second only to the Bible. Luther and Melanchthon also refer to Lombard jocularly as the "Meister von hohen Sinnen" (the master of deep meanings), which was a German pun on his Latin title "magister Sententiarum." Tetzel may be here enjoying some German-Latin word play of his own: *Hoenszyn* = Master of Gaul = *Haehnchen* (German, "little cock") = *gallus* (Latin, "cock").

19. "Of whom many are saints, etc." Tetzel uses this phrase several times to strengthen his case for the absolute reliability of certain "modern" doctors, most notably St. Thomas Aquinas, the first University of Paris doctor to be canonized and a fellow Dominican. Thomas's system of theology has acquired quasi-official status in the church through repeated formal endorsement by various popes.

that the holy Roman Church agrees with them concerning the three parts of penance. It has neither found fault with them, but accepted them all as truthful; nor has it admitted or proven that they have written a single dissentient word contrary to scripture and the four doctors of the church.[20] Rather, they have been recognized as true interpreters of holy scripture and of the ancient holy doctors.

For such reasons it should be assumed publicly and supported by all believing Christians that these following articles of this presumptuous *Sermon* are suspect, erroneous, entirely misleading, and contrary to the holy Christian church, as I intend to prove with the help of God by refuting each of the articles individually and in depth.

I bring this rebuttal to the judgment of his Papal Holiness, the pope, the whole Christian church, and all universities.[21]

I.

A Sermon concerning Indulgences and Grace, etc.

Its first erroneous article reads as follows. "First, you should know that various new teachers such as the Master of the Sentences, St. Thomas, and their followers ascribe three parts to penance, namely contrition, confession, and satisfaction. And although this distinction (as they conceive it) is with difficulty or not at all to be found substantiated in holy scripture or in the ancient holy Christian teachers, nevertheless we will let it stand now as it is and speak in their manner."[22]

Rebuttal

This erroneous article is rebutted thusly in a Christian manner and on solid foundation: First, it is erroneous and unfounded, because it claims that the

---

20. The four doctors of the church, Saints Ambrose (340–397), Jerome (340–420), Augustine (354–430), and Gregory the Great (540–604), were proclaimed "Doctors of the Church" by Pope Boniface VIII on September 20, 1295. The title recognized them as the preeminent teachers of the Christian faith.

21. Tetzel employs a variation of this sentence to conclude each rebuttal. It expresses succinctly and unmistakably his stance on the importance of papal authority and emphasizes his own legitimacy as representative speaker for accepted church teaching, doctrines which at that very time are being articulated by "trustworthy" academic theologians (cf. n. 33 below).

22. In each of the twenty articles, Tetzel quotes Luther's sermon first and then proceeds to refute it.

three parts of penance are not founded on holy scripture and on the ancient Christian teachers, wherein the truth is compromised. For scripture and the ancient and modern holy doctors, of whom there are many thousand, maintain that Almighty God wishes to have repayment and satisfaction for sin. For Christ our Lord commands sinners in the Gospel, "Bear fruit worthy of repentance." [Matt 3:8] This is interpreted and understood by all the holy doctors of the whole world to mean satisfying penance.

For this reason, too, God sent his only son into the world to make sufficient satisfaction for the sins of humankind, even though Adam and Eve repented most profoundly of their sin and yet for which they were cast forth from paradise into penance. However, that the Lord Jesus released Mary Magdalene, the adulteress, [Luke 7:37–51; John 8:1–11] and the paralytic man [Matt 9:1–8; Mark 2:1–12; Luke 5:18–26] from all their sins without imposing any kind of penance does not support the idea that God desires from the sinner only contrition and the carrying of the cross. For Christ recognized that the contrition of the persons just mentioned, which he himself gave them, was sufficient. Moreover, he himself forgave them, and he released them perfectly by means of the excellent power of the key, that is by the power of 'going beyond.'[23] Priests, however, can neither recognize a person's contrition nor give them contrition. They possess merely the key of their ministry. Therefore, no matter how greatly a person repents of his sins or carries the cross, if he scorns confession or satisfaction as elements of the sacrament of penance, the pain due his sins will never be forgiven him.

Submitted to the judgment of the holy papal see and of all Christian universities and doctors.

II.—III.

The second and third erroneous articles of the sermon read as follows.

"Second, they say that an indulgence does not remove the first or second part, i.e., contrition or confession, but rather the third part, namely satisfaction."

"Third, satisfaction is divided further into three parts: that is praying, fasting, and giving alms. Prayer includes all kinds of works that are

23. *Potestas (clavorum) excellentiae* was a Thomist idea to explain how Christ, during his earthly ministry, had the power to produce the effect of a sacrament without there being a sacrament. This power "excelled" that of his disciples and their successors, who were given only the routine *potestas ministerialis*, as Tetzel correctly goes on to point out.

concerned with the soul, such as reading, writing, hearing God's word, preaching, teaching, and similar practices. Fasting comprises all kinds of works of the mortification of the flesh, such as night watches, physical labor, uncomfortable bed, clothing, etc. Giving alms comprises all kinds of good works of love and mercy toward one's neighbor."

Rebuttal

They are rebutted thusly in a Christian manner: First, both of them are erroneous and entirely misleading, since in them the truth is silenced. For in the holy Council of Constance it was once again confirmed that whoever wishes to earn an indulgence must, in addition to contrition, have gone to confession according to the ordinances of holy church or seriously intend to do so according to the ordinances of the church. This instruction is found in all papal bulls and letters of indulgence. But in the first article such confession is implicitly, that is secretly, separated and severed from genuine contrition, though erroneously.

Submitted to the judgment of His Papal Holiness and of all Christian universities and doctors.

IV.

The fourth article of the erroneous sermon reads as follows.

"Fourth, it is unquestioned by all of them that indulgence takes away those same works of satisfaction obligated by or imposed for sins. Thus, since it is supposed to take away all of these works, there would remain nothing else good for us to do."

Rebuttal

It is rebutted in this Christian manner: The plenary indulgence remits the works of satisfaction to this extent: whoever is granted complete remission of punishment is freed through papal power so that he is no longer obligated to do those works of satisfaction noted in article three, which had been imposed upon him for repented and confessed sins. Yet after the complete forgiveness of sins and pain, a person is no less tempted by the devil, his own flesh, and the world than he was before forgiveness. And evil habits and the possibility of falling quickly into sin again remain after forgiveness of sins and punishment. Therefore, in order to resist the devil, the flesh and the world and to subdue evil, sinful habit, inclination, and the possibility of falling quickly into sin again, a man, after complete forgiveness of sins and suffering, dare not refrain from penitential works that are salvific for him and a medicine for his spiritual weakness and also helpful toward gaining eternal life.

Also, no papal or episcopal brief of indulgence maintains that people who earn an indulgence should refrain henceforth from good works and from making satisfaction. In fact, we owe it to the honor of the eternal Godhead to do good works, even had we not sinned, solely because of his creation of us. And when we have accomplished all the good works that are possible for us, then we should [still] say, "We are useless servants of God." [Luke 10:17] For this reason, this article is completely erroneous and misleading, and fabricated solely to the disadvantage of indulgences.

Submitted to the judgment of the holy Roman see and of all Christian universities and theologians.

V.

The fifth erroneous article of the sermon reads as follows.

"Fifth, for many people there has been an important and as yet unresolved question whether indulgence also removes something more than such prescribed good works, that is, whether indulgence also removes the suffering that divine justice demands for sin."

Rebuttal

It is rebutted thusly in a Christian manner: First of all, it is completely erroneous and deceptive. For the plenary indulgence remits also the suffering that divine justice requires for sins, when they have been repented of and confessed and the penance imposed by the priest is insufficient. For the Papal Holiness follows St. Peter in the throne and papal office and also possesses, like St. Peter himself, the authority and the power to remit all sin. And it possesses this power from the words of the Lord, "All that you loose on earth will be loosed in heaven, etc." [Matt 16:19] Now because the pope can forgive all sins, he can also remit, through indulgence, all the suffering due sin. For all the pain that people deserve to suffer for their sin is imposed and conferred on them as just punishment, first and foremost by God, against whom all mortal sin is directed.

Concerning the second point and following, suffering is imposed upon the sinner by priestly authority in God's stead. Thus, this authority should exercise the greatest diligence in imposing the penance ordered by the canons of the law, called *canones penitentiales,* in order to be in conformity with divine justice. For this reason no one should consider it merely an *unresolved question* that indulgences remit the pain demanded by divine justice for repented and confessed sins but for which the priest imposed insufficient penance. For the holy Roman church observes this custom, as do all Christian theologians of whom there are thousands; and this custom, [as mentioned in the fifth article], has never been repudiated by the Roman church. Therefore, this article is erroneous and intended to deceive people.

Submitted to the judgment of the holy Roman see and of all Christian universities and doctors.

VI.

The sixth erroneous article reads as follows.

"Sixth, I leave their opinion without condemnation for the moment. I say that no one can prove by a single word of scripture that divine justice desires or demands any sort of suffering or satisfaction from the sinner other than his heartfelt and genuine sorrow or conversion, with the intention to bear the cross of Christ from now on and practice the work mentioned above (even if not imposed by anyone). For thus he speaks through Ezekiel, "If the sinner repents and does right, then I will never remember his sin." [Ezek 18:21; 33:14–16] Furthermore, he himself absolved everyone—Mary Magdalene, the paralytic, the woman caught in adultery, etc. And I should very much like to hear who would prove otherwise, in spite of the fact that some theologians have thought so."

Rebuttal

It is rebutted accordingly on the basis of holy scripture: First, it is entirely erroneous, unfounded und misleading, fabricated to the detriment of indulgences. For holy scripture, both the Old and the New Testament, indicate that God demands satisfaction for sin. One finds this in Deuteronomy in the twenty-fifth chapter. [Deut 25:1–2; 32:49] The ancient holy Christian teachers say the same thing, in particular St. Gregory in his Thirty-Second address to layfolk or Homily, "The heavenly physician, Our Lord Jesus Christ, prescribes for every specific vice valuable medicine."[24] Also St. Augustine says, "God has given no one license to sin, and he mercifully forgives the sins that are committed, as long as the fitting and necessary satisfaction for the sin is not omitted."[25] God forgave David his adultery, yet as satisfaction he had to suffer a war, the disgracing of his wives, and after his remorse and confession the death of his child. David also felt great sorrow for his sin regarding the census of his people. But he still had to offer satisfaction to God for that sin in addition to his remorse, for the angel slew 70,000 men at God's command because of it, as the Book of Kings relates in detail. [2 Samuel 24]

Years ago, with the same wording and message of this sixth article, the heretics Wycliffe and Jan Hus also sought to maintain that confession and satisfaction are unnecessary. That is why in several countries persons who go to confession are given no penance by the priest. Rather, he says to them, "Go forth and determine never more to sin."[26] This article is erroneous and not to be believed.

Submitted to the judgment of His Papal Holiness, of the holy see in Rome and of all Christian universities and theologians.

VII.

The seventh erroneous article reads as follows.

"Seventh, one does indeed observe that God punishes some persons according to his righteousness, or forces them toward contrition through suffering, as Psalm 88 says, "If his children shall sin, I will punish their transgression with the rod, but I will not turn my mercy from them." [Ps 89:30–34] But to remit this suffering lies in no one's power except God's alone. Indeed, he will not remit it; rather he promises that he will impose it."

24. This is Homily 25 in modern editions: Gregory the Great, "Homilia XXV" *PL* 76:1188–96, quote from 1195. For an English translation, see Gregory the Great, *Forty Gospel Homilies*, translated by David Hurst (Kalamazoo, MI: Cistercian Publications, 1990), 187–99, quote from 197.

25. Augustine, "De utilitate agenda poenitentiae (Sermo 351, 10)" *PL* 39:1545–47.

26. Refers to the practice of the Hussites, followers of the doctrine of Jan Hus, still viable in areas of Europe at the time of the Reformation.

Rebuttal

It is rebutted in Christian manner thusly: First of all, it is trite prattle and mirror tricks. For God who says, "If my children shall sin, then I shall punish their sin with the rod, yet I shall not turn my mercy from them," has granted the fullness of his power to St. Peter and to every legitimately elected pope who reigns over holy church in such a manner that the pope has the power to do all things necessary, in the holy church that are for the salvation of the holy church and of humankind.

For this reason the pope has the power, by means of plenary indulgences, to remit the suffering imposed by God upon sinners for their sin, as long as it has been repented of and confessed by them. That a person is absolved from the suffering that God has imposed and decreed as judgment for his sin should, after contrition and confession, the punishment and penance imposed by the priest, be insufficient for his repentance and confession) serves that person quite positively for his soul's salvation. It is also a tremendous act of God's mercy that his vicar, the pope, releases people from the suffering of their sin by means of an indulgence. For this reason, David's words are cited as a subterfuge in this erroneous article without their true Christian meaning. Thus this article should be read with critical eyes and not be expounded blindly and obscurely.

When God says that he will punish the sins of his children with the rod, that is, to force them through pain to repent, it means that an indulgence is not useful against this kind of pain, but rather only for the pain of repented and confessed sin. For one finds it written in holy scripture that at times God inflicts pain upon men to increase their merit, as with Job; at times to test their virtue, as with St. Paul; at times as chastisement for sins, as with Miriam, the sister of Moses; at times for the honor of God, as with the man born blind; and at times as the beginning of the suffering of eternal punishment, as with Herod. To impose such God-willed chastisements and sufferings on a person remains solely in God's power. Nonetheless, the pope can with a plenary indulgence remit the pain imposed by God for those sins that have been repented of and confessed but assigned insufficient penance by the priest. Consequently, this article is erroneous and deceptive.

This submitted to the judgment of the holy papal see and of all Christian universities and doctors.

VIII.

The eighth erroneous article reads as follows.

"Eighth, therefore, no one can assign this so-called suffering a name. And no one knows what it is, if it is neither this punishment nor the above-mentioned good works."

Rebuttal

It is rebutted in Christian manner thusly: First, it is erroneous because the suffering that God's righteousness imposes on a person for his sin, if insufficiently repented of or insufficiently acknowledged through the priest in confession, is called a retribution of God and the worthy fruit of contrition. Satisfaction for this cannot be made by just any kind of contrition but only by profoundly compensatory satisfaction. St. Augustine and all theologians of Christianity say this. What the particular name of such suffering exacted by God will have in purgatory is known [only] to those people suffering it now, along with the ones who will suffer it because of their wretched deception of poor believers in Christ, if indeed they don't go to hell instead!

Submitted to the judgment of the holy Roman see and of all Christian universities and doctors.

IX.

The ninth erroneous article reads as follows.

"Ninth, I say, 'Even if the Christian church right now would decide and declare that indulgence removes more than the works of satisfaction, it would still be a thousand times better, if no Christian would buy or desire an indulgence but would rather do the works and bear the suffering. For indulgence is nothing else, and cannot become anything else, than a release from good works and wholesome suffering. Men should rightly welcome these rather than avoid them, in spite of the fact that some modern preachers have invented two kinds of suffering: remedial and satisfactory, that is, some suffering is for satisfaction, some for amending one's ways. But we have more freedom to disdain this and all such prattle (thanks be to God!) than they do to invent it. For all suffering, indeed everything that God inflicts, is beneficial and useful for Christians."

Rebuttal

It is rebutted thusly in a Christian manner: It is deceptive because the holy Roman church maintains and decides by means of its tradition and practice that a plenary indulgence removes not only the works of satisfaction imposed by the priest or by law but also by God's righteousness, if the sins are insufficiently repented and the priest in confession has imposed insufficient satisfaction. For St. Augustine declares that the customs, which the people of God or Christians exercise, and the statutes of the church fathers are to be considered as law, even though holy scripture says nothing specific of such customs and matters. It is therefore by law (because the Roman see observes it as a custom) that the pope can remit all the aforementioned suffering through a plenary indulgence.

This erroneous article also indicates that no person should desire an indulgence even if the indulgence remits more from that person than the penance imposed by priest or canon law. These words contradict Christian truth. For with them the article maintains that a person may have an indulgence without contrition. Thus, it also separates the indulgence from contrition and the production of the good work for which indulgence is given. That in truth can nevermore be substantiated in Christian doctrine. For those who earn an indulgence are living in a state of genuine contrition and in the love of God, which state does not allow them to remain lazy and slothful. Rather, it enflames them to serve God and do great works to honor him. For it is as clear as day that Christian, God-fearing, pious people, and not loose and lazy persons, earn indulgences with fervent desire.

For this reason this article is full of poison and by its argument wants to make indulgences, which are most necessary and salutary for poor sinners, disgusting to people. Indeed, God's great unconstrained mercy appears to us most clearly in the granting of indulgences. For through his mercy God chooses to let Jesus's own satisfaction satisfy for all the suffering due to persons who have not repented sufficiently of their sin and for which sins insufficient penance was assigned by the priest. In this way papal authority applies Christ's own satisfaction to their guilt.

It is also Christian to believe that when anyone gives alms, prays, visits churches, undertakes pilgrimage, fasts, or does other good works that earn indulgences and does them with the same love of God in which one would do such works, if not graced with indulgences, that [then] these named indulgenced works are far better and more meritorious for people than others [not so graced]. For this reason this article is miserably formulated to lead people astray.

Submitted to the judgment of the holy papal see and of all Christian universities and doctors.

X.

The tenth erroneous article reads as follows.

"Tenth, it is vacuous talk to say that there is so much suffering and so many works that a person cannot accomplish them due to the brevity of life, for which reason indulgences are necessary. I counter that as unfounded and pure fantasy. For God and holy church impose on no one more than is possible for him to bear, just as St. Paul says, that God does not allow anyone to be tempted by more than he can bear. [1 Cor 10:8] And it contributes not little to Christianity's shame that one blames it for imposing more than we can bear."

Rebuttal

It is rebutted in a Christian manner thusly: An indulgence is not granted solely because the brevity of a person's life does not let him complete the required works of satisfaction. It is as clear as day that the greatest sinner can satisfy God's justice for all the penance incurred by his through genuine, complete contrition, provided of course that he not disdain sacramental confession and penance. When these two things are disdained, all contrition is null and powerless. For this reason it is untruthfully imputed to us sub-commissioners and preachers of grace that we defame God and Christianity by supposedly saying that God and the church impose impossible things upon a person. Such words are incomprehensible! For indulgences are granted at times for almsgiving; at times because of personal accomplishments, such as when one goes on crusade against the infidels and heretics, builds bridges, and repairs roads. At times the precariousness of life prompts earning indulgences, such as when persons travel overseas to the Holy Land, as our sacred laws clearly mandate. Therefore, indulgences are not granted solely on account of the brevity of human life that could prevent a person from completing his assigned penance.

Submitted to the judgment of the holy papal see and of all Christian universities and doctors.

XI.

The eleventh article reads as follows.[27]

"Eleventh, even if acts of penance as established by canon law were now in effect, mandating seven years of penance for each mortal sin, Christianity would still have to abandon such regulations and not impose anything more than a person could bear. All the more, since such canon law is not now in effect, one must take care not to impose more than any person can possibly bear."

Rebuttal

It is to be exposed as an unfounded statement as follows: Even though the statutes of canon law establishing acts of penance for human frailty are not now in effect, people are not thereby given greater license to sin, nor are the sins punished by divine justice with less penance than the penitential canons stipulated, or the equivalent punishment acceptable to God. For whoever does not carry out the penance imposed by canon law must suffer something different, which God's justice accepts as equally valid fruits of penance. Also, when the priest is absolving the sinner, he must consider not only the contrition, as he is imposing the penance on him for repented of and confessed sin. Rather, he must also take very seriously the scale of penances set out in the penitential canons so that he does not—as much as possible—act contrary to the divine justice spelled out by the canons, as stated in canon law. And when he has taken into account the penitent's contrition and the satisfaction imposed by canon law, he should then assign the penitent satisfaction in confession.

In this manner and not according to their whims, priests are to assign the sinner a penance in confession for repented of sins. The penance imposed by the priest in confession profits the absolved sinner in that he does not sin, if he does not observe the penance for his sin spelled out in canon law. However, if the priest assigns too little penance, then God will demand of a person the remaining part, either here or in the next world. Whoever teaches people otherwise, that person deceives them.

Submitted to the judgment of the holy papal see and of all Christian universities and doctors.

---

27. Tetzel omits in the introductory formula for rebuttals 11–12 his usual "erroneous" jab at the sermon's articles.

XII.

The twelfth article reads as follows.

"Twelfth, one indeed says that the sinner should either be sent to purgatory with the remaining suffering or directed to an indulgence. But there are indeed more things said without foundation and proof."

Rebuttal

It is refuted in Christian manner thusly: It is first of all completely erroneous and is set forth without any validity and proof of holy scripture, and also without any recourse to legal judgments, as though its subject matter were appropriate for the holy Gospel, although in truth they are as different as night and day.

Besides, it is Christian and true to know that the sinner should be sent either to purgatory with the remaining suffering or to an indulgence. For the holy Christian church and the community of all ancient and modern theologians teach that God is so merciful that he forgives guilt and sin, [but] that he nevertheless remains just in not letting these go unpunished. Therefore, if one's inner contrition is insufficient to count as punishment for sin, and external satisfaction is not undertaken and completed, then God, who knows the extent and number of sins, will demand that the remaining penance and satisfaction not performed by the person in this life be completed in purgatory.

Further, as Anselm says in his book, *Cur deus homo* [*Why God Became Man*], "A person can do enough for his sin solely through good works, which could not be demanded of a person unless he had sinned."[28] And in any case people are obligated to do the good works of God's commandments because they are his creatures, so that God also demands them of people, even if they had not sinned. Thus, this twelfth article is erroneous and misleading, since satisfaction must take place in this life or in the next.

Submitted to the judgment of the holy papal see and of all Christian universities and theologians.

---

28. St. Anselm of Canterbury (c. 1033–1109) describes in his *Cur deus homo* Christ's death on the cross as an act of satisfaction, returning to God the honor stolen by human sin. This passage is found in Anselm, *Opera II*, 48.74–84.101f., as cited in *Dokumente zur Causa Lutheri*, 353n52.

XIII.

The thirteenth erroneous article reads as follows.

"Thirteenth, it is a great error that anyone would think that he would himself make satisfaction for his sins, since God forgives those same sins at all times for free, out of his inestimable grace, demanding nothing but that one live well from thence forward. Christianity, to be sure, does demand something, thus it can and should also cease doing this and not impose difficult and unbearable things."

Rebuttal

It is rebutted in Christian manner thusly: First, it is unfounded and misleading, for God, along with the church, as shown repeatedly above, desires satisfaction for sins. This has been the conclusion of the ancient and modern doctors of holy church, of whom there are thousands and of whom many count among the saints in heaven. They all say that no matter how great contrition is, if a person scorns confession and acts of penance, then contrition alone will not help. To be sure, for a mortal sin no one can be reconciled with God without the help of Christ's sufferings, as St. Augustine also believes. Indeed, if the author of this article had considered St. Augustine, this error would not have been promoted. For St. Augustine says, "For God does not look with license on our sinning, although in his mercy he may blot out sins that are already committed, if appropriate satisfaction is not neglected."[29] However, this erroneous article does not count as new, for Wycliffe and Jan Hus also maintained this error: specifically, the idea that confession, in which acts of satisfaction are imposed upon a person, is not necessary. And for this reason Jan Hus was burned at the stake by the ecumenical Council of Constance and Wycliffe died as a heretic.

Submitted to the judgment of the holy papal see and all Christian universities and theologians.

---

29. "*Nemini enim dedit laxamentum peccandi deus, quamvis miserando deleas [sic] iam facta peccata, si non satisfactio congrua negligatur.*" Cf. Augustine, *De poenitentia*, ch. 18 (Augustinus, Ench. c. 70, as cited in *Dokumente zur Causa Lutheri*, 354 n.54).

XIV.

The fourteenth erroneous article reads as follows.

"Fourteenth, an indulgence is allowed for the sake of imperfect and lazy Christians who do not want to practice good works earnestly or who are sickly.[30] For an indulgence does not spur them on to improvement but tolerates and allows their imperfection. Therefore, no one should speak against indulgences, but neither should anyone speak in their favor."

Rebuttal

It is rebutted in Christian manner thusly: Even though a person earns every indulgence, he should still not refrain from penitential works. Thus says Pope Innocent, for after the forgiveness of sins and of all penance through indulgence, there remains in a person the tendency to sin again.[31] A person must medicate himself against this tendency by means of good works. If after the forgiveness of sin and penance by God he also wants to gain and increase his merit, then he dare not omit painful good works. Rather he must bear the cross of Christ to the very end. An indulgence does not remove this but rather inflames a person toward the cross and makes him not "lazy" but ready and eager to perform painful works.

Therefore, this article is erroneous and mere prattle, because it announces that no one ought to speak against indulgences, which nonetheless occurs in almost every article of the sermon. That one should "not speak in their favor" is against the custom of the holy Roman church which permitted the holy Jubilee Year, celebrated in Rome, to be announced and proclaimed long before he came on the scene.[32]

The article also contradicts the practice of all those individual Christian churches throughout the whole world, which always allow papal indulgences as well as those of their own bishops to be proclaimed. For example, when a crusade is undertaken by Christians against heretics and infidels, people are urged and admonished with great diligence to participate, not

30. As for Luther's word, *unleyedlich* ("who are sickly") could refer either to someone's physical incapacity (sickliness) to practice good works or to a mental or spiritual indisposition (those who find them intolerable).

31. Pope Innocent III (1198–1216); cf. *PL* 217:691–702.

32. Luther refers to the Jubilee Indulgence in thesis twenty-six of his ninety-five theses, and Tetzel addresses that topic in thesis thirty-three of his *106 Frankfurt Theses*. For details, see W. Lurz, "Heiliges Jahr II," *Lexikon für Theologie und Kirche* (1993), 4:1325.

least because of the plenary indulgence that crusaders gain. Hence, the concluding words of this article are declared contrary to all truth.

This submitted to the judgment of the holy Roman see and of all Christian universities and theologians.

XV.

The fifteenth erroneous article reads as follows.

"Fifteenth, it would be far more positive and beneficial for a person to give to the building of St. Peter, or to whatever project is named, solely for the sake of God than to get an indulgence for so doing. For it is dangerous to make such a gift for the sake of an indulgence and not for the sake of God."

Rebuttal

It is rebutted thusly in Christian manner: First, it is totally bare and naked and fabricated without any proof based on holy scripture, when it implies in its conclusion that a person could give alms merely for the sake of an indulgence and not for the sake of God. As though anyone would give alms for the sake of an indulgence without thereby also praising God! For just as surely as a person gives alms for an indulgence, so too he gives it for the sake of God. Indeed, all indulgences are given first of all for the glory of God. Thus, whoever gives alms for the sake of an indulgence is also giving it principally for the sake of God, aside from the fact that no one earns an indulgence unless he has true contrition and love of God. And whoever does good works for the love of God is dedicating them to God and his praise. Therefore, Christians should not believe this article in the least.

This submitted to the judgment of the holy Roman see and of all Christian universities and theologians.

XVI.

The sixteenth erroneous article reads as follows.

"Sixteenth, far better is the good work shown a needy person that than given to a building. It is also far better than the indulgence granted for it. For as it is said: 'Better is a good work done than much remitted.' The indulgence, however, is the remittance of many good works, or else nothing is remitted.

Indeed, so that I instruct you correctly, pay attention. You should above all things (considering neither St. Peter's nor indulgence) give to your poor neighbor, if you want to give anything. But if it should happen that there is no one else in your city who needs help (which unless God will it, will never happen), then you should give as you will, to the churches, altars, jewels, chalices in your city. And when that too is now no longer necessary, then and only then may you give as you will to the building of St. Peter's or to anything else. Nonetheless, that also you ought not do for the sake of indulgences. For St. Paul says, 'Whoever does not do good to his closest neighbor is no Christian and worse than a heathen.' [1 Tim 5:8] And keep this in mind: whoever tells you otherwise is deceiving you or is really seeking your soul in your purse. And if he finds a penny therein, he would prefer that to every soul.

If you then declare, 'Then I will never more buy an indulgence,' I reply, 'I have already said earlier that my will, desire, request, and advice are that no one seek an indulgence. Let lazy and sleepy Christians buy indulgences. You go your own way.'"

Rebuttal

It is rebutted in Christian manner thusly: First, it is unfounded and entirely obscure, since it considers one matter and leaves the other matter unmentioned. For giving alms to a poor person is more beneficial for the earning of salvation, yet buying a plenary—or indeed any indulgence—is more beneficial for the speedier satisfaction of punishment due to sin. Further, everyone should know that buying an indulgence is also a work of mercy. For whoever buys an indulgence takes pity on his soul and makes himself well-pleasing to God thereby. Therefore, this article concludes erroneously in saying that buying an indulgence is not an act of mercy, and it concludes in a quite un-Christian manner in maintaining that an indulgence is the omission of many good works. For it substantiates that with no passage of scripture, nor will one ever be found, which could confirm such a thing. Besides, anyone who earns an indulgence must be living in a state of love for God, and where that love is in a person, that person does many good and great works. [Cf. Wis 7:14]

This erroneous article also contradicts the contents of all indulgence bulls and briefs, all of which proclaim unanimously that indulgences are given to spur people on to contrition and confession and good works. Therefore, this erroneous article should be entirely discounted.

Pronounced in acknowledgment of the holy Roman see and of all Christian universities and doctors.

This article also implies that people are given true teaching in the erroneous sermon. That corresponds not at all with the truth. Rather, it "is wished, implored, and advised" in this article "that no one should buy an indulgence," advice which is detrimental to salvation. The article says further that only "lazy and sleepy Christians" should purchase an indulgence, which cruelly misleads Christianity. Consider that a person does himself much better in purchasing the indulgence he needs, than in giving alms to a poor person who is not in a state of utmost need. For the alms or the good work with which someone is earning the indulgence functions just as meritoriously toward eternal life, since it is done for the love of God, as do the alms given to a poor person.

Furthermore, because a person who earns an indulgence by giving alms is released quickly and speedily from the suffering due him for his sins, it is better for him to earn an indulgence than to give alms to poor persons not in a condition of extreme need. Also, the Lord Jesus says in Luke, the eleventh chapter, "Whatever is superfluous, give alms therefrom" [Luke 11:41], which means to those who are not in a condition of utmost need. God does, however, command us to give alms to those who are in a condition of utmost need, even of those goods needed to maintain our nature and status. Therefore, St. Paul is improperly quoted in this article. For St. Paul says, "Whoever does not act well toward the members of his household is no Christian and worse than a heathen." [1 Tim 5:8] He does not, however, forbid a person to do good for himself sooner than for his household members who are not in a state of utmost need. Each person should also observe the order of charity in giving alms; that is, he helps himself sooner than his relatives, as discussed above. Therefore, Christian believers should grant no credence to the plain, naked, unsupported words of this article, for the article is not established on the basis of any reliable substantiation of holy scripture.

This submitted to the judgment of the holy Roman see and of all Christian universities and doctors.

XVII.

The seventeenth erroneous article reads as follows.

"Seventeenth, an indulgence is not required, also not recommended but rather is one of those things that are tolerated and allowed. Therefore, it is not a work of obedience, is also not meritorious, but is rather an excuse from obedience. Therefore, although one should not prevent anyone from buying an indulgence, so too one should draw Christians away from doing so and instead should stimulate and strengthen them for the works and sufferings which indulgences omit."

Rebuttal

It is rebutted in true Christian manner thusly: True, there is no command to earn an indulgence. It is, however, most truly advised by Their Holinesses the Popes, by the revered holy ecumenical councils, by all devout prelates of holy church who grant indulgences for the sake of practicing good works, to the honor of God and for the good of Christendom and for the merit of an individual (since he does good works for the sake of the indulgence) and for the good of the person so that he is freed from the suffering due his sins, as mentioned above. Therefore, an indulgence is not one of those things that are merely "tolerated and allowed."

This article claims further that earning an indulgence is not a meritorious work but rather a way out of obedience, which for all eternity can be as little justified by any shred of holy scripture as all the other articles. For the works that are graced with an indulgence are always better than the same ones accomplished with the same love but without an indulgence. Thus, this article contradicts the freedom of the holy Roman see, for God has entrusted to his vicar, the pope and the papal see, the prime leadership of the things that serve humankind for salvation.

This submitted to the judgment of the holy Roman see and of all Christian universities and theologians.

XVIII.

The eighteenth erroneous article reads as follows.

"Eighteenth, whether souls are drawn out of purgatory by indulgences, I do not know. Still, I do not believe so, although various modern scholars say so. But it is impossible for them to prove it, and furthermore, the church has not yet come to a conclusion. Therefore, for greater certainty it is better that you pray for them and labor for them. For this is more proven and is certain."

Rebuttal

It is refuted thusly in Christian manner: First, it is full of malicious guile, when it claims that the church has not concluded that souls can be delivered from purgatory through indulgences. For the tradition of the holy Roman church does maintain that souls are delivered from purgatory by an indulgence. There are also very many altars, churches, and chapels in Rome, where souls are released by celebrating Masses or by doing other good works. This is so because the popes have granted plenary indulgences to these very places to release souls, whenever Mass is celebrated there or other good words are carried out, as is the practice in Rome. The pope and the Roman church would not permit this release of souls in such manner in Rome, if it were not thoroughly established. For the pope and the holy see, as well as the papal office, do not err in matters that concern the faith.

Now indulgences also concern faith, for whoever does not believe that the pope can grant indulgences and plenary indulgences to the living and the dead—in a state of love for God—that person maintains that the pope has not received the plenitude of power from the Lord Christ over Christian believers, which contradicts sacred canon law.

This article also announces that various modern theologians say that souls can be delivered from purgatory through indulgences, but that it is impossible for them to prove it. In this regard one should know that the revered modern theologians have indeed established it very well and have never been condemned for that by the holy Roman church. Accordingly, they must well have proven it. Especially is this the case with St. Thomas, whose teaching on faith and salvation of souls Popes Urban and Innocent have accepted and affirmed his teaching as Christian and true.[33] Furthermore, up to now, no pope has ever condemned his teaching. Because the teaching of St. Thomas is accepted as Christian, the truth of this article is truly questionable. Also St. Jerome says, "Because the faith of His Papal Holiness is accepted as right and good, since he occupies the throne and faith of Peter, so then that person who reproves his [the pope's] faith proves himself to be ignorant, or evil, or a heretic."[34] And this is how that person is to be judged who reproves St. Thomas's teaching of the Christian faith as unsubstantiated.

33. Urban IV (Pope 1261–1264, French) never resided in Rome. Innocent VI (Pope 1352–1362, French) acted severely toward the Spiritual Franciscans. Aquinas served as theological counselor to this papal court in Viterbo.

34. St. Jerome, "Epistula ad Damasum (No. 15)," CSEL (Vindobonae: Verlag der Österreichischen Akademie der Wissenschaften, 1996), 54:62–67.

This submitted to the judgment of the holy see and of all Christian universities and doctors.

XIX.

The nineteenth erroneous article reads as follows.

"Nineteenth, in these points I have no doubts and they are sufficiently grounded in scripture. Therefore, you should also have no doubt and let the scholastic doctors remain scholastics. Taken all together they are not enough with their opinions to substantiate a sermon."

Rebuttal

It is refuted in Christian manner accordingly: First, this article and all the articles cited are totally ungrounded in scripture. For the articles contradict the custom of the holy Roman church and the teaching of all modern, venerable Christian teachers. If St. Augustine together with the three other ancient, venerable doctors of the church had foreseen that the authority of the papal office and of the Roman church concerning indulgences would be so despised by erring persons, they would certainly have forestalled it with their writings. Modern revered theologians have, however, experienced and heard how malicious men have been speaking, preaching, and writing against the pope and the validity of indulgences, and they have challenged this, based on solid Christian foundation. Nor has the holy Roman church rebuked or censored them for doing so.

This article also states, "One should let the '*doctores scholasticos*' remain 'scholastics,' for taken all together, they with their opinions are unable to substantiate a sermon." [And further,] ignorant people hold this opinion of the venerable scholastic doctors, for these venerable "*doctores*" uncover and oppose all new errors. Therefore, wrong-thinking people deride them. However, the holy Roman church together with the whole community of sacred Christendom are in unanimous agreement that the revered venerable "*doctores scholasticos*" buttress the holy Christian faith against the heretics with their truly salvific teaching based on solid Christian doctrine. And what is more, they are certainly able to preach a sermon! Thus this article makes sport of them quite unfairly and shamefully and contrary to all reason and truth.

Further, all the erroneous articles are characterized by abruptness and obscurity, perhaps because they are intended to be interpreted however one will and in any direction. The great scandal that they elicit, however, ought to have been considered beforehand. For because of them many people will hold the *magisterium* and jurisdiction of His Papal Holiness and the holy Roman see in contempt. The works of sacramental satisfaction will also cease. People will no longer believe preachers and theologians. Everyone will want to interpret holy scripture according to his own whim. Through this, all of holy Christendom must come into great spiritual danger, since each person will believe what best pleases him. In time, as the deceptive article announces, the modern revered theologians, in whom for many centuries Christianity has placed great confidence, shall no longer be considered credible. For these reasons this article is entirely erroneous.

Submitted to the judgment of the holy Roman see and of all Christian universities and theologians.

XX.

The twentieth erroneous article reads as follows.

"Twentieth, whether some people reproach me as a heretic (for such a truth is quite injurious for their money boxes), I pay little heed to such babblings inasmuch as no one does so except some muddled brains who have never sniffed a Bible, have never read the Christian teachers, have never understood their own teachers but rather are decaying in their riddled and fragmented opinions. For if they had understood them, they would know that they should defame no one without hearing and challenging him. Nonetheless, may God give them and us right understanding. Amen."

Rebuttal

It can be refuted in a Christian and well-grounded manner: First, it is totally erroneous and demands to know without a riddled brain who is a heretic. Therefore I, Brother Johann Tetzel, Order of Preachers, am forced to produce several other teachings and positions here, which I intend, with God's help, to discuss and prove correct in a Christian manner at the respected University of Frankfurt an der Oder on a date to be arranged.[35] That disputation will make anyone with half a brain able to learn and recognize who is a *Heresiarcha, Hereticus, Sismaticus, Erroneus, Temerarius, Malesonans,*

---

35. Tetzel is referring to his forthcoming, Latin disputation-document, "50 Positiones," which is a second series of fifty theses that he (rather than Wimpina) had written. Reprinted in *Dokumente zur Causa Lutheri*, Text 12, 369–75.

etc., (which is translated: *an archheretic, a heretic, a reprobate, erroneous, a blasphemer or slanderer, etc.*) and who is truly a Christian believer or not, granted of course that they have considered this treatise of mine as well as my previous treatise and [also] the sermon of twenty erroneous articles, as well as the treatise which begins, "*Amore et studio elucidando veritatis,*" and concludes in the last thesis, "*Ac sic magis per multas tribulations intrare celum quam per securitatem pacis confidant.*"[36]

From all this it will also become clear who "has a confused brain, who has never sniffed a Bible, never read the Christian masters, has never understood his own teachers." Therefore, I offer all of this rebuttal and my position that I have written regarding these matters for the consideration and judgment of His Holiness the Pope, the holy Roman church, all trustworthy Christian universities, and doctors[37] with sure trust in the truth, with the commitment to suffer whatever they judge just, [if any of it be heretical], be it through imprisonment, the stocks, drowning, or burning at the stake.

I write this as true Christian fraternal admonition, so that from now on no one should believe the sermon of the twenty erroneous articles nor the theses that begin, "*Dominus et magister Magister noster Jhesus Christus dicendo penitentiam agite etc.,*" and end, "*Ac sic magis per multas tribulations intrare celum etc.,*"[38] [that is to say], unless their author were to submit to the consideration and judgment of the His Papal Holiness, the holy Roman church, and all trustworthy Christian universities and shall have proven such submission through his actions. For I am confident that without such submission, the sermon of the twenty articles and the recently mentioned theses would be neither sermon nor wholesome teaching but rather a seduction and a perversion of the people. For Christ himself says, "Whoever hears not the church, that one shall be to you as a gentile and a publican." [Matt 18:17]

And if that person who wrote and distributed the erroneous sermon of the twenty articles should maintain anything publicly against this rebuttal of mine without the evidence of holy scripture, of canon law, and of

36. Luther's *Ninety-Five Theses.* Tetzel quotes the opening words of the "Introduction" ("Out of love and zeal for the truth"), and the complete thesis ninety-five ("And thus be confident of entering into heaven through many tribulations rather than through the false security of peace").

37. Note Tetzel's subtle but crucial variation of his concluding formula, from "all Christian" to "all trustworthy Christian" (*unvordechtig* = trustworthy, above suspicion) and his insertion of it three times into the body itself of rebuttal twenty. Note also his inclusion of the formula (unchanged) within the body of rebuttal sixteen above.

38. In this final reference to Luther's *Ninety-Five Theses,* Tetzel omits the opening phrase quoted in paragraph one above and cites instead the beginning of the first thesis ("When our Lord and Master Jesus Christ said, 'Repent'").

theologians, or without consideration of sufficient cause and reason, then no Christian should be upset by him, for it is mere prattle. And if this person does not submit his fabrication publicly and in writing to the judgment of His Papal Holiness, of the holy see, and of all trustworthy Christian universities, then I will not write against him again, considering it all unworthy of response and rebuttal. To which I do herewith publicly give my witness.

Submitted for the praise of God, for the salvation of humankind, and to the honor of the holy papal see.

3

Johann Eck

Response on Behalf of Hieronymus Emser[1]

—DAVID BAGCHI

INTRODUCTION

AFTER THE LEIPZIG DISPUTATION ended in July 1519, the chaplain to Duke George of Saxony, Hieronymus Emser, wrote a pamphlet entitled *The Leipzig Disputation: To What Extent Did It Support the Bohemians?* The purpose of this pamphlet was to dispel any suggestion that the majority Hussite Church in Bohemia could find succor in the apparently pro-Hussite statements Luther made during the debate. Emser's treatment of Luther in this pamphlet was outwardly courteous and consistently played down any culpability on his part. Luther's reply, *The Addition to Emser's Wild Goat*, was very different in tone.[2] The reason for Luther's hostility is not clear. It is possible that an earlier meeting with Emser in July 1518, at a dinner party that ended badly, had convinced him that the court chaplain was not to be trusted.[3] Equally, it is possible that Emser's close connection to Duke George, who had reacted so explosively to Luther's defence of Hus at the

---

1. *Johannis Eckij pro Hieronymo Emser contra malesanam Luteri Venationem responsio* (Leipzig: Landsberg, 1519).

2. *Ad aegocerotam Emserianum additio* (1519) (WA 2:658–79).

3. See the account in Martin Brecht, *Martin Luther: His Road to Reformation, 1483–1521* (Minneapolis: Fortress, 1985), 240–41.

disputation, rang warning bells. For whatever reason, Luther convinced himself that Emser's apparently friendly pamphlet was a trap.

At the end of 1519, Luther's opponent at Leipzig, the Ingolstadt professor Johann Eck, published a defence of Emser in the form of an open letter to Emser's ordinary, the Bishop of Meissen.[4] His intention in writing the *Response on Behalf of Hieronymus Emser against Luther's Mad Hunt* was to undermine Luther's public reputation as a heroic underdog by portraying him instead as a demented bully, who had launched a vicious and unprovoked "mad hunt" of Emser, who is here presented as a model priest—saintly, scholarly, and sincere. More generally, he wished to negate the advantage that the Wittenberg cause had gained from the post-disputation pamphlet campaign. Eck may well have won the debate itself by cornering Luther into defending a heretical position, but in the ensuing media battle he had been presented as an obscurantist and a scholastic, while Luther had been held up as a champion of humanism. At a time when the Reuchlin controversy was reaching its climax, this was disastrous for Eck's public reputation amongst humanists. His *Response* therefore bristles with satirical wordplay and classical allusions calculated to appeal to the humanist reader. Equally prominent are the repeated, derogatory references to Luther's status as a friar, ridiculing his habit and even his tonsure. This, too, was an attempt to reduce Luther's stock among humanists by associating him with the monastic and fraternal obscurantists traditionally satirized by the belletrists, not least by Erasmus himself. A final ploy was to portray Luther as someone "who prefers the branches to the roots," and therefore fundamentally opposed to the humanist *ad fontes* principle.

Eck was not a natural satirist, and his attempts at wordplay are generally pedestrian and lacking in humor. His forte lay elsewhere, in the forensic dismantling of an opponent's case by inexorable logic and by an almost total recall of the relevant authorities whether from scripture, the fathers, or canon law. (As the notes to the translation show, the accuracy of Eck's citations is remarkably good by the standards of early sixteenth-century debate.) The heaping-up of authorities is, however, neither attractive nor practical in pamphlet warfare, which is why Eck is obliged repeatedly to refer the reader to the fuller treatment of these issues in a forthcoming treatise, the three-volume blockbuster, *The Primacy of Peter*.

Johann Eck's *Response* exists in two editions, with several examples from each still extant in research libraries around the world. The example in the Kessler Collection is a first edition, printed by Martin Landsberg in

---

4. For further information on Eck, see the introduction to his *Address* in this volume.

Leipzig in 1519. It is set in an attractive and highly legible roman typeface, and the title page is decorated with the firm's stock border decoration. This displays the logotype of Landsberg's printing house in the top panel, with the initials "M.H.A.V." ("Martin of Würzburg and Augsburg"—the towns in which he had worked previously), and in the bottom panel the arms of Leipzig. Putti, in various poses, decorate the side panels. The second edition, which was also printed by Landsberg in Leipzig, was issued the following year. In appearance it is almost identical to the first edition but contains a number of typesetting errors and other departures from the original. This suggests that the original formes for the 1519 edition had been broken up, possibly because the demand for a second edition was not anticipated and Landsberg needed the type for another job. A copy of the first edition was then evidently used as a guide for the compositor of the second edition, who followed it almost exactly, except for some lapses here and there.

The text has not been translated into English before, to the best of my knowledge, but it has been rendered into German on at least two occasions. The first was by J. G. Walch in his monumental series *D. Martin Luthers Sämtliche Schriften*, vol. 18 (Halle: Gebauer, 1746), cols. 1090–1114. (This translation was evidently based on the second, 1520, edition.) A more recent translation by Peter Fabisch can currently be found on the late Vinzenz Pfnür's Reformation history website, in the edited collection of Eck's letters.[5] I am indebted to both translations, but have been obliged to depart from their readings occasionally. I have also felt justified in ignoring the original punctuation marks where to do so would make Eck's meaning less intelligible. The signatures of the 1519 edition have been included in this translation as a guide for anyone who wishes to consult the original.

A feature of the *Response* is the extensive use of marginal notes. They are of two types. Some are designed to indicate to the reader, at a glance, the salient points being discussed, in much the same way as modern books use subheadings. The other is to provide fuller references, as we would use footnotes. I have relegated all the marginalia to the footnotes, where the references, in particular, can be expanded. Square brackets indicate that the reference has been expanded or supplied where it was lacking in the original.

As noted above, the point-by-point approach adopted by Eck meant that he referred very frequently to Luther's original attack on Emser, the *Ad aegocerotam Emserianum additio*. Unfortunately, the *Additio* has yet to be translated into English, and so I have cited it in the notes in the standard

---

5. Available at http://ivv7srv15.uni-muenster.de/mnkg/pfnuer/Eckbriefe/No96.html.

Weimar Edition of Luther's works (WA 2:658–679). References to the text
of Emser's *De disputatione Lipsicensi* are to the standard edition by F. X.
Thurnhofer.[6]

TRANSLATION

[Ai[r]] The Response of Johann Eck on Behalf of Hieronymus Emser against
Luther's Mad Hunt.

To God alone be the glory.[7]

[Ai[v]] In the name of the Lord Jesus, Johann Eck wishes the most reverend lord, Lord Johann von Schleinitz, most worthy bishop of the illustrious
church of Meissen, his worshipful lord, salvation in the Lord Jesus.[8]

The holy council of Elibitanum soundly decreed that no bishops,
priests, or deacons should take part in hunting (as is reported in the Decretals under the heading of the council of Aureliensis).[9] And Saint Augustine
declared the art of hunting to be the most evil of all, as did Bernard [of
Clairvaux].[10] Jerome on Psalm 90 [Vg.; Psalm 91, EVV] states: "Esau was
a hunter because he was a sinner, and we do not find anywhere in the holy
scriptures any hunter who was holy. We find fishermen who are holy."[11]
These authorities are pertinent, reverend bishop, because Martin Luther—
priest, theologian, and monk—has become a hunter. He does not pursue
wild boars, stags, or little mules through fields, groves, and sunny meadows.
Instead, an innocent man is hunted: Hieronymus Emser, conspicuous in
God's church for his integrity, wisdom, and learning. And he hunts him

6. *Hieronymus Emser: De disputatio Lipsicensi, quantum ad Boemos obiter deflexa
est,* CCath 4 (Münster: Aschendorff, 1921), 29–40.

7. In an earlier exchange of pamphlets, both Luther and Eck had accused the other
of seeking, through the Leipzig Disputation, his own glory rather than God's. See Eck's
Expurgatio adversus criminationes F. Martini Lutter (1519) and Luther's counter-blast,
the *Epistola super Expurgatione Ecciana* (1519), *passim*. This dedication was clearly
meant to remove any doubts about Eck's priorities.

8. Johann von Schleinitz (c. 1470–1532) served as bishop of Meissen from 1518
until his death. He was to become an implacable foe of Luther's. See Traugott Bautz, ed.,
Biographisch-Bibliographisches Kirchenlexikon 9 (Herzberg: Bautz, 1995), cols. 271–72.

9. Marginal note: "Concilia." Eck's slightly mangled reference is to the synod of
Eliberitanum (Elvira), near Granada, which took place in the early fourth century. Eck
has taken the chain of anti-hunting references that follows from canon law.

10. Marginal note: "Augu[stinus]." For the reference, see Gratian's Decrees, Pars I:
D. 86, c. 9, in Emil Friedberg, ed., *Corpus iuris canonici*, 2 vols. (Leipzig: Tauchnitz,
1879–81), 1:300.

11. Marginal note: "Hiero[nymus]." For the reference, see Gratian's Decrees, Pars I:
D. 86, c. 11, in *Corpus iuris canonici* 1:300.

not with baying dogs nor with slavering Molossian hounds, but with miserable writings, slanderous words, impudent insults, trifles, nonsense, lies, and other fearful monstrosities of this sort.[12] For by these arts—detraction, slander, and satire—Luther intends to make his name great, regardless of his order and his vows.

You ask, most worthy prelate, "Why does Luther sharpen his Theonine tooth against my priest, a man known for honesty and sound morals?"[13] I reply as follows. Your neighbors, the schismatic and heretical Bohemians (I do not speak here of the faithful Bohemians, who are worthy of all praise), think that they have found a champion of their errors. They pestered God with their little prayers in public for Luther to emerge from the Leipzig Disputation victorious over me. But God does not hear sinners. They even infiltrated some men of their own type to attend the Leipzig Disputation. Luther then said, at the urging of these most villainous sycophants, that some of the Hussite articles condemned by the Council of Constance were most Christian and evangelical. But Emser, fearing [Aijʳ] that heretics and schismatics would have cause to insult the faithful or to congratulate themselves on having found such a champion, sent a letter to the administrator of the Catholic Church in Prague, by which this good man, a most faithful upholder of the truth of the faith we hold in common, might have something with which to encourage and stir up his brethren and suppress the vainglorious boasting of the schismatics.[14] But Emser wrote with such seriousness and modesty that no good and prudent man could disapprove of his writing. Yet how did Luther respond to this? If he were concerned with saving as many souls as he has sent to their destruction, he ought to have been extremely grateful. But the impatient friar, stirred up by his customary malice, wrote biliously against him, and the matter descended into tragedy and fable. In so impudently hunting this Aegocerota, against all brotherly love, he also exposed our faith to Bohemian ridicule.[15] Other Wittenbergers

12. Marginal note: "Luther's custom."

13. Eck alludes to a verse from Horace, in which the "Theonine tooth" indicated sharp, insulting wit. If the expression refers to a satirist or wit, no firm identification with any known Theon of antiquity can be established. See *Epistles* 1.18.82 in Horace, *Satires, Epistles and Ars Poetica* (London: Heinemann, 1926), 374.

14. Marginal note: "Why Emser wrote."

15. Eck here echoes the name-calling of the Emser-Luther dispute. Luther had referred to Emser as a wild goat (*aegoceros* in Latin), which he had resolved to hunt. This image was inspired by Emser's heraldic arms, prominently featuring a wild goat, which appeared on the title page of his published letter. Emser would eventually repay Luther in kind by referring to him as the bull (*Stier* in German) of Wittenberg: see the translation of Emser's *To the Bull in Wittenberg* in this volume. Eck (who like Emser was a secular priest) instead chose to draw attention to Luther's status as a friar, referring to

wrote most mordantly against me with weapons dipped in poison.[16] But they always say, "Do not touch me" [John 20:17] and refuse to be engaged with in the slightest. But then this monk, the most biting of all, readied himself to hunt me as well. But he will need dogs to catch me, for he cannot follow my tracks. I have determined to destroy this hunt of Luther's[17] and to entangle him in his own snares, ropes, and nets, putting my hope in him who will deliver us "from the snare of the hunters and from a sharp word."[18]

Luther claims to marvel that Emser has become his champion, by excusing him from Eck's accusation that he [Luther] had championed the Bohemian faction. But Emser, in his letter, had no intention of championing the lying monk. Rather, concerned for the position of the Bohemian Catholics vis-à-vis the schismatics, he explained that Luther had condemned the Bohemians' break with the Roman church. Therefore, Emser is the champion of the faith, not of Luther. He should not be compared with Joab. And utterly intolerable is this comparison: on the basis of such a serious, sincere, and Christian letter, Luther dares to equate this blameless and upright priest to the traitor Judas.[19] This man, commissioned in the army of Christ, wrote for the benefit of the faith, for the encouragement of the faithful, and for the destruction of schismatic error. But the Cuculla in his festering malice ascribes it to Emser's "envy," who out of hatred for Luther gave his soul to the devil. What will this unrestrained monk not dare to do? [Aijᵛ] Emser certainly had no wish to harm anyone in his letter, but to be of use to the faithful. Yet the Bardocuculla attacks him with enough acerbity to challenge Lucian himself.[20] In typical fashion Luther quite histrionically jests that Emser has left his wild goat without hay, and that therefore his pedigree must be faulty. This is the sort of silly game any fool can play with any prince, no matter how noble. But believe me, Luther, Emser can put hay on his horns when the need arises.[21]

---

him in this pamphlet as "Cucullus" ("the cowl-bearer") after his habit. Another insulting name, "Bardocucullus," referred to a longer variant of the cowl of Gallic ("*bardic*") origin. The gender shift to "Cuculla/Bardocuculla" was a further insult, and reflected Luther's own alternative nickname for Emser—"*aegocerota*," or wild nanny-goat.

16. This is presumably a reference to Melanchthon, whom Eck attacked in his pamphlet *Excusatio Eckij: ad ea quae falso sibi Philippus Melanchton . . . super theologica disputatione Lipsica adscripsit* (1519).

17. Marginal note: "The reason for writing."

18. Marginal note: Ps [90:3, Vg.; 91:3, EVV].

19. Marginal note: "Luther should be compared to a slanderer."

20. Lucian of Samosata was a satirist of the second century famed for his biting wit.

21. Marginal note: "Emser's Aegoceros." The wordplay concerning hay and horns refers to the heraldic arms that appeared on the title page of Emser's *The Leipzig Disputation*. An accompanying verse declared Emser's wild goat to be *sine foenu*—without

Then he imagines that he is "between a rock and a hard place." But I know that he has already been swallowed by Scylla and Charybdis, when he was forced to concede to me the title of champion of Catholic truth and pass on the torch.[22] God grant that when a favorable judgment is issued by the University of Paris, he will admit defeat (not to Eck, for I do not seek my own glory, but to the truth) and leave off misleading simple Christians and filling them with errors.[23] He seems to appoint himself master and head of all the faithful, when he says, "My Christ lives and reigns."[24] That is true. But Luther will feel this "living and reigning" even more clearly, when Christ punishes him for the many heresies, scandals, and perverse doctrines he has caused to arise in the church—unless he should repent. How dare Luther suggest that Christ is the author of this insane hunting and cursing? As if our gentle master would ever teach such unrestrained cursing and abrasive slander!

Then he says, "My Emser, I shall ignore your false flattery and your Judas kiss." He dared to say the same thing of me, falsely, namely that at Leipzig I had not cited any texts from holy scripture and could not deal with those that were cited. But once the disputation proceedings, taken down by extremely accurate notaries, are published, the verdict of the famed University of Paris will reveal how falsely the arrogant friar has spoken. Then he argued that Emser, by calling him "Catholic," wished to prevent Lutheran doctrines from being approved by the Bohemians.[25] In objecting on the basis of *partibus ex puris*—a schoolboy error—the hunter creates for himself an imaginary syllogism, purely so that he can attack Emser the more freely.[26] But the candid reader will understand Emser's letter well enough:

hay. This was an allusion to the ancient practice of covering the horns of fierce bulls with straw to prevent damage or injury. It achieved proverbial status through Horace's line, "He has straw on his horns—run far away!" (*Satires* I:4, 33). Luther's implication was that a truly noble heraldic beast would be undomesticated and therefore have hay on its horns.

22. Here Eck refers back to Luther's reply to Emser, taking a hypothetical admission of defeat at face value. See WA 2:660.7–9.

23. The text reads "*deus dei*," but this must be a typesetter's slip for "*deus det*" ("May God grant"). This error was retained in the second edition. Marginal note: "What Eck seeks."

24. Marginal note: "Christ reigns." See WA 2:660.18.

25. Marginal note: "Luther described by Emser as Catholic."

26. The "puerorum *partibus ex puris*" fallacy of which Eck accuses Luther was to make the first statement of a syllogism of particular rather than universal application: putting the universal statement, "all men are mortal," first will lead to a valid syllogism, but putting the particular statement, "Socrates is a man," first will not. The fallacy was usually designated "*ex puris particularibus (nihil sequitur)*," but Eck may have had the version cited by Peter of Spain in mind, "*Partibus ex puris sequitur nil*." See Petrus

he did not want heretics to insult the faithful by boasting that they have the Catholic doctor Luther as a champion of their faction, and so he reported how insistent Luther was in denying the fact at Leipzig.

Luther then accuses Emser of using as a touchstone the principle that "whatever [Aiij^r] pleases Bohemians is heretical."[27] With lies like this Luther inverts and corrupts the words of a priest of God. It is how he treats holy scriptures as well. Emser never said any such thing in his letter. It is all in Luther's dreams, so that with the greater shamelessness he can insult an innocent man. This is how the boastful Thraso struts and captures the public ear.[28] We know well enough that no one is so weak (or so erroneous) in spirit that nothing that is good can please him, as Emser and Bede state.[29] For this reason the Bardomonachus should attribute his inventions not to "Eckian or Emserian dialectic" but to Lutheran ravings and lies.[30]

We need not defend ourselves against "reasoning" of this sort.[31] But he invents this foolishness and then attributes it to us, so that he can pass himself off as a learned man and us as mere blockheads. It is idiotic to ask, as you do, why you are not equally known as "the champion of the Jews."[32] I answer Luther thus: if I had found him describing any articles of the Jews, that had been condemned by the church, as "Catholic," I would have described him as being a champion of the Jews, as much as I described him as a champion of the Bohemians. So it is in vain that he keeps harping on the fact that everything that pleases the Bohemians is heretical, and everything that displeases them is Catholic. No one could come to that conclusion unless they were as thick as a plank, just as Luther is.

He says that letters are sent to him from various parts of the world by distinguished supporters of his arrogance, begging him not to recant. They will soon see for themselves how fully this makes them "champions of error" as well. For it is not only those who do evil but those who consent, who are

---

Hispanus, *Summulae logicales* (Hildesheim: Ohms, 1981), 122.

27. Marginal note: "What pleases the Hussites." See WA 2:661.24–27.

28. Thraso was the braggart soldier in Terence's comedy *The Eunuch.*

29. Marginal note: "Bede." The Venerable Bede had declared that heretics typically include orthodox truth in their writings, in order to snare the unwary into accepting their falsehoods: "*nulla porro falsa doctrina est, quae non aliqua vera intermisceat.*" See Bede's commentary on Luke 17:12 in J. A. Giles, ed., *Venerabilis Bedae Commentaria in Scripturas Sacras* (London: Whittaker, 1844), 5:244–45.

30. WA 2:661.27–31. "*Bardomonachus*" is a play on "*bardocucullus*" (see above). Luther was of course an Augustinian friar, not a monk, but the insult allows Eck to align himself with humanist criticism of monastic obscurantism.

31. WA 2:662.1.

32. WA 2:662.5f.

worthy of death.[33] For Emser was moved to write not by mere suspicion but by factual evidence. It is notorious that the Bohemians offered public prayers for Luther. It is notorious and evident that they rejoiced over Luther. It is notorious that they sent Luther congratulatory letters. This barrack-room lawyer ought to have remained silent rather than exclaim that theologians oppose heresy only out of fear and mistrust.[34] This mighty hunter Nimrod (whom the interlinear gloss on Gen 10 describes as "a deceiver of souls") invents his prey at will.[35] And so he hunts goat-deer and other such figments of his imagination.

False also is the claim that theologians use two points of reference, namely what pleases heretics and what displeases them.[36] But it is true that what the all too puffed up and arrogant monk said at the Leipzig Disputation—that some Hussite articles [Aiij^v] condemned by the holy general Council of Constance are most Christian and evangelical—is a sacrilege and a diabolical championing of the errors of heretics. What faithful person does not understand that this will only please the heretics and let them boast, while insulting Catholics?[37]

This is what Luther, the new doctor of grammatico-theology, teaches with his new theology: that he is the one and only true theologian, while Eck and others are not theologians. The Bardocuculla once again hallucinates that I have no knowledge of scripture.[38] In his usual, histrionic, manner, he accused me of having adduced no arguments for three weeks other than from the Hussite articles. The masters of Leipzig University and all future readers of the disputation proceedings will recognize that as slanderous invention.

Then the scheming hunter unleashes a Molossian hound. He alleges that when Master Emser wrote, he did not condemn all Luther's teachings but only those erroneous ones that please the Bohemians, which are falsely attributed to Luther.[39] But Master Emser never put this in his letter. Luther dreamt this while sleeping on his straw bed. But let us examine the horned dilemma of this horned hunter. He posits that Emser wished to say that other teachings had pleased the Bohemians than those that they had read in Luther's books, and that Luther published half-baked and erroneous

33. Marginal note: "Paul to the Romans" [Rom 1:32].

34. WA 2:662.24–28.

35. Marginal note: "On the book of Ge[nesis]."

36. WA 2:662.33–36.

37. Marginal note: "Why the Hussites still persist."

38. WA 2:663.3.

39. WA 2:663:6–8. Marginal note: "Luther's erroneous teachings."

books and sermons and circulated them to seduce the poor people.[40] Emser, however, makes these claims nowhere in his letter. Luther invented them in order to create his horned argument by lying—I mean "hunting." Luther says, if it is true that the Bohemians support his teachings, and if Emser claims that they do so wrongly, because Luther has refused to champion the Bohemians, then one of two things follows: either Emser is an impudent liar or Luther must revoke his teachings.[41] But David says, "I will break the horns of sinners but the horns of the righteous shall be lifted up."[42] Therefore, this mighty hunter's goat horns will be broken, for it is certain that Emser has not lied.[43] But let us see if Luther has not lied. He denies that he is the champion of the Bohemians, and yet he both says and writes that the most damnable articles of the Hussites are "most Christian." This he has repeated so often with his blaspheming mouth that the monk dares to write this quite shamelessly, despite the fact that I proved that such a statement amounted to defending the heresy of Hus. He writes that he wishes that his words might be pleasing [Aiv^r] to Bohemians and even to Turks and Jews. It is certain that they are, at least when you show contempt for the Roman pontiff and make him equal in status to that of any little mass-priest.[44] But what praise, Luther, might be pleasing to the wicked? And what will you do, if you are also found well-pleasing to the devil, who prowls around like a lion, seeking whom he may devour [1 Pet 5:8]? But he raises another horn which, as in Daniel, makes war with the saints.[45] If the Bohemians are of the same mind as me, he says, then they are of the right mind.[46] On the contrary, I say if the Bohemians are of the same mind as you, then they are of the same mind as they have always been. (Or does he deny that the Bohemians are heretics? I hear that he has been pouring out poison of this

40. WA 2:663.9–11.

41. WA 2:663.11–14.

42. Marginal note: Ps [74:11, Vg.; 75:11, EVV].

43. Here Eck further develops Luther's notion of himself as the hunter and Emser as a goat in a playful but rather confusing way. Alluding to the common notion of the "horns of a dilemma" (two equally unacceptable alternatives between which a disputant must choose), Eck describes Luther's dilemma as "goat-horned" (*capricornus*). Again, Eck's description of Luther as "a mighty hunter" (*robustus venator*) equates him to Nimrod (Gen 10:9), where the description is not complimentary.

44. In his *Additio*, Luther argued that the monarchical high priesthood of Aaron found its fulfilment in the New Testament in Christ's priestly office, not in the Petrine succession (see WA 2:669.24–34). For Eck, this relegated the pope to the status of an ordinary mass-priest (*sacerdos sacrificulus*).

45. Marginal note: Dan [7:21].

46. WA 2:663.27.

sort along with his friend Philipp Melanchthon.[47] "It is no heresy to disbe-
lieve indelible character, transubstantiation and the like":[48] this is how the
Wittenbergers argue, so that among them are no heretics, even though they
say that in the holy sacrament of the altar one eats the element of bread,
just as one does ordinary food!)[49] Therefore, this foolish hunter confuses
Bohemian and Catholic articles, and the rejected and the condemned. So
it is certain that the Bohemians boast that in these articles, in which they
dissent from the Catholic Church, they have Luther as their champion—and
indeed that he is the most Hussite of them all.[50]

There is no need for Master Emser to be granted "a memory of Eckian proportions" in order to enable him to remember his own line of argument.[51] His own powers of memory, together with his genius and erudition,
easily overshadow Luther's. May you be a witness, Bishop Johann, most
beloved of God, of the powers of memory that Emser demonstrated when
he preached so fluently at your consecration. Eck could, however, afford to
spare Emser such memory as Luther's colleague Karlstadt possesses—and
still have a better memory than Luther![52] (But any glory or honor for my
powers of memory should be accorded not to me but to the God who made
me.)

Luther is a dreamer. Not the one of whom the patriarchs said, "Behold,
a dreamer comes,"[53] but he of whom the Lord God said, "Do not listen to
the words of that dreamer."[54] He dreams that Master Emser wishes that
the Bohemians might boast of their foreign doctrines and errors in Luther's name. I see no such thing in Emser's letter. But he would detest that

47. Eck had been involved in a quarrel with Melanchthon as a result of the latter's
report on the Leipzig Disputation addressed to Johannes Oecolampadius, which had
been critical of Eck.

48. This thesis is cited verbatim from the list of propositions debated by Melanchthon as part of his examination for the degree of *baccalaureus biblicus*. This disputation
took place on September 9, 1519. See Robert Stupperich, ed., *Melanchthons Werke in
Auswahl*, 1:25, ll.1–2.

49. Marginal note: "It is a new heresy to believe that one can deny transubstantiation without heresy."

50. Marginal note: "Champion of the Hussites."

51. WA 2:664.4–5.

52. Marginal note: "Karlstadt's memory." Eck criticized Karlstadt for wishing to
consult his books during the Leipzig Disputation rather than relying on memory. See
Erwin Iserloh, *Johannes Eck (1486–1543): Scholastiker, Humanist, Kontroverstheologe*,
Katholisches Leben und Kirchenreform im Zeitalter der Glaubensspaltung 41 (Münster: Aschendorff, 1981), 34.

53. Marginal note: Gen [37:19].

54. Marginal note: Deut [13:3].

Lutherine boasting, which claims that "many very Christian French, Italian, English, German, and Spanish people" also boast of his teachings.[55] So what? Birds of a feather flock together, and everyone has their own poison.[56] On the contrary, most gracious bishop, I respond that I am ready to dispute Luther's errors at the universities of Rome, Naples, Bologna, Paris, [Aiv^v] Toulouse, Louvain, Cologne, or Vienna.[57] Let Luther decide the location and the procedural details. If I lose, I shall pay all the costs, plus the expenses incurred by the Lutheran side. But it is Luther who will lose. He alone should revoke his errors, lest there be scandals in the church of God, and lest the people of God be led astray. This is the royal way by which I shall hunt Luther so that, in accordance with Jeremiah's prophecy, the wild desert donkey—one should have said "the donkey in the desert"—may become a lion's prey.[58] And thus it will become plain which one of us is the "son (and lord) of darkness."[59]

Our hunter then unleashes other hounds. Luther shamefully denies the fact that the schismatic Bohemians offered up public and daily (though profane) prayers for him, when he fought me at Leipzig, but it is true and beyond any shadow of doubt.[60] He knows this well enough. Who doubts that the Bohemians supported Luther over the specific points debated at Leipzig? Only someone more stupid than Coroebus.[61] He criticizes Emser

55. WA 2:664.20–22.

56. The Latin proverbs that Eck uses are "*mulus mulum scabit*" ("one mule scratches another," a reference to mutual flattery) and "*similes habent labra lactucas*" ("as the lips, so the lettuce").

57. Marginal note: "He will dispute." In 1516 Eck had debated at Bologna the question of whether charging interest at 5 percent was usurious and had attempted to repeat the performance at Vienna (see Erwin Iserloh, *Johannes Eck*, 20–22). He clearly thought that his stock was still high in these places.

58. This short sentence is rich in allusion and wordplay. Eck is referring principally to Sir 13:23 ("As the wild donkey is the lion's prey in the desert, so are the poor devoured by the rich"), here misattributed to the prophet Jeremiah. In Christian interpretation, the "wild donkey in the desert" (*onager in heremo*) became the *onager heremita*, a type of the hermit monk who seeks solitude in the desert. See for instance Eucherius of Lyons's *Liber de spiritalibus formulis*, a spiritual glossary of biblical terms (Eucherius of Lyon, *Commentarij in Genesim, et in libros Regum* [Rome: Paulus Manutius, 1564], 330). The term could easily be used pejoratively, especially as Jerome, for instance, glossed the depiction of Ishmael (the "wild man whose hand is against everyone and every man against him" [Gen 16:12]) as an onager. (See Paul de Lagarde, ed., *Jerome: Quaestiones hebraicae in libro Geneseos* [Leipzig: Teubner, 1868], 26, ll.14–20). Eck builds on this association of images to continue the idea of hunting, while also ridiculing Luther, who was an Augustinian "eremite" or hermit, as a donkey.

59. WA 2:664.29.

60. WA 2:664.39–665.1.

61. According to Erasmus, Coroebus was a man so lacking in wits that he undertook

for having written that Luther was "Catholic."[62] If, Luther, you consider the
name "Catholic" to be unworthy of you, then I reply that we ought to give
you a name that suits you, namely, "Hussite." Are you not already baptized
with this worthy name? But how has Master Emser sinned? He did not say
that you had defended the condemned Hussite articles (for that Hussite pu-
trefaction and filth flows from you), but that you had said (at least openly,
though perhaps you think differently in your heart) that it displeased you
that the Bohemians had broken with the unity of the church, and that in this
they had acted evilly. If deep down in his heart Master Emser really does
believe you to be a heretic, then I swear by this right hand that he is not far
from the truth. Nonetheless, he observes the tenor of your words, as they
are written, in which you deny that you are a champion of the Bohemians.
But call a halt to your poisonous hunt, while you consider this, Luther: do
those words of yours really come from the heart, or do they come only from
your lips? For it is you, Luther, who will be like that man who from the same
spring drinks water both sweet and bitter.[63] Luther calls Emser his Rufinus,
thus likening himself to Jerome.[64] If he wishes he can make himself King of
Beans![65] Rufinus, as Gennadius said, was a great doctor of the church—although I must say that, like Giovanni Pico della Mirandola, I have always
preferred Jerome to him.[66] However, it is evident that Emser is innocent and

an impossible task (to count the waves in the sea) with insufficient resources (he was
unable to count beyond five). See *Adages* 2.9.64.

62. Marginal note: "Luther honored with the name 'Catholic' by Emser." WA
2:665.8–13.

63. Luther had accused Emser of this (WA 2:665.13–14). The allusion is to Jas 3:11,
though Eck alters the image from that of a spring impossibly pouring forth both fresh
and salt water.

64. Marginal note: "Luther wishes to be Jerome." Luther makes this equation repeatedly. See WA 2:664. 6, 8, 29; 665.2, 19, 28; 666.2. The church historian Tyrannius
Rufinus (Rufinus of Aquileia, c.345–c.410) was originally a friend of Jerome's. They fell
out when Rufinus, in his preface to a translation of the work of Origen, claimed that
Jerome was strongly influenced by the Alexandrian. For Jerome, this was tantamount
to being accused of heresy. See Henry Chadwick, "Jerome and Rufinus: controversy
about Origen," in Chadwick, *The Church in Ancient Society: From Galilee to Gregory
the Great* (Oxford: Oxford University Press, 2001), 433–45. Luther believed that Emser
was accusing him of heresy under the guise of defending him from that same charge.

65. The *rex fabarum* was a lord of misrule appointed by lot at Christmas. Often
associated with educational establishments, the tradition was particularly strong at the
English universities. See John Brand, *Observations on Popular Antiquities* (London:
Knight, 1841), 1:17.

66. Marginal note: "Rufinus. Gennadius. Pico." In claiming that "*Ruffinus fuit
magna pars doctorum ecclesiae*," Eck takes a slight liberty with Gennadius of Constantinople's more modest claim: "*Rufinus, Aquileiensis ecclesiae presbyter, non minima pars
doctorum ecclesiae.*" See Ernest Cushing Richardson, ed., *Hieronymus, Liber de viris*

never [Bi^r] contradicted himself, and that this ridiculous Cucullus is just shadow-boxing. Master Emser does not persecute dream-Bohemians, but those who have set themselves against the Roman church as schismatics and heretics—unless Luther impudently declares the entire church itself to be a dream.[67] But why should he so captiously and sophistically assume that Master Emser would judge Lutheran doctrine to be true? He makes jests like this, but he will be caught by his own nets. Where—anywhere—does Emser claim your teachings to be true? I believe that if he were asked to give his considered opinion on your perverse doctrines, he would at once judge them on the basis of his learning to be sacrilegious and damnable. The madness of this Cucullus is to be marvelled at, when he claims that we will be found unjust liars for regarding the Bohemians as heretics.[68] In that case the entire Christian world would be a liar, together with the Catholics in Bohemia and others who also regard the Hussites as heretics. Luther should stop his lying accusations against a decent and learned man like Emser. There is no lie so big that it would make Luther blush to tell it. Nor does he write privately, so that the birds of the air may carry his words to Emser [Eccl 10:20].[69] But through the printing press he publishes his letter in a thousand copies. Why should he not proclaim himself a new prophet, seeing that God must have endowed him with the discretion of spirits, the mind of Christ, and the deepest divine mysteries?[70] For who has known the mind of the Lord, and who has been his counsellor [Rom 11:34]? The law and the prophets were until John the Baptist [Luke 16:16; cf. Matt 11:13].[71] But I judge that Luther, by his foul, monstrous doctrines will plumb the depths of Hell sooner than he will come to any knowledge of the discretion of spirits and of the depths of God.

Emser asserted on the authority of Bede that heretics mix truth and falsehood. Augustine, Jerome, and Gregory say the same.[72] Thus even Jan Hus, of damnable memory, did say some things that are true. But Luther rises up as if Emser had contradicted the holy Council of Constance and declared some of the Hussite articles wrongly condemned.[73] He should

---

inlustribus; Gennadius, Liber de viris inlustribus (Leipzig: Hinrichs, 1896), 67, ll.28–29.

67. Luther had accused Emser of attacking "Bohemians formed by him in his sleep" (WA 2:665.24–25).

68. WA 2:665.37.

69. WA 2:666.7.

70. Marginal note: "Luther the prophet."

71. This verse concludes, "since then, all have entered the kingdom of God violently," and Eck may have cited it as an implicit condemnation of Luther.

72. Marginal note: "Bede. Augustine. Jerome."

73. WA 2:666.12–17.

show us where Master Emser ever said this, where he is supposed to have challenged the holy council. He must think that there are others as obstinate and impudent as he, who reject the church fathers, the decrees of the Roman pontiff, and canons of the holy councils as freely, or rather as casually, as he does. But as far as I am concerned, he alleges two lies against me. First, that I showed contempt for the Council of Nicaea.[74] In this he most clearly slanders me. As [Biᵛ] was recorded by the notaries and as the whole of Leipzig knows, throughout the entire course of the disputation, not only did I never reject or contemn any council, but I never rejected any of the holy doctors. Let us consider who has more respect for the ecclesiastical doctors. Is it Luther, who rejects them so casually and elevates his own opinions over the saints of old, contrary to the final canon of Saint Clement?[75] Or is it Eck, who honors their words and venerates their authority? (I grant, however, that I do reject the teaching of a holy doctor, where it conflicts with the teaching of the majority.) The second slander is that I dared correct the Holy Spirit and re-interpret the Council of Constance.[76] This is absolutely untrue: the articles cited by me were manifestly above board. I do not believe that Luther has ever seen the declaration made by those deputed by the council to examine the articles, but I have both seen and read it. As always, Luther prefers the branches to the roots.[77] If he had seen it, he would know that although only thirty articles of Hus and Jerome of Prague were condemned, the council examined and discussed almost three times that number of errors in their writings. This appears in Henry of Piro's report.[78] Similarly, forty-five articles of John Wycliffe were condemned, but 223 articles had previously been examined at Oxford in England, a copy of all of which I have with me.[79] Luther has made a rod for his own back. If I had re-inter-

74. Marginal note: "The Council of Nicaea." WA 2:666.23–24.

75. Marginal notes: "Eck venerates the ecclesiastics whom Luther contemns" and "Clement." For the reference to Clement V, see Gratian's Decrees Pars I: D. 37, c, 14, in *Corpus iuris canonici* 1:139.

76. WA 2:666.24–25.

77. Marginal note: "Luther's knowledge." The Leipzig Disputation was portrayed by the Wittenbergers as a clash between humanists and, in Eck, a scholastic obscurantist. Here Eck portrays himself as a better humanist than Luther, who did not consult the primary sources.

78. Marginal note: "Henry of Piro." Henricus Henrici de Piro (d. 1438) was a canon lawyer trained at Cologne and Bologna, who took part in the Council of Constance. He is not to be confused with his more famous nephew, the Carthusian Henricus Brunonis de Piro (1403–1473), who was still a child when the council sat. See Robert Feenstra, "Henricus Brunonis de Piro († 1473): professeur de droit civil et Chartreux," *Tijdschrift voor Rechtsgeschiedenis* 64 (1996), 3–46, esp. 2–3.

79. Marginal note: "Wycliffe's articles."

preted even one article of the council, he would have accused me of daring
to correct the Holy Spirit, which suggests that you believe that the Council
of Constance was directed by the Holy Spirit.[80] Why therefore do you dare,
under the devil's influence, to call "most Christian and evangelical" articles
that have been condemned under the direction of the Holy Spirit? What
Erinys has seized you? What Furies drive you? What blaspheming lust has
puffed you up? The present age will judge between our writings, and future
ages will do so even more happily. For my book on *The Primacy of Peter* will
shortly appear, and daily I see quires of Luther's trifles being carried away in
boxes from perfume shops.

But let us examine the beautiful argumentation of the grammatico-
theologian. He says to Emser, "You admit that I am Catholic. If so, you must
equally admit that my teachings are Catholic."[81] But consider the case of
Cyprian, and you will soon see how mangled and invalid this statement is.
Cyprian was a Catholic martyr; but you would not regard his teaching, that
those baptized by heretics should be re-baptized [Bijʳ], as Catholic. Master
Emser was too trusting of Luther's craftiness in making out that he did not
assert his teachings obstinately and that he was prepared to recant them if
anyone could offer better. This he claimed in his writings. This he spoke
with his own mouth. And this was why Master Emser judged him to be
Catholic, even though his teachings were perverse, so Bernard.[82] Augustine
purges Cyprian from suspicion of heresy in book two of *Against the Donatists Concerning Baptism*.[83] See, reverend Bishop, how imperfect Luther's
understanding of such matters is!

When Master Emser reported that the Bohemians had in public offered up to God daily (though profane) prayers in support of Luther, Luther

80. Marginal note: "The Council of Constance." In this sentence Eck begins by referring to Luther in the third person but soon changes to the second person.

81. WA 2:667.5–6. Marginal note: "Luther's feeble inference." The word translated
"feeble" is *frigida*, the Latin for "cold," but used in this context to mean "unconvincing."
Eck had taken strong exception to Luther's use of this word to characterize the decrees
of canon law that supported papal primacy: "*probatur ex frigidissimis Romanorum
Pontificorum decretis*." See Luther, *Disputatio et excusatio adversus criminationes D. J.
Eckii* (1519) (WA 2:161.35–36). This clear allusion to an earlier dispute he had had with
Luther suggests that Eck may have prepared at least some of the marginal notes himself.

82. The definition of heresy in canon law was not doctrinal error alone, but the
obstinate assertion of error. Among many iterations of this point in Bernard of Clairvaux can be found this one from Ep. 193: "[Abelard] proves himself to be a heretic not
so much by his error as by his pertinacious defence of error." See Jean Mabillon, ed., *S.
Bernardi abbatis primi Clarae-Vallensis opera omnia, nova editio*, in PL 182:359.

83. Marginal note: "Augu." See Augustine, "De baptismo contra Donatistas," in
Michael Petschenig, ed., *Sancti Aureli Augustini scripta contra Donatistas*, CSEL 51
(Vienna: Tempsky; Leipzig: Freytag, 1908), 177–78.

became incandescent with his customary rage.[84] He reproved Emser for
calling sacred things profane and divine worship mendacious. This doctor
of grammatico-theology seems unaware that the holy things of any sect
should be called "most execrable." But every Catholic is well aware of the
solemnities by which heretics celebrate, confect, baptize, and so on—these
"holy" things are in reality profane, as the Lord said through the prophet,
"I will curse your blessings."[85] Master Emser's words ring loud and clear,
but Luther corrupts and perverts them with such calumny of God to satisfy both his envy and his lust for blasphemy. Why, Luther, do you boast
that you pray for Eck and Emser?[86] Christ commanded, "Let not your left
hand know what your right is doing."[87] Yet here he is, boasting of prayers
said by him for his enemies. I made diligent inquiries whether Luther ever
celebrated Mass at Leipzig, since many great feast days occurred during the
disputation. I cannot be certain that he celebrated Mass even once during
these three weeks, though in this respect he is to be praised, if he abstained
in observance of the *sententia* of the Supreme Pastor, Leo X.[88] But my prayer
is that Luther's prayers do me no harm: God, the searcher of our hearts [Cf.
Rom 8:27], knows what is in our prayers for one another. But Luther invites
prayers for his errors even from the Turks.[89] Such are his intercessors and
such are his doctrines—erroneous, impure, temerarious, scandalous, and
heretical. This vainglorious Thraso, this sacrilegious huntsman, boasts that
he has captured the Aegocerota by tracking him with Molossian hounds, as
once he was tracked by Albanian dogs (which the histories tell us are the
most ferocious of all).[90] If only that had happened! This huntsman has so

84. WA 2:667.10–13.

85. Marginal note: Mal [2:2].

86. Marginal note: "Luther's boasting." The reference is to WA 2:667.12–18, where
Luther admits that "there is no one for whom I more ardently pray than for Johann
Tetzel, the author of this tragedy (may his soul rest in peace), and for you [Emser] and
for Eck and for all my adversaries." Luther spoke only of praying for his opponents, not
of saying Mass for them. Eck, as a secular priest, would naturally have associated intercession with the saying of Mass; Luther, as a religious, would perhaps more naturally
associate regular intercession with the daily offices, outside a eucharistic context.

87. Marginal note: Matt [6:3].

88. Marginal note: "Luther is to be praised." I have not been able to identify the
sententia to which Eck refers.

89. WA 2:667.18–20.

90. WA 2:667.22–25. Several ancient historians, including Pliny, Strabo, and Solinus, recorded that Alexander the Great was given one or more dogs of extraordinary
fierceness and size by the king of Albania (not the modern Balkan state but a kingdom
bordering the Caspian Sea). It was reported that an Albanian dog was able to kill a lion
or even an elephant. See Solinus, *Polyhistor* (Cologne: Cervicornus, 1520), xxxixv.

far breathed only threats, or has become a goat-stag, with a horn upon his
nose.[91] Whoever fears him should flee: this Lutheran evil spews forth its
immodesty and all kinds of disease, wishing to capture, disembowel, and
flay our Aegocerota.

But Master Emser, as befits someone who is outstandingly learned in
sound theology, provides well-rounded arguments in his letter to persuade
[Bijʳ] and convince the reader that primacy over the church is by divine
right, just as much as it was in the synagogue under Aaron. This argument
is adequately developed in our book *The Primacy of Peter*. There is no need
for me to provide additional help for someone who is already victorious; but
I consider that, on the question of the upper and the lower millstone, Master
Emser was following the Interlinear Gloss, which interprets the lower millstone as fear and therefore as the Old Law, since it was a law based on fear.[92]
(I remember reading a great deal about this. However, this hunter, with
his biting hounds, needs to be captured today.) For in truth the synagogue
was passive and weighed down with great burdens,[93] when compared with
the church, the bride of Christ.[94] So Master Emser is right to state that, as
Aaron was appointed prelate over all the priests, so in the church (which is
greater than the synagogue) there should be a high priest set above all others. But then envy enters the heart of the obsessed Luther, so that he finds
fault with Emser for not making the new priesthood superior to the old, the
fulfillment of the sign superior to the sign itself, or the truth superior to
the prefiguration of the truth.[95] But these are mere dreams and nightmares,
which you will not read in Emser's letter. Luther has willfully invented them
out of his disease-ridden imagination. Why can it not be that primacy over
priests once existed in figure and in sign and exists now in fullness and
truth? To this, Luther has no answer other than insults, injuries, and strange
verbal monstrosities that allow him to evade the truth and in his mindless
folly to drink deep of the cup of vanity. This is the whole reason why he
avoids the judgment of his case: for he fears that his cunning, trickery, and
impostures, which now he wretchedly covers with his excessive verbiage
of scurrilous insults, will be exposed when subjected to judgment.[96] The

91. The goat-stag (*hircocervus*) was an example used by the classical philosophers of
a creature that could be imagined but did not exist. Luther had already accused Emser
of being a non-entity in this way. Eck repays the compliment, adding for good measure
a rhinoceros horn to the already composite animal.
92. Marginal note: Deut [24:6].
93. Marginal note: "The Synagogue."
94. Marginal note: "The Church."
95. WA 2:668.15–29.
96. Marginal note: "Luther fears a judgment."

statement of the apostle, that Christ is the true high pontiff and Aaron but a shadow, is very well known to us.[97] But Emser developed this idea to argue that though the primacy then existed only in a shadow of what was to come, it was nonetheless a true primacy. The magnificence of priestly vestments is merely an outward matter, though I certainly do not disapprove of the use of costly garments by priests in divine worship.[98]

The hypocrite then ties a Gordian knot: in the Old Testament there was one high priest, but now there are two, Christ and his vicar.[99] Luther raves like this in a continual delirium. As if a master and his representative should be counted as two! It in no way compromises Christ's headship but rather complements it, allowing him to communicate with the faithful in a tangible manner.[100] Then Luther most damnably [Biij^r] insults the "new theologians" for disdaining to regard the holy Son of God as a monarch.[101] There never was such a theologian, and no one ever disdained any such thing—outside the imputations of this manufacturer of lies. He then adds an argument worthy of Lutheran ingenuity, for I know the man well, who misleads himself and his supporters with sophisms like this: "It is impossible," he declares, "for all people on earth to seek to have their bishops confirmed at Rome."[102] O Luther, most stupid of men! Who was ever so foolish as to say that, by divine right, all bishops ought to be confirmed at Rome, in the way Luther understands it? But I shall consider this matter in my book *The Primacy of Peter*, where I deal with Luther's fantasies at greater length.

97. Marginal note: Heb [7–9].

98. In his original letter, Emser had argued that the divine institution of the Aaronic high priesthood was confirmed by the fact that Christ himself did not blush to subject himself to the high priest Caiaphas, even to the point of death. Luther objected to this line of argument on the grounds that it accorded too much honor to the Old Testament priesthood and not enough to the high priest of the New Testament, namely Christ. Emser had also cited the gorgeous decoration worn by Aaronic priests as proof of divine institution: "Therefore, it cannot be denied that Aaron's pontificate was instituted by God. And it was added by the same God, to the glory and ornament of that priesthood, that it should be adorned with robes twice-dyed in purple, the finest linen, and silver, jewels, and gold." To this, Luther objected that such pomp and ceremony was inappropriate to the followers of Christ, who urged those who would be great to be the least of all. For Emser's argument, see Thurnhofer, *Hieronymus Emser: De disputatio Lipsicensi, quantum ad Boemos obiter deflexa est*, 37. For Luther's response, see WA 2:668.21–669.16. (Cited above, n5.)

99. Reading "*sum, sacerdos*" as "*sum[mus] sacerdos*." For Luther's argument that the Aaronic priesthood cannot presage both Christ's primacy and the pope's, see WA 2:669.24–29.

100. Marginal note: "Christ the head of the Church."

101. WA 2:669.29–34.

102. WA 2:669.35–39.

This monk needs a dose of mind-medicine, for he is constantly raving in perpetual madness of this sort. For instance, Master Emser said that the papacy is established as much by the interpretation of sacred councils as by the command of Christ to "Feed my sheep."[103] At this, Luther goes completely mad, raving because he denies any council created the divine right of the papacy.[104] But Emser never said that a council created the divine right of the papacy. He said that a council *declared* the papacy to be by divine right. In the same way, the Council of Nicaea declared the Son's consubstantiality with the Father, against Arius's treachery: it did not create the consubstantiality.[105] This is why the very learned Master Emser said that councils had declared the papal monarchy to be by divine right. To this he quickly added the divine institution itself, namely the command, "Feed my sheep." [John 21:17] But there is much more about that verse in my book *The Primacy of Peter*. Because I deal appropriately with his carping sophistries in that book, I shall not detail here Luther's perverse insults or his interpretations, which are contemptuous of all archbishops and bishops.[106] But I wish that you, most worthy Bishop Johann, and all you bishops, who are most beloved of God, may continue to discharge the great spiritual government committed to you, in such a way that this upstart monk will never be able to convict those invested with the pontifical regalia of either tyranny or neglect. But you will see the extent of Luther's ignorance set out in my book *The Primacy of Peter*. And if God grants him a better spirit, he will repent of the blasphemy, the impudence, and the error of his farrago of words.

Next, this mad huntsman makes a mountain out of a molehill (or rather out of his mouldy little thoughts), namely that the church of Christ existed for twenty years after the crucifixion before the church at Rome was founded.[107] But this is dealt with in my book *The Primacy of Peter*, where the falsity of his assumptions is first detected, and then the weakness of his arguments is utterly [Biijᵛ] laid bare and reduced to ashes—except perhaps in the island of the Hussites, which is defended by such enchantments that it is not possible to burn it by fire.[108] Then Luther solemnly charges Mas-

---

103. CCath 4:37–38.

104. WA 2:670.1–5.

105. Marginal note: "Nicaea." The word Eck uses for the consubstantiality formula is the Greek word *homoousion* transliterated.

106. WA 2:670.7–18. Here Luther argues that the dominical command to Peter, "Feed my sheep," implies a ministry of service to the Christian flock, not domination and primacy over it.

107. WA 2:670.37–671.4.

108. Marginal note: "The Hussite island incombustible." The designation of landlocked Bohemia as an island of Hussites is startling, but it would have rung true for

ter Emser with self-contradiction, for first declaring Peter's primacy to be by divine right, and then by saying that in human affairs matters proceed slowly.[109] Friar, remove the stupidity from your shaven head! Can you not see that the dignity of the Roman pontiff is a human matter, but that this power has been sustained by divine right? And do these facts contradict one another, you "weeder and sower of villainies?"[110] For this power is indeed a human matter in that it pertains to human salvation, but the granting of this power is a divine matter. The histrionic huntsman considers it unworthy that Master Emser should give the example of the penitent thief.[111] Perhaps it was not the most apposite example, but I can prove his point that delay does not always make things worse. Caiaphas and Balaam are terrifying examples for Luther, who resists with such singularity and obstinacy the truth revealed by the Holy Spirit in sacred scripture and the sacred councils, so that it can be said of him that he is the singular wild beast who has ravaged the Lord's vineyard.[112]

German Catholics. In his coloured broadsheet map for pilgrims to Rome, printed at the turn of the century, Erhard Etzlaub represented Bohemia as a tinted circle in the middle of German lands, carefully demarcated by forests and clearly a destination to be avoided by pious travellers. See Etzlaub, *Das ist der Rom-Weg von meylen zu meylen* ([Nuremberg], c. 1500). Johannes Cochlaeus (who would later rank alongside Eck as one of Luther's most dogged opponents) also drew attention to Bohemia's isolation in his historical geography of Germany written for schoolboys: "The Bohemians are surrounded on all sides by German peoples, but they themselves do not speak German. . . . The Hercynian forest encircles it completely, like a natural wall. . . . The region itself is defended by the might of noblemen, innumerable fortresses, and even the very forest, so that it is impossible to root out this treacherous progeny of heretics who—in addition to their other thoroughly abominable and execrable practices—even frequent public baths, where they defile themselves in promiscuity." See Karl Langosch, ed., *Johannes Cochlaeus: Brevis Germanie descriptio (1512)* (Darmstadt: Wissenschaftliche Buchgesellschaft, 1960), 110–12.

109. WA 2:671.5–7.

110. Eck's insult, "*sartor satorque malorum*," seems to be a misremembering or adaptation of "*sartor satorque scelerum*," from Plautus's comedy *The Captives* (Act III, scene 5), so I have shown it as a quotation. "Sartor" here is a contracted form of "*sarritor*," unrelated to the more common word "*sartor*" meaning "patcher" or "mender." See Charlton A. Lewis and Charles Short, eds., *A Latin Dictionary* (Oxford: Oxford University Press, 1879), s.v., "Sartor I. and II."

111. WA 2:671.14–15.

112. Marginal note: Ps [79:14, Vg.; 80:13, EVV]. "Singularity" is a charge Eck frequently levelled at Luther in his writings of 1519. This reference to the *singularis ferus* ("the singular wild beast" in the Douai-Rheims translation of the Vulgate) is an early adumbration of the preamble of the papal bull of condemnation against Luther, which Eck would be entrusted with promoting in Germany in the following year, *Exsurge Domine*.

In his usual way, Luther also falsely accuses Master Emser of saying that Peter's primacy was idle for twenty years. This he never said. Rather, Emser proposed that it was no hindrance to the Roman church, if for twenty years Peter were delayed from giving it its preeminence. Who but a demented person could infer from this that Peter's primacy was idle, when it was being exercised in Jerusalem and then in Antioch? (There is more about this in my book *The Primacy of Peter*.) But to this he adds the destructive argument, which he did not shrink from adducing at Leipzig either, that Saint Peter suffered himself to be sent, as an inferior, in Acts 8[:14].[113] Such was the argument of the most treacherous Arius, when he declared the Son to be less than the Father, because he was sent by the Father.[114] Luther appealed to the invalid defence that Peter gave an account of himself in Acts 10, as if a superior must never explain himself, even for the avoidance of scandal.[115] This is how the doctor of grammatico-theology mistreats holy scripture. And this is how our falsifier corrupts a third text of holy scripture, when blasphemously he dares to assert that Peter's judgment was altered or confirmed on the authority of James [Acts 15:13–21].[116] Not even a grammatical theologian could take this to mean that any aspect of Peter's judgment was altered. Jerome put the matter well when he said that Peter was the principal in this decree concerning the Jewish laws.[117]

I consider unimportant the jests that this buffoon spews forth concerning these wrongly and most foully understood places of scripture. [Biv^r] Let Luther meet me in a debate before judges, and then we will see whose opinions concerning the divine right are more in accordance with holy scripture.[118] For Luther is a fine debater when he has a pen in his hand, with which he can defend his poisonous propositions; but he runs away from the prospect of judgment. His most impudent lie of all is his claim that his proposition concerning Peter's primacy is identical with that of the Council of Nicaea.[119] Here he is a bigger liar than any Thessalonian or Cretan, because he has never even seen the canons of the Nicene council. I, on the other hand, prove in my book *The Primacy of Peter* that the Roman

113. Marginal note: "Luke" (as author of the Acts of the Apostles). WA 2:671.30–31.

114. Marginal note: "Arius."

115. WA 2:671.31–32.

116. WA 2:671.32–35.

117. Marginal note: "Jerome." Here Eck quotes verbatim Jerome's words from Letter 112, ch. 8, to Augustine. See Isidore Hilberg, ed., *Sancti Eusebii Hieronymi Epistulae. Pars II: Epistulae LXXI–CXX*, CSEL 60 (Vienna: F. Tempsky; Leipzig: G. Freytag, 1912), 375, l.28; 376, l.1.

118. Marginal note: "Eck's offer."

119. WA 2:672.5–6.

pontiff was granted primacy over the universal church by the authority of the Nicene council.[120] In the book I refer the candid reader, for the better comprehension of Luther's lie, to the canons of that council, to the epistle of Julius I against the Arians, and to the acts of the Sixth Council of Carthage. With equal mendacity he croaks that I avoided this point at Leipzig.[121] The whole of Leipzig knows this remark to be pure Lutheran, that is, pure fiction. This is why I have shut his wicked mouth, with respect to the holy Council of Nicaea, in my book *The Primacy of Peter*.

I have often said it before and I say it again: Luther can never engage with any matter in a truly sound way, because he clings to the branches more than the roots. I met with equal arrogance, when Luther's grammarian, Philipp Melanchthon, declared that the books of Maccabees had been declared non-canonical by a formal decision of the church, when he had never so much as looked at any church canon relating to which biblical books are to be received: if they were not so arrogant and were prepared to be taught by Eck, they might learn something. If not, let them show me the canon. To my knowledge, there isn't one. He says nothing to the point when he says, "I do not fear your very strong and very noisy Eck."[122] If that is so, let us meet and dispute before judges, who will give a decision on the spot. It is equally pointless to accuse me of being unable to teach holy scripture well.[123] It is enough for Luther that he is, unfortunately, well able to teach errors, scandals, heresies, and all that is most pestilential. He boasts that he has been quite worn down by the scholastic doctors:[124] I doubt that he has ever understood even one of them. How very true are those words of Jeremiah [49:16a], "Your arrogance has deceived you."[125] But though as a scholar Luther is weak, as a biter he is strong.

Finally he gets to the nub of the matter and would show Emser that he did not spew forth at Leipzig all the material that he had at his disposal.[126] But compare his (error-strewn) book on the power of the pope with the record of the disputation, and you will see that he had indeed vomited up all that he had to say about the Acts of the Apostles and about councils.[127]

---

120. Marginal note: "The Council of Nicaea."

121. WA 2:673.34–35.

122. Marginal note: "Luther." WA 2:672.31–32.

123. WA 2:672.36–38.

124. WA 2:673.1.

125. Marginal note: "Jeremiah."

126. WA 2:673.34–36.

127. Eck is presumably referring to Luther's *Resolutio Lutheriana super propositione sua decima tertia de potestate papae* (WA 2:181–240).

Nor does it matter that this fraudulent champion lied that I presented my case against him for four days on end, [Biv^v] for the truth of the matter will be obvious when the disputation report is read, namely that that sophist and Proteus, while he was acting as respondent, cleverly took the part of opponent and turned all his stronger weapons against me, so that when finally it was his turn to defend, what little ammunition he had left was weak. I refer to the notaries' reports. With no less arrogance he plays the Cretan, when he describes my arguments as hollow and trivial, and me as unworthy of Karlstadt, who brought forth such productive answers to my "trivial" objections.[128] How dare you lie so openly, you threefold thief who deserves a good thrashing? What web of deceit is this, that you now call this man Karlstadt "productive," when you had earlier deplored his sterility? Why did you permit a man so weak, so unconvincing, and so forgetful to descend into the arena of battle? Ask anyone in Leipzig, and they will tell you about the extent of Karlstadt's ability—not his ability in learning, which is small, but his ability to read out of books, in schoolboy fashion. Both Luther and his lying will be exposed when the disputation is published. But I am absolutely convinced that Luther himself never wanted a disputation, from which he would rather have fled.[129] We know who it is who hates the light and who flees the judgment. And certainly I had hoped to hear the meaning of holy scripture set out, but instead I was forced to listen to an exposition of the Hussite articles. And I believed that I was to dispute with a Catholic and religious doctor of theology, but instead found that my business was with a Hussite.[130]

Then the plague-ridden Luther vomits up something else, daring to claim that to this day the argument concerning the Council of Nicaea has not yet been resolved, because the fathers there made a decree contrary to an article of the Council of Constance. Good God! Is there nothing that this desperate and mad monk dare not do? He characterizes the most sacred councils as making decrees that conflict and oppose each other. How contrary to the Holy Spirit, who led and taught both councils? I have already said that the Bardocuculla has never seen the decrees of Nicaea. I shall add to that and say that the primacy of the Roman church is most clearly approved by the Council of Nicaea and that the article of the Council of Constance affirmed it, as is more fully demonstrated in my book, *The Primacy of Peter.*

128. WA 2:673.36–674.7. I take *cretisat* to mean "he plays the Cretan," i.e., "he lies."
129. Marginal note: "Luther flees from disputation."
130. WA 2:674.5–10.

Here it will be evident that the Council of Nicaea is not Luther's Tydeus:[131] if he wants a champion, he would do better to ask some apostate Arian!

He abuses holy scripture with such malice, arguing that primacy among the apostles was held first by Judas and then by Matthias, that this Cuculla is worthy only of pitch, brimstone, and fire [cf. Isa 34:9].[132] Why would anyone try to follow such absurd and profane thinking? In the same way it shames me to repeat his view that the Roman [Bvʳ] pontiffs sought this primacy in order to have tyrannical power for themselves.[133] If so, by that power (which was given only for edification) they would have destroyed rather than built. This I firmly believe, with holy mother church, that Peter was constituted by Christ as pastor of the universal church. I believe that this power is also possessed by all who sit in Peter's chair. Again, I honor the Lord God's command, "You will not curse a ruler of your people, for whoever curses a prince will die."[134] It does not please me at all when an erring pontiff is flattered: he should be warned and gently corrected. For in all things, Christ is to be preferred above any mere human. So Paul reprehended Peter, and Jethro was wiser than Moses [Gal 2:11–13; Exod 18:24].

131. In his *Addition*, Luther had claimed that the Council of Nicaea was his "Tydeus" against all arguments in favor of divine right defences of Roman primacy (WA 2:674.15–16). Tydeus was a warrior whose legendary defeat of all the commanders of the city of Thebes in single combat is recalled in Book 4 of the *Iliad*. Luther's appeal to the council was based on Canon 6, which confirmed only that Rome had primacy over neighboring Italian churches "by ancient custom" (i.e., not by divine right) and recognized that the sees of Alexandria and Antioch exercised similar metropolitan jurisdiction by custom. See Giuseppe Alberigo et al., eds., *Conciliorum Oecumenicorum Decreta* (Bologna: Istituto per le Scienze Religiose, 1973), 8–9. In his *Explanation of the Thirteenth Proposition*, Luther cites as his source an ecclesiastical history (presumably one of the numerous continuations of Eusebius), thus supporting Eck's contention that Luther had not seen the text of the Nicene Council itself. Luther's summary of the canon is however accurate. See *Resolutio Lutheriana super propositione XIII de potestate papae*, 1519 (WA 2:238.3–11).

132. Marginal note: "Judas the first apostle, according to Luther." In the section of the *Addition* to which Eck refers, Luther satirizes Eck's scholastic way of arguing by proposing and defending an absurd notion following similar logic: Matthias was the last and least of the disciples; but Jesus said that the last shall be first; since Matthias replaced and therefore succeeded the traitor Judas, then Judas must have been the first and foremost disciple before him. See WA 2:674.25–675.15.

133. WA 2:675.27–30.

134. Here Eck joins to Exod 22:28 some of the wording of Exod 21:17, but substituting "prince" for "your father and mother." The commandment to honor one's parents was commonly assumed throughout the Middle Ages and beyond to enjoin respect for all in a position of authority, and so Eck would have seen this alteration as consonant with the spirit, if not with the letter, of scripture. See Pierre Janelle, ed., *Obedience in Church and State: Three Political Tracts by Stephen Gardiner* (Cambridge: Cambridge University Press, 1930), 180.

But what Luther babbles forth with such temerity, that there is no power in the church except for the curtailing of sin,[135] is utterly false, for this power is as much for the promotion of the good as for the inhibition of evil. If it were not, how could any innocent boy be confirmed, or any righteous youth be ordained? The penitent, who had made satisfaction for sin, will no longer seek to receive the holy sacrament of the Eucharist. It is of the greatest importance that the abuses of the Roman curia be discussed openly, for they are rampant, as Luther says.[136] But his manner of correcting them is not acceptable, for up to now he has never voiced his criticisms of the Roman pontiff privately to his face but has straightaway told the church.[137] Here he would do well to observe the apostle's command, "Rebuke not an elder but entreat him as a father" [1 Tim 5:1], which he ignores. At length he pours out his usual poison, arguing that there is no distinction of degree (*maioritas*) in the church.[138] He bases this on Christ's words, "Whoever would be great (*maior*) amongst you must be your servant" [Matt 20:26], but he understands them wrongly, as I demonstrated at the Leipzig Disputation and in my book *The Primacy of Peter*.

Finally Luther, worn out by hunting, complains that the Leipzig Disputation resulted only in the fruits described by the apostle in 1 Timothy 6. But let Luther (or one of his canons who disseminate Lutheran errors) tell me: whose fault is that if not Luther's and his supporters?[139] Why did they not await the judgment of the illustrious University of Paris in silence? Had you been concerned with the truth of faith, you would have done so. What you aimed at was not that but wisps of transitory glory, popular acclaim, and empty show. And since this did not happen, [Bvᵛ] you decided to expunge the ignominy you received and adopt this most bitter and envious style of writing! May God and all the saints be my witness that I—entirely unvanquished in the disputation—have merely repaid his insults. For myself, I wished for nothing more than that the whole truth might be laid bare by the judgment of Paris. I disputed so that I did not have to write. But things turned out quite differently. Because I have disputed, it has become the more important for me to write, lest the errors, heresies, and perverse

135. WA 2:676.16–21.

136. WA 2:676.22–30.

137. Eck appears to be alluding to Matt 18:15–17, which sets out a procedure for correcting erring brethren: a private stage ("*corripe eum inter te et ipsum solum*": Eck has "*arguerit Romanum pontificem inter se et illum*"); a semi-public stage involving witnesses; and the public stage in which the entire church is involved ("*Dic ecclesiae*": Eck has "*dicit Ecclesiae*").

138. WA 2:678.3–7.

139. Marginal note: "The unlearned Lutheran canons."

doctrines broadcast by the Lutherans gain a fictitious victory and lead the simple folk astray. But listen to what this professed monk has to say: "We did not know that we were in the midst of wolves." In whose midst was Luther at Leipzig? Councillors of the illustrious prince and lord George, duke of Saxony, and the senate of Leipzig University! This most blasphemous of all men dared to call them wolves and to liken them to dogs and pigs.[140] And the vice by which he strives so officiously to gain glory for himself, he attributes to others. I—may God be my witness—have sought only the truth, and therefore, I have awaited the judgment. The Cuculla does not seek the truth but glory. The evidence is his many biting, slanderous, and arrogant writings with which this boastful Thraso sings of his victory before it is awarded. I would rather he had remained quiet in a spirit of gentle humility and (like me) awaited the judgment of Paris in perfect tranquillity. He could and still can find in Eck a man who is ready to make peace, if only he would in silence await the determination of the truth of our statements by the Christian masters of that Athens of the Christian world, namely the University of Paris.

I would like, most magnificent bishop, to touch briefly in passing on the way in which I have seen Master Hieronymus Emser suffer such mockery and injury at Luther's hands. Neither his wide-ranging and deep learning, nor his integrity of life (which is well known and evident to you), nor the honor of his priestly status, nor his careful foresight, deserved such impudent and biting invective. The unbiased reader, having seen Emser's letter, will readily endorse all that I have just said. And so you will forgive me, all who read the present work, and above all you, most worthy bishop, if Luther the biter has himself been bitten, for there is no other way to deal with such a wild and hateful huntsman. I have had to force myself to use greater violence against him than my kindheartedness would normally allow. May God almighty achieve that which he promised through the prophet, [Bvjʳ] namely that, having been reprimanded, that huntsman Luther will be mollified, and that hunters after peace and salvation will follow on his heels. "I will send them," says Jeremiah [16:16–17], "many hunters, and they will hunt them from every peak and from every hill and from every rocky cavern, for my eyes are upon all their ways."

Farewell, worthy bishop. From Ingolstadt, 28 October, in this year of grace 1519. Finis.

140. Marginal note: "Luther calls the Leipzigers wolves." The reference is to WA 2:678.27–31, where, in disgust at the Leipzigers' partisanship, Luther cites Jesus's command not to give holy things to dogs nor to cast pearls before swine (Matt 7:6).

4

Hieronymus Emser

To the Bull in Wittenberg

—ARMIN SIEDLECKI

INTRODUCTION

HIERONYMUS EMSER WAS BORN in Weidenstetten near the Swabian city of Ulm in 1478. He studied in Tübingen and Basel, where he received a humanist education, and in 1504 he lectured at the University of Erfurt, where Martin Luther was among his students. In 1509 he entered the service of Duke George of Saxony, of the Albertine line of the House of Wettin. In contrast to the Ernestine line, which included Frederick the Wise and John the Steadfast, who were among the earliest supporters of Martin Luther, Duke George favored the Catholic Church. Emser served as Duke George's court chaplain in Dresden until his death in 1527. He was succeeded in his post by Johannes Cochlaeus, another of Martin Luther's most vehement critics.[1]

1. On Emser, see especially: Agostino Borromeo, "Emser, Hieronymus," in *OER*, 2:42–43; Hieronymus Emser, "An den Stier zu Wittenberg," in *Flugschriften gegen die Reformation* (1518–1524), edited by Adolf Laube and Ulman Weiss (Berlin: Akademie Verlag, 1997), 221–28; Ludwig Enders, ed., *Luther und Emser: Ihre Streitschriften aus dem Jahre 1521* (Halle an der Saale: Max Niemeyer, 1890–1892); Marc Mudrak, *Reformation und alter Glaube:Zugehörigkeit der Altgläubigen im Alten Reich und in Frankreich* (Berlin: De Gruyter, 2017); Heribert Smolinsky, *Augustin von Alveldt und Hieronymus Emser: Eine Untersuchung zur Kontroverstheologie der frühen Reformationszeit im Herzogtum Sachsen*, RGST 122 (Münster: Aschendorff, 1983); Heribert Smolinsky, "Hieronymus Emser (1478–1527)" in *Katholische Theologen der Reformationszeit* (Münster: Aschendorff, 1984), 1:37–46; Christoph Volkmar, *Catholic Reform in the Age of Luther*.

Given their humanist training and approach to theology, there was much that Emser and Luther had in common, and their relationship was initially quite sympathetic. In his correspondence Luther himself had even occasionally referred to the other as "Emser *noster*" (our Emser). Even in the work translated here, Emser invoked his correspondence with Willibald Pirckheimer, Peter Mosellanus, Philipp Melanchthon, and Johannes Lang to contradict Luther's claim that all scholars had turned against Emser, pointing to the continued existence of a network of biblical humanists with their own program of loyal reform within the church.[2] A change in the relationship between Emser and Luther came in 1519 with the Leipzig Disputation, where Andreas Karlstadt and Martin Luther debated with Johann Eck on the authority of the pope and questions of free will, divine grace, and the legitimacy of indulgences. Emser had attended the disputation and saw certain similarities between Luther's argumentation and points raised by Jan Hus, who had been condemned as a heretic and burnt at the stake a century earlier. In an open letter to Johann Zack,[3] church administrator in Prague, he issued a warning that the Bohemian church should not be led astray but at the same time expressed doubt that it was Luther's intention to return the teachings of Hus to Bohemia. Luther took this concern to be a feigned expression of friendship, intended to back him into a corner and force him to either renounce his position or to acknowledge publicly that he shared Hus's heretical views. He responded accordingly with a strongly worded open letter, *To the Goat Emser*,[4] which Emser republished along with his original letter.[5] Almost a year later, when Luther received (before its publication) the first few pages of Emser's critique[6] of his *Address to the Christian Nobility of the German Nation*,[7] he wrote his arguably best known work against Emser—*To the Goat in Leipzig*.[8] The appellation "goat" is a reference to the goat's head in Emser's family crest.

Duke George of Saxony and the Church, 1488–1525, SMRT 209 (Leiden: Brill, 2018).

2. Mudrak, *Reformation und alter Glaube*, 89.

3. Hieronymus Emser, *De Disputatione Lipsicensi: quantum ad Boemos obiter deflexa est* (Leipzig: Melchior Lotter the Elder, 1519).

4. Martin Luther, *Ad Aegocerotem Emserianum* (Wittenberg: Grunenberg, 1519); WA 2:656.

5. Emser, *De Disputatione Lipsicensi . . . Ad Aegocerotem Emserianum* (Augsburg: Otmar, 1519).

6. Emser, *Wider das unchristenliche Buch Martini Luters Augustiners an den Teutschen Adel außgangen* (Leipzig: Landsberg, 1521).

7. Luther, *An den christlichen Adel deutscher Nation von des christlichen Standes Besserung* (Leipzig: Melchior Lotter the Younger, 1520); WA 6:397.

8. Luther, *An den Bock zu Leipzig* (Wittenberg: Melchior Lotter the Younger, 1521);

The work translated here is Emser's reply to Luther,[9] written before the publication of Luther's *To the Goat in Leipzig*. It appears that Emser had access to a draft of Luther's work, since he responds specifically to some of the points raised in it, such as Luther's reaction to receiving the first page of his critique of Luther's address to the Christian nobility. His reference to Tomasso Radini Tedeschi's book, on the other hand, responds to a charge made by Luther in his first letter in Latin, *To the Goat Emser*, but absent in the final published version of the German *To the Goat in Leipzig*. The controversy continued throughout 1521[10]—before Luther broke off all contact with Emser in 1522—but is perhaps best exemplified by a joint reading of Luther's *Goat in Leipzig* and Emser's *Bull in Wittenberg*.

TRANSLATION

As you, Brother Luther, have offered me your greeting at the beginning of your letter, there is little difference between your greeting and the kiss of Judas. For you let it be known far and wide that you are a spiritual father and Christian teacher, but your teaching resembles the gospel as much as an ass resembles a lion, for the gospel says that whoever calls his brother a fool is guilty of the fires of hell, and you call me not only a fool but also an ass. Since I do not have ears that would make me resemble a donkey, and Aristotle, Thomas [Aquinas], Bonaventure, popes, cardinals, and bishops—living and dead—would also be asses according to you, I shall prefer to remain in my ass' stable (in one of which even Christ was born) rather than your raven's nest. Formerly, I was hopeful that one would find in both our writings who was in fact the ass, but you were already set to take from this marksman festival (before it even occurred) the prize bull. Since, the first leaf had you up in arms and the goat had struck, what would a quarto or twenty of them that come after it do to you? In these I demonstrate to our lay brothers what kind of bird you are and how true to Christ and the holy Gospels your teaching is.

Allow me to defend myself before the reader against the affront you present to me in your letter, since you—as peasants often do—cut me off before I was finished speaking: just as God has given to each animal natural defenses and weapons to protect itself against other who would hurt it, talons to birds, tusks to boars, to vipers their tongues (of which you too have

---

WA 7:260, LW39:105–15.

9. Emser, *An den Stier zu Vuitenberg* (Leipzig: Landsberg, 1520).

10. See Enders, ed., *Luther und Emser: Ihre Streitschriften aus dem Jahre 1521* (Halle an der Saale: Niemeyer, 1890–1892).

one in your mouth), and the like, he has also given to this goat horns, which he is careful not to use against anyone except those who willfully provoke him. For God is my witness, that I am justified in defending myself against the unchristian, slanderous book that you wrote against me with no fault of mine and with no just cause. For I had resolved to keep my peace soon after Leipzig,[11] that I might devote myself to the holy scriptures and to my prayers. But you and many others who wished to curry your favor have since published no book in which Emser is not made sport of, and the goat becomes a scapegoat for you. Who would think ill of him, if he, following your example, should strike you on the head? For religious and civil law grant everyone the right to defense and protection.

But far be it from me to undertake this task or to write anything else against you because of your slander and taunting (in which no one takes pleasure), if I did not feel pity for the pious Christian people, whom you mislead so pathetically and divide and separate, and if my own conscience did not compel me to submit to you the Christian truth (for the sake of which every Christian should be willing to die). While you do not consider me worthy enough and say you do not hide even from those who have more ability and intellect in a single hair than I do in my entire body and soul, you would have done well to hear my words and then to judge. But your condescending spirit, with which you receive my quartos before the ink is dry, cannot tolerate that anyone says or writes anything contradictory, and does not want to hear anyone or to owe to anyone its attention or explanation, but itself. I will not speak of priests who from childhood on were no less accustomed than you to dealing with the scriptures, but even your Augustine was not ashamed to learn from a child. Therefore, it is not the spirit of the Lord that is upon you, but another [spirit], for the prophet says that the spirit of the Lord is upon no one except those that are humble, peaceful, and placid. Now it is well known throughout the land that you are like a wild beast, who day and night has neither peace nor rest himself, nor can he leave others in peace, but who like fortune and waves beating against a ship, you rub against one then another and search for what you shall eventually find.

But I cannot remain silent that you as an insult to me make the common person believe that I wrote three books against you out of anger and such hatred that you are astonished, that I slanderously chastised you and spread lies about you, so that you can win people over to your side with artful speech and rhetoric and make them not want to believe this fourth one nor even read it. First I say by my priestly faith in place of an oath that I have not had nor have envy or hatred against you in my heart on account

11. The Leipzig Debate of 1519.

of your person, but leave it to the strict judgment of God, who shall judge you and me. But I have always been opposed to your presumptuous plans against our mother, the holy Christian church, your false teaching, and your obstinate interpretation contrary to all Christian teachers, and moreover you are concocting ever greater follies every day. So I have given you three brotherly warnings and have implored you for God's sake to spare the common people who are obviously bothered by this matter, and you responded eventually with these words, "May the devil strike! The matter was not begun for God's sake and it shall not end for God's sake."[12] Whether this is Christian or un-Christian talk (for the apostle says that whatever we do, we shall do and begin in the name of the Lord), I leave up to each Christian to decide, but it is to be understood that since this conflict did not begin with God, what good can come from it?

For I have already noted that you are going down the wrong path, to teach us Germans the long condemned heresy of Jan Hus and to inflame an old, extinguished fire from the ashes. For it brought the Bohemians little joy, and other poor Christian people of our faith who were among them were greatly despised and persecuted because of it, so that I recently comforted the remaining Christians with a Christian letter and let them know that the situation is not so bad and that you yourself admitted in the [Leipzig] Disputation that the Bohemians had done wrong and should not separate themselves from the holy see and its authority. In this letter I did not offend you in any way, but made greater allowances than you deserve, but that you vilified and mocked me without warning against God's honor and justice, when you received this letter, is well attested in your slanderous book and is still fresh in my memory. I refuse to believe that I, having presented the same book as a necessity in defense of my honor and have applied the same measure to it, have become the enemy of all scholars. For the letters that they wrote to me in response, namely Willibald Pirckheimer, Peter Mosellanus, Philipp Melanchthon, and Johannes Lang of your own order, contain nothing unkind but that they would all like to see that the two of us be at peace with each other. So, thus I have concluded on the basis of their writings alone, but you have since needled me in your books and have tried to coax me into a fight with your unchristian writings.

You accuse me of writing Thomas Radini's[13] book against you and having it printed in Rome, so that no one would find out. I ask you first, how

---

12. This comment likely refers to a verbal comment made by Luther within the context of the Leipzig Disputation. Cf. Adolf Laube, ed., *Flugschriften gegen die Reformation: 1518–1524* (Berlin: Akademie Verlag, 1997), 226–27n15.

13. Tomasso Radini Tedeschi (1488–1527), a Dominican theologian, had written an oration in the style of Cicero against Martin Luther (*In Martino Lutherum . . . Oratio*

highly do you think of me that I should compose such an eloquent and noble book? Why then do you call me an ass, if this book contains more eloquence, rhetoric, philosophy, and correct theology as well as discipline, reason, and wisdom than can be found in all your books? Furthermore, while you conclude on the basis of these quartos (which made their way to you through treachery, before I could publish my book) how much I am afraid of you, why should I go through the trouble of sending it to Rome, if I have access to printers right here? Indeed, no one who is not completely deluded as you are would judge that it is my style or composition, and he who wrote it would undoubtedly come to you and would not be ashamed of his name.

Since you would like for me to stop lying and to write truthfully, you shall know for certain that all my life I have never favored a lying man, and no decent person can truthfully say that I have ever lied to him. As I have always written truthfully, so I write now and would like to keep it that way. I submit most respectfully to the consideration and judgment of any reasonable and impartial reader that if you think that I have offended you anywhere before my rightful judge and you are justified in accusing me, I shall answer you immediately. I ask in return of you that you submit to the same measure and not rebuke me with despicable falsehoods (which is not Christian, and which no decent person could abide). So that if one has made a human error in one's writing, it should be countered with reliable, documented reasons and not with insults and abuses.

As you continue to threaten me with many angry words and let your mind run unrestrained against me, a strong Christian faith shall serve me as holy water to exorcize an evil spirit, and before this threat I shall put on no other armor than the breastplate of faith and drive you back with my sword, that is scripture and the word of God, even if you have seven evil spirits in you. But you should not misconstrue my words, as you already begin to say that I hang scripture on goose feathers but the teachers of the church on chains. Save your truth, for with Augustine I give first place to the proven and canonical scriptures, the second to the tradition of the Christian church, and only the third and last to the interpretation of the upright and honest reason of the holy teachers, and I say again with Augustine: no Christian

---

[Leipzig: Melchior Lotther the Elder, 1520]). In response, Philipp Melanchthon wrote an oration in defense of Luther: *Didymi Faventini adversus Thomam Placentium, pro Martino Luthero Oratio* (Basel: Petri, 1521). Radini then issued another oration: *In Philippum Melanchthonem Lutheranae haereseon defensorem oratio* (Rome: Mazochi, 1522), which Luther suggested was written by Emser.

would argue against scripture, no peaceful person against the tradition of the church, and no intelligent person against reason.[14]

Finally, you should not think that you are so pure and innocent or untainted that you were first tarnished by me, as your drunken verses claim; as your name Luther is not sincere,[15] I also know that you are not worth as much as a false penny. Therefore, it was never my intention to go on arguing with you, as is the custom not of learned and devout, but of thoughtless people. I do want to convey to you in writing that you have turned your face away from your mother, the Christian church and have followed in the footsteps of Hus,[16] Wycliffe,[17] Dolcino,[18] Faustus,[19] Pelagius,[20] Vigilantius,[21] Arius,[22] Bardesanes,[23] the Armenians,[24] Lampecius,[25] and all other old and new heretics and wanted to instruct us in long condemned heresies and errors. I believe I have said this in plain enough language without hesitation or babbling. Leave me, therefore, alone and do not obstruct me with your interlocutions, for you do not intimidate me with them, even if—according to your words (I shall be repaid what was borrowed from me)—you or your followers would do me violence to prevent my writing, God would give his spirit to another and would not leave his church. Therefore, I counsel you in Christian love and faithfulness, give up this foolishness, and even if you

14. "*Contra rationem nemo sobrius, contra Scripturas nemo christianus, contra Ecclesiam nemo pacificus senserit* [Against reason no sober person would judge, against the scriptures no Christian and against the Church no peaceful person]" (Augustine, *De Trinitate* 4,6).

15. A play on words (*dann deyn nam Luter, nicht lauter ist*), linking *Luter* (Luther) and *lauter* (sincere).

16. Jan Hus (ca. 1369–1415), Bohemian reformer, burnt at the stake during the Council of Constance.

17. John Wycliffe (ca. 1320–1386), English theologian and Bible translator, posthumously condemned as a heretic.

18. Fra Dolcino (Dulcinus; ca. 1250–1307), leader of the Dulcinian reformist movement, burnt at the stake on charges of heresy.

19. Faustus of Mileve (fourth century), a Manichean bishop and contemporary of Augustine.

20. Pelagius (ca. 360–418), British monk and opponent of Augustine.

21. Vigilantius (active around 400), presbyter of Aquitaine and opponent of Jerome.

22. Arius (256–336), North African presbyter, denied the consubstantiality of Father and Son for which he was condemned by the Council of Nicea.

23. Bardesanes (or Bardasain) (154–222), Syrian gnostic and founder of the Bardesanites.

24. Probably a reference to the adoption by Armenian Christians of Monophysitism, the doctrine that asserts Christ only had one nature, which was divine.

25. Lampetius (or Lampecius; fifth century), leader of the Euchites (also known as Messalians) an allegedly fanatical and ascetic sect in Syria and Armenia.

have made sport of faith on account of glory, envy, or any other reason (since you said yourself it is not for God's sake), recant it and the two of us shall be good friends, and I shall help you to work against the corruption that is rooted not only in the priesthood in Rome but also among us Germans, as I have written to you before. With this, I commend you to God.

5

Augustin Alveldt

A Sermon in which Brother Augustin of Alveldt Expresses His Complaint

—KURT K. HENDEL

INTRODUCTION

Augustin Alveldt (ca. 1480–ca. 1535)[1]

AUGUSTIN ALVELDT (AUGUSTINUS VON Alveldt) was a Franciscan friar whose chief sphere of activity was Ducal Saxony. Relatively little is known about the specifics of his life. He was apparently born in Alfeld, a town near the north German episcopal city of Hildesheim. Since no matriculation records have been discovered, it is likely that he received a monastic education. His writings indicate that the ideals of Renaissance humanism attracted him. He was acquainted with the biblical languages and was an able Latinist, familiar with both classical and humanist literature. He was, therefore, intellectually prepared to defend the church against the challenges of Luther. In addition to his apologetic vocation, he became a leader within the Franciscan community. In 1520 he was appointed biblical lecturer in the Franciscan cloister in Leipzig, and in 1523 or 1524 he became the guardian

---

1. The biographical sketch in this introduction is based largely on three Alveldt biographical essays: Carl Ruland, "Alveld, Augustin," in *ADB* 1:375–76; Paul Lehmann, "Alveldt (Ahlfeld, Alfeld, Alefeld), Augustin (von)," in *NDB* 1:230–31; and Henry G. Ganss, "Augustin von Alfeld," in *The Catholic Encyclopedia* (1907) (http://www.newadvent.org/cathen/02079a.htm).

or superior of the Franciscan community in Halle. In 1529 he was elected the provincial head of the Franciscans in Saxony and served in this role until 1532.

Context for the Sermon

Luther's critique of the papacy reached the public sphere with the publication and rapid dissemination of the *Ninety-Five Theses* (1517),[2] and it was expanded in the *Explanation of the Ninety-Five Theses* (1518).[3] The reformer broached the subject again in a direct way in the *Resolutio Lutherana super propositione sua decima tertia de potestate papae*[4] (1519) and in the *Babylonian Captivity of the Church* (1520),[5] his critical analysis of the church's sacramental theology and piety. While Luther's focus in the latter treatise was on the sacraments, he also challenged the sacerdotal system of the church, which inevitably involved a critique of the papacy.

Alveldt's initial response to Luther's challenge of papal authority was his *On the Apostolic See,*[6] which he published in 1520. Luther did not respond to this treatise but encouraged his student and fellow Franciscan, Johannes Lonicer (c. 1497–1569), to do so.[7] Alveldt prepared another tract, *A Poultice Newly Best Prepared,*[8] and in order to reach a wider audience, he issued the work in German with minimal changes as *A Very Fruitful and Useful Pamphlet.*[9] Luther now became convinced that Alveldt's writ-

---

2. See *LW* 31:17–33.

3. *LW* 31:77–252.

4. See WA 2:180–241.

5. *LW* 36:3–126; see also *De captivitate Babylonica ecclesiae praeludium* (WA 6:484–573).

6. See Alveldt's *Super apostolica sede an videlicet diuino sit iure nec ne, anque po[n]tifex qui Papa dici caeptus est, iure diuino in ea ipsa pr[a]esideat, no[n] paru[m] laudanda, ex sacro Biblior[um] canone Declaratio.* See the work in the Bayerische Staatsbibliothek (Münchener DigitalisierungsZentrum Digitale Bibliothek), Res/4.ref.259, VD16 A 2105.

7. Lonicer's response was his *Contra Romanistam fratrem Augustinum Alveldensem, Franciscanum Lipsicum Canonis Biblici publicum lictorem et tortorem eiusdem.* See the work in the Bayerische Staatsbibliothek (Münchener DigitalisierungsZentrum Digitale Bibliothek), 4 Polem. 2498, VD16 L 2437.

8. See *Malagma optimum per fratrem Avgvstinum Alueldensem ordinis minorum de obseruancia nuper Confectum Contra infirmitatem horribilem duorum virorum, fratris Iannis Ioniceri theologiste, Et fratris Martini luteri ordiis ememitani de vicariatu, vt sanetur ad p[er]cuciendam Vituperij citharam.* See the work in the Staats- und Stadtbibliothek Augsburg, 4 Th H 78.

9. See Alveldt's *Eyn gar fruchtbar vnd nutzbarlich buchleyn vo[n] de[n] babstlichen*

ings required a response from him, and so he published *On the Papacy in Rome Against the Most Celebrated Romanist in Leipzig*[10] in 1520. Alveldt responded by defending himself and rejecting Luther's anti-papal arguments in *A Sermon in which Brother Augustin of Alveldt Expresses his Complaint.*

This sermon is available in two extant editions. The first was printed in Leipzig by Wolfgang Stöckel in 1520 and is translated here. No other English translation of the sermon has been identified. A slightly revised and expanded version was also published but without including publisher or publication date.[11] The second edition includes only minor editorial changes to the original sermon. However, the content of the sermon is expanded significantly by an addendum that addresses various aspects of Luther's sacramental teachings, particularly the assertions that the mass is Christ's testament, that the eucharistic vestments are of human creation, that the mass is not a sacrifice, that the mass should be celebrated in the vernacular, that the sacrament is intended for the living and does not benefit souls in purgatory, and that both elements should be distributed to the communicants.

Content of the Sermon

Alveldt's sermon consists of three main sections. The first is a self-defense and a reprimand of Luther, particularly because of the reformer's use of derogatory names for Alveldt. The second section accuses Luther of heresy by placing him in the company of condemned heretics—particularly John Wycliffe and Jan Hus—by noting that Luther has defended these and other heretics, and by asserting that Luther's theological perspectives are often consistent with those of the heretics. In the third section Alveldt addresses Luther's challenge of papal power and authority by insisting that Christ specifically chose Peter and his successors to be his vicars and to feed and nourish the sheep of Christ. The papal office is, therefore, a divine

---

stule, vn[d] von sant Peter, vnd von den dye warhafftige scheffleyn Christi seynt, dy Christus vnsser herre, Petro beuolen hat, yn seyne hute vnd regirung/ gemacht durch bruder Agustinu[m], Alueldt. Sant Francisci ordens/ tzu Leyptzk (Leipzig, 1520). See the work in the Bayerische Staatsbibliothek (Münchener DigitalisierungsZentrum Digitale Bibliothek), Res/4.ref.259, VD16 A 2092.

10. WA 6:277–324. *LW* 39:49–104.

11. The revised, second edition of the sermon (VD16 A2099) has the following publication information provided by VD16: Leipzig: Landsberg, 1520. It is accessible electronically at the following sites: http://resolver.staatsbibliothek-berlin.de/SBB0001C3A500000000; http://www.mdz-nbn-resolving.de/urn/resolver.pl?urn=urn:nbn:de:bvb:12-bsb10688301-8 (damaged, incomplete text); http://www.mdz-nbn-resolving.de/urn/resolver.pl?urn=urn:nbn:de:bvb:12-bsb10168066-7.

institution and is essential for the wellbeing of the church. He supports this argument further by defending his assertions in previous writings and by responding to Luther's comments in *On the Papacy in Rome Against the Most Celebrated Romanist in Leipzig* with a lengthy interpretation of the significance of the relationship between Moses and Aaron for papal authority within the church. Alveldt concludes the sermon by promising to engage Luther in other writings.

TRANSLATION

A sermon in which Brother Augustin of Alveldt, of St. Francis's Order, who[12] was insulted and dishonored with many shameful names in [the writings of] Brother Martin Luther, of the Augustinian Order, expresses his complaint; and how Augustin has the intention to write further against Martin (in order [that people might] recognize how sound his teaching is).[13]

> 1 Pet 3[:13–14]
>
> "Who can harm you if you follow what is good? However, blessed are you if you suffer something for the sake of righteousness. You should neither be distressed by nor fear their threat."

A German Sermon

"See, then, that you walk circumspectly, not as fools but as wise, redeeming the time, because the days are evil. Therefore do not be foolish but understanding what the will of God is."[14]

---

12. The original reads *des*, but the context suggests *der*.

13. The edition of the Alveldt sermon included in the digital holdings of the Bayerische Staatsbibliothek (Münchener DigitalisierungsZentrum Digitale Bibliothek), 4 Polem. 49, VD 16 A 2099, adds: "Which [the sermon] has been newly corrected and defended by him; it had been seen in this form by the printer beforehand. An addition concerning some matters Martin Luther has recently written concerning the sacraments has also been made for the solace and improvement of the common, simple people." As this expansion of the original title indicates, the revised, edited, and expanded edition of Alveldt's sermon also includes a section on the Eucharist. This sacramental section is not fully reproduced in the digital version, however. The incomplete text of the expanded sermon can be accessed at https://www.digitale-sammlungen.de. The complete text of this edition is available at http://digital.staatsbibliothek-berlin.de.

14. Left Margin (hereafter, LM and Right Margin, RM): Paul to the Ephesians in chapter 5 [Eph 5:15–17]. The translation is from the Latin in the original text.

St. Paul (the chosen instrument)[15] certainly knew from the Holy Spirit that after his times many will appear who are not children of the light but of darkness. They will present a hidden poison through beautiful teaching with inflated, crafty, and subtle words and will appear among the people who believe in Christ. Therefore the preceding, presented Latin words, written as a warning, state: "See to it that you walk safely, not like the foolish but like the wise who seize the time again (because these are evil days now), so that you do not become foolish but recognize God's will, etc." (Eph 5:15–17).[16]

It is the will of God that we should tolerate and suffer persecution, humiliation, lies, and vilification—indeed, not only evil words but also blows and everything that such an evil tyrant inflicts on a true Christian—with a gentle understanding because of the love of God.[17] Since, then, these same wicked people appear in the most terrifying fashion in the last days, during which the faithful Christians are also persecuted most violently, I might, indeed, have thought that the antichrist—who now appears to be nearby—should not be born for a long time yet. However, he wants to discern immediately that his forerunners are already noticed in our times.

¶[18]Since the little Latin book[19] about the office of St. Peter and his descendants [appeared], I published a little German book[20] about the same matter in response to the command and desire of the reverend in God the Father, serene, right honorable prince and lord, Sir Adolph,[21] bishop of Merseburg, prince of Anhalt, etc., my gracious lord. I have only sought to

15. The original reads *das vasz der erwelung.* The meaning of the word *vasz* is not clear in German. Alveldt is likely referencing the Vulgate and its use of *vas electionis* in Acts 9:15.

16. The translation is from the German in the original text.

17. The original reads *von wegen der liebe gottes.* This phrase could be interpreted to refer either to God's love for us or to our love for God. It is likely that Alveldt meant to convey the latter.

18. The original does not indicate that a new paragraph should begin here. However, the change of topic suggests that this is advisable. Hereafter ¶ will mark such instances; in cases where this symbol actually occurs in the text, a footnote will note this.

19. See Alveldt's *Super apostolica sede an videlicet diuino sit iure nec ne, anque po[n] tifex qui Papa dici caeptus est, iure diuino in ea ipsa pr[a]esideat, no[n] paru[m] laudanda, ex sacro Biblior[um] canone Declaratio.*

20. See Alveldt's *Eyn gar fruchtbar vnd nutzbarlich buchleyn vo[n] de[n] babstlichen stule, vn[d] von sant Peter, vnd von den dye warhafftige scheffleyn Christi seynt, dy Christus vnsser herre, Petro beuolen hat, yn seyne hute vnd regirung/ gemacht durch bruder Agustinu[m], Alueldt. Sant Francisci ordens/ tzu Leyptzk* (Leipzig, 1520).

21. Adolf II (1458–1526) was the prince of Anhalt-Köthen and also served as the bishop of Merseburg. Although he appears to have appreciated Martin Luther's doctrine of justification, he remained loyal to Rome and opposed the emerging Lutheran reform movement.

reveal the truth of these matters in it, and, with the exception of the false, cursed heretics and Beghards[22] Conrad Schmidt,[23] Wycliffe,[24] and Hus[25] (to-

22. The Beghards were groups of men who did not take monastic vows but lived together in communities, shared their possessions, and promoted the spiritual formation of their members. Their chief ministry was the care of the poor. They flourished especially in Northern Europe, particularly in the Netherlands, and were often suspected of heretical theological perspectives. Groups of women, who promoted similar ideals, were known as Beguines. John Wycliffe and Jan Hus were not members of these lay communities, though they were both condemned as heretics.

23. Conrad Schmidt was the leader of a group of flagellants in Saxony. He was an apocalyptic preacher who apparently challenged the church's sacramental theology, including the real presence of Christ in the Eucharist. It is not clear whether Sangerhausen was his home, although Alveldt makes this claim. He may have been burned at the stake in Sangerhausen in 1414. See Friedrich Schmidt, *Geschichte der Stadt Sangerhausen* (Sangerhausen: Selbstverlag des Magistrats der Stadt Sangerhausen, 1906), 858–64; Gordon Leff, *Heresy in the Later Middle Ages. The Relation of Heterodoxy to Dissent, c. 1250–c.1450* (Manchester: Manchester University Press, 1967), 492.

24. John Wycliffe (ca. 1330–1384) was a theologian, reformer, and advocate of the translation of the Bible into English. He earned the doctorate at Oxford, was ordained, and served in a number of parishes. As he pursued his ecclesiastical vocation, he also defended the prerogatives of temporal authorities in their conflicts with the church, especially with regard to fiscal matters. However, his chief interests were scholarly. He is viewed as a forerunner of the Reformation because of his critique of the wealth and corruption of the institutional church and its leaders and because of his theological assertions. In his ecclesiological writings Wycliffe envisioned the church as the community of all the saints or the elect rather than as a hierarchical institution. He also addressed the church's sacramental theology and rejected the scholastic doctrine of transubstantiation. Although he was accused of heresy and ultimately condemned as a heretic at the Council of Constance, he inspired the Lollard movement, which focused its attention on still another of Wycliffe's interests, namely, the translation of the Bible into English.

25. Jan Hus (ca. 1369–1415) inspired an ecclesiastical reform movement in his native Bohemia and is viewed as a precursor of the sixteenth-century Reformation. He was educated at Charles University in Prague where he earned a Master's degree in 1396 and where he also taught and served as dean of the theological faculty and as rector. Hus was an ordained priest and became a popular reforming preacher at Bethlehem Chapel in Prague. During his ministry, he emerged both as an ethical and theological reformer. He urged the church to abandon its quest for wealth and power and criticized the papacy, bishops, and clergy for their moral laxity and temporal interest. Influenced by Wycliffe, he also envisioned the church primarily as the community of saints. In his sacramental theology, Hus insisted that all of the people receive both elements in the Eucharist and thereby inspired the Utraquist movement, which flourished in Bohemia after Hus. He was also a Bohemian or Czech patriot; contributed to the development of the modern Czech language; and promoted the political power of the Bohemian contingent of instructors and students at Charles University, both for theological and patriotic reasons. As a result, many students and instructors from other parts of Europe left the university in protest. This exodus led to the establishment of the University of Leipzig. Hus was, therefore, not a popular figure in Leipzig. Alveldt was likely aware of this, and his linking of Luther and Hus was an effective polemical strategy. After being

gether with their supporters and defenders), I have mentioned no person by name in the same little book or harassed anyone in my writings. However, I have addressed the heretics mentioned above in the little book so that those who perhaps have not known very much about this error before might see and experience how damnable their teaching was, [and] how it was burned and dismissed by the holy, Christian church.

¶Now Brother Martin Luther (who calls himself a doctor and has considered it an iniquity on my part that I call myself a reader of holy scripture), together with his supporters,[26] has concerned himself with my writing, and as reader of holy scripture (which, after all, no one is ultimately forbidden to read) he has not just interpreted the same title in an evil manner, but in a wholly evil manner. He has also[27] disparaged, maligned, and reproved me much in Latin and German, and has no less imprecated, ridiculed, and cursed me, in opposition to God and all brotherly love. In addition, he has laughed at and despised me and called me a donkey, ox, ape, frog, heretic, liar, and goat and has not skipped anything that he could invent in a vituperative and reviling manner against me. Rather, as far as it was possible for him to extend it, [he did so] by developing it in the hearts of people with several polemical booklets,[28] so that he created anger and a reason for rebuking me in them (as I fear). In this way he has skewed, changed, and falsified my words in Latin and German and has ascribed to me what I have never thought, much less spoken or written. This has been the impetus for

---

excommunicated in 1410, primarily because of his challenge of the church's authority and his demands for ethical reform within the church, Hus was eventually summoned to appear before the Council of Constance. While he was given a safe conduct by King Sigismund (1368–1437), the safe conduct was revoked. He was subsequently condemned by the council and burned at the stake on July 6, 1415. His reforms continued to be promoted by the Utraquists.

26. Johannes Lonicer (ca. 1497–1569) was, no doubt, one of the supporters to whom Alveldt is referring. Lonicer published his *Contra Romanistam fratrem Augustinum Alveldensem, Franciscanum Lipsicum Canonis Biblici publicum* in response to Alveldt's *On the Apostolic See*. See footnote 7. Another supporter of Luther who opposed Alveldt was Johannes Bernardi von Feldkirch (ca. 1490–1534), also known as Velcurio, whose *Confutatio inepti et impii libelli F. August. Alueld. Franciscani Lipsici: pro d. Mar. Luthero* was published in 1520. See the work in the Bayerische Staatsbibliothek (Münchener DigitalisierungsZentrum Digitale Bibliothek), 4 Polem. 2498, VD16 B 2036.

27. The transitional word used in the original is *sunder*, which is generally translated "but." The word is not included in the translation since it is unnecessary to convey the meaning of the two sentences. *Auch* or "also" functions in the transitional role.

28. *Scheltbuchlein*. It may be that Alveldt is referring to the works of Lonicer and Bernardi as well as to Luther's *On the Papacy in Rome Against the Most Celebrated Romanist in Leipzig*.

me to indicate to some degree with this,[29] also in the German tongue, what I have said and written and what I still desire to write with God's help. (I have set aside [fear of] Brother Martin, whom I have called a brother in accordance with the words of our Savior that we are all brothers and under one master, Christ, and also all other fear.) Therefore, I place myself under the judgment of all reasonable Christians,[30]—spiritual, temporal, noble and not noble, burghers and peasants, old and young—who can recognize the truth or who only want to regard God's truth in order to see and hear what I have written and taught and whether Brother Martin has something enduring to bring up against it of which he is aware. I will await this from him here in Leipzig and will also have the indubitable hope in God and the glorious Mother of God that he will not pull out even one of my hairs, much less prove what he imposes on me in such an evil manner on the basis of my little book, in contradiction to Christian modesty. He will also not deter me with what he threatens (as one is accustomed to do with fools), [namely,] to decorate me with flowers and send me home, as if such a petty threat (which would surely not be seemly for Christian and spiritual and also well-educated people, as he is considered to be) would be becoming and not against the holy gospel. Thus I would indeed (though it be far from me) wish to decorate him[31] in turn with box tree (which does not dry up quickly like flowers). This would, however, be acting against the teaching of Christ and Paul and in accordance with the common practice of some frivolous people, who would be given sufficient reason to respond with rebuke with two calumnious names of arguably a hundred that they have hung on me. However, I want to remunerate them with the words of my dear Lord Jesus,[32] who said: "Father forgive them for they do not know what they are doing." This short sermon has been given simply as a plea and warning and offered to all of you so that you would not have a longing [for it], for I am thinking of publishing several little books very soon concerning the reception of the noble sacrament in both kinds and other matters that are useful and necessary to know. I will not let Brother Martin's rebuking hinder me from doing so, for I am surely able to endure as much as he can ever rebuke. However, how well the rebuking befits him I entrust to the discernment of all people who are godly and who love God.

29. Alveldt is referring to his sermon.

30. *Cristenn menschen.*

31. The original includes no pronoun. However, the edition in the Bayerische Staatsbibliothek adds *yn*, which is deemed an appropriate addition in light of the context.

32. LM: Luke in his Gospel, in the twenty-third chapter [Luke 23:34].

¶In response to such things one might, indeed, ask what reason Brother Martin had for being so ardently concerned about my writing, particularly the matters that I wrote concerning the papal office, because there were, after all, other much more saintly doctors who have also written concerning this topic.[33] As a result, he will have to answer one or both of the following.

¶First, [he claims] that he does not wish to see, much less endure and tolerate, the sin, evil, and shame that occur in Rome, none of which [are considered to be] too excessive in that place; likewise, the abuse of indulgences and their trade; in addition, the [sale of the] archbishop's mantle and the improper practice of the ban, together with other similar matters. However, that he says he supports the Beghards and Conrad Schmidt from Sangerhausen or Wycliffe, Hus, and other befouled, cursed, and damned heretics or that they have suffered injustice (which has already come up for discussion), that is speaking well, etc.

To the first [matter],[34] (you most-beloved, obedient people of Christ our dear Lord, who loved holy obedience so much that he affixed himself to the glorious cross for us), I say that (without doubt) I fully anticipate that one will not find anywhere in my previously mentioned writing that I have ventured to champion Rome even with one letter [of the alphabet] or to excuse the wicked, inexcusable life, which may be led there, although it is to be hoped, without doubt, that there are also many Christian and godly people there. However, I am heartily[35] sorry that many evil people are mixed in, and I testify to this before[36] God, who knows all hearts. I do not desire to see anything more on earth than that such simoniacal abuse, greed, and pride together with other punishable dealings that are found there[37] and in all of Christendom might be eradicated, reformed, and improved. However, what can I contribute to this, since this authority is committed to me as little as it is to Brother Martin Luther, and [the work of] reforming is far beyond our power? This is also not the way to change such things. To use such profanity, rebuking, and condemnation boldly, publicly, and persistently with the accompanying derision and disdain (as if this were not against the holy gospel of Christ and as if it were commanded to do this in Brother Martin Luther's gospel) seldom improves matters. Thus, unconditional and proper rules about how one should punish evil and who should do so are also

33. LM: A question.

34. RM: Answer.

35. Though the original reads *herlich*, it should read *hertzlich*, as the edition in the Bayerische Staatsbibliothek confirms.

36. The text reads *mit*.

37. Rome.

established for us by our Savior Christ and his holy Apostle Paul. However, Brother Martin did not follow these rules, perhaps because he has oriented himself more according to his than according to Christ's gospel.

¶However,[38] [he will also have to answer] whether he touches on the second matter, which is to be noted hereafter, in order to defend, support, or follow Hus or other declared heretics (who have introduced such cursed opinions and suspicious views and who have dared to topple the papal seat or office, that is, [the office] of feeding and ruling the little sheep of Christ, together with the pope, that is, the vicar of Christ, although they have not accomplished it) and, finally, to direct the matter to this end.

¶[This toppling of the papacy is desired] so that one may rule the holy, Christian church without a vicar of the highest head, Christ, in order that everyone can do or not do what he likes and believe and live as he wishes. This might eventually also awaken disobedience in the secular realm (about which I am, however, not commanded to write). With his assertion that one should have Christ alone as a lord, Brother Martin seeks this, and nothing else, in order to adorn it and to paint it with another deceptive color. Thereby the holy Christian church becomes a murdering pit and the sleeping chamber of the devil, although the heavy hand of God deservedly frightens the declared heretics and has driven them from this erring way. Indeed, it should also still turn them away now.[39] Perhaps they find cause in the saying of the wise man for persisting in their blindness, because he says: "The final judgment against the evil has been long delayed. Therefore, the children of humans sin without fear and freely." It is also daily apparent that the Lord God is not quick to revenge, although the one who depends on this is a fool. For this reason I have produced my little Latin book about the papal office so that thereby I might again direct the person, who may be striving against the truth in such a manner (which has happened to the declared heretics but never to a godly person) and wandering on the same wrong way, to the correct way, which I soon[40] want to explicate further and make clear on the basis of the truth with the help of God und Mary.

Because I now notice that Brother Martin Luther defends the declared, condemned heretics and scoundrels and in part walks in their ways, even as it was also his manner to reject his opponents with profaning, reproving, and cursing, so I want (with strengthened hope in God) to reveal briefly and prove publicly that Brother Martin Luther seeks nothing else than that

38. LM: Answer.

39. LM: In the book of Ecclesiastes the eighth chapter [Eccl 8:11].

40. The original reads *ehelanhs*. The meaning of the word is unclear. It has been interpreted to mean *ehe lang* and has, therefore, been translated as "soon."

he might make Meissen, Saxony, and Thuringia like Bohemia and that he might accomplish this. For these people[41] believed and lived as the declared, condemned Beghards and heretics believed and lived. The latter received a part of their reward physically from the holy church with the knowledge of the leaders of the spiritual and the temporal swords in praiseworthy, large numbers, no doubt through the inspiration of the Holy Spirit. Thus the most illumined and the illumined and right honorable Electors and Dukes of Saxony, etc., ancestors of praiseworthy memory, without doubt as godly princes who loved God, have burned the declared heretics of Sangerhausen to ashes.[42] The princes have retained this praise until now and have still not acted unjustly, although some say now that Wycliffe and Hus experienced an injustice. However, this is not surprising, for no council has ever taken place that was pleasing to heretics, just as the Council of Nicaea was also opposed to the condemned heretic Arius with his supporters. Therefore, it was called the devil's council by him, just as their followers[43] have now unfortunately called the Council of Constance in a tyrannical manner, because they burned Jan Hus there and broke the safe conduct that they supposedly promised to him. If these people had read about the council and all of the proceedings in the matter, then they would have discovered what was the nature of the safe conduct, and that berating of the council might perhaps have remained unwritten[44] so that, in the opinion of the wise man, it would not have been expressed in indecent words.[45]

Therefore, I also still intend to publish in German the articles of:
the heretical and not the godly Greeks,
the Beghards,
Conrad Schmidt of Sangerhausen,
John Wycliffe of condemned remembrance, [and]
Jan Hus, the harmful heretic
so[46] that every Christian person might see and notice how Brother Martin stated several of his articles and a part of his teaching and preaching in

41. The context suggests that Alveldt is referring to the Bohemians, specifically, the Utraquists who were followers of Jan Hus.

42. A number of heretics were burned at the stake in Sangerhausen in 1414. See footnote 23. Friedrich Schmidt gives an account of this event in the pages noted.

43. Alveldt is likely referring to the followers and defenders of Hus and Wycliffe, but he may also be intending to link the latter with the Arians.

44. The original reads *in der feddern bliben*.

45. RM: In the book of the Spiritual Discipline, in the fifth chapter [Eccl 5:2–3]; LM: Promise of what he still intends to write.

46. Although there is a paragraph sign at this point in the text, the content of this section does not warrant a new paragraph.

agreement with them. In the same way, he based the little book that he wrote against the Romanist on them.[47] [I also intend to publish the articles] in order that one might recognize the difference between the gospel of Christ and that of Brother Martin Luther (which do not agree anywhere) and might guard oneself and watch out for the hidden poison of Luther's gospel that is covered with gold (which has lain dormant for almost 400 years and has now been produced again). For it is based significantly on the Islamic law[48] and pieced together of five parts in such a manner that it has almost become five essences (as the alchemists say), which the followers of Martin call a spiritual body;[49] also the spiritual church or the spiritual realm. [I do so further], because, as promised above, I then want to clearly examine and manifestly bring to light with God's help and on the basis of the intercession of the highly praised Queen Mary that Brother Martin's foundation is basically not beneficial at all. In addition, I have translated my first treatise concerning St. Peter's office more clearly into German and have published it (in order that one may see how wrongly he interpreted and explained it for me).[50] [I did so] with the hope that what I have written and what I will still write will surely not be shot down by him. Although, they scold me as a foolish, blind donkey, while being ignorant of the fact that Christ wants to ride such a donkey (as it has been written)[51] and as David also desires: "I am like a beast before you, etc." Paul clarifies this for us with these words: "Seek the experience of Christ who speaks in me and who is not weakened in you, etc." [cf. 2 Cor 13:3]. Therefore, these highly learned doctors should allow me to remain that same donkey.

47. Alveldt is referring to Luther's *On the Papacy in Rome Against the Most Celebrated Romanist in Leipzig*. The *Romanist* is, of course, Alveldt.

48. The original reads *Machometischen ehe*. It is unclear why Alveldt makes this claim, and he provides no defense of his assertion.

49. The original reads *lieb*. However, the context suggests that it should read *leib*.

50. Alveldt is referring to his *Eyn gar fruchtbar vnd nutzbarlich buchleyn vo[n] de[n] babstlichen stule, vn[d] von sant Peter, vnd von den dye warhafftige scheffleyn Christi seynt, dy Christus vnsser herre, Petro beuolen hat, yn seyne hute vnd regirung/ gemacht durch bruder Agustinu[m], Alueldt. Sant Francisci ordens/ tzu Leyptzk* (Leipzig, 1520).

51. LM: David in the seventy-second Psalm [Ps 72:23, Vg.; 73:22, EVV]; 2 Cor 13[:3].

The Reason for my Attention [to this Matter] Now Follows Hereafter with Brief Words [and] without Delay until the Promised Little Books Will Follow.

Christianity is the assembly of one faith under [the authority of] the trust-worthy holy scripture of the Old and New Testaments and of the seven holy sacraments. However, the head of this assembly is Christ. Nevertheless, it is necessary for this assembly and it must be that they have a sovereign who is a vicar of Christ, not that he is above Christ, but [that he is] like him, though under Christ, so that everyone is not unencumbered and free to interpret the faith, scripture, and the seven sacraments wrongly and to pollute them as he wishes. For this reason it has always been and it still is so difficult and against their will for the useless heretics to be under [the authority] of the vicar or deputy of Christ. Some of these heretics have said and say that the vicar was established by and came from God. However, this office has ended, and there is no pope since the time of Urban VI.[52] Rather, those who have occupied this office since then were worthless antichrists. The others have said and still say that the pope or the vicar of Christ is not established by God but by humans. They want to assert thereby that it is not neces-sary to obey the command of the church. I respond to this together with all holy doctors (of the church, many of whose life was so holy that it has been adorned and confirmed with great miraculous signs, even after their death) that the pope or vicar of God has been established by God since he said publicly to Peter, once and a second time,[53] not privately but at supper in the presence and hearing of the other apostles: "Peter, tend or feed my little sheep." However, the third time [He said]: "Peter, you shall rule my little sheep."[54] These are the manifest and transparent words of our savior, without any annotation or falsification. This same dear Lord of ours has also spoken further:[55] "I am a good shepherd and have sheep that are not from this sheep stall" of the law of Moses, for the Gentiles are excluded. No other people were united with the law of Moses. These Gentiles, who lived according to reason, are also little sheep of God, but as it is stated above, not from the law of Moses. He has rejected these little sheep as Jews and Gentiles. However,

---

52. Urban VI (ca. 1318–1389) was the first pope elected after the Avignon Papacy and served as Bishop of Rome, 1378–1389. His papacy marks the beginning of the Great Schism in the Western church.

53. RM: As John says in his Gospel in the twenty-first chapter [John 21:15–17].

54. While Alveldt claims that Jesus commanded Peter to "rule" his little sheep the third time, in fact the Vulgate uses the same verb in all three instances of Jesus's com-mands to Peter.

55. RM: John in the tenth chapter [John 10:11, 14, 16].

later on he became a cornerstone and through his holy suffering and dying
has brought them together in one sheep stall under one shepherd[56] and has
commended them to St. Peter, and no one else, as the vicar and governor
of Christ with apparent, expressed, and clear words (which the heretics
dared to interpret but which do not tolerate any interpretation). However,
they are not his [i.e., St. Peter's] possession, but he [i.e., Christ] placed them
into his care and protection so that he would feed and rule them with the
words: "Guard and feed my little sheep, not yours, but my little sheep. You
shall guard, preserve, and rule them as my shepherd and vicar so that they
receive no poison or something else that is harmful in the pasture, that is,
in the faith of holy scripture and in the seven sacraments";[57] in faith, when
the righteous person lives through faith; in holy scripture, when a person
lives not by bread alone but by every word that proceeds from God's mouth;
in the seven sacraments, when life and also Christian strength are given in
baptism; the same in confirmation; in the blessed body of Jesus Christ the
sustenance and sweetness of divine comfort; and in penance and confession
true medicine for health to those sick in sins; in addition, in ordination
a true instruction regarding the service of God and the soul's[58] salvation;
for the Lord says: "I have chosen and established you so that you should
bear fruit, and your fruit shall remain" [John 15:16]; in the estate of marriage a chaste life is achieved; in addition, in the unction a certain departing
from this miserable and sorrowful life, etc. This is the food of nourishment,
feeding, pasturing, and life of the little sheep of Christ pastured under the
authority of St. Peter and his successors. In this situation these same, godly
little sheep have now remained fed, fresh, healthy, and unharmed for 1,486
years. However, those who have departed from this assembly and have run
away from the protection, care, rule, and preservation of St. Peter together
with his successors have universally become befouled, errant, and heretics.
Yet, for the sake of the pope's office (which the Lord God has established
and secured against the portals of hell, that is, the devils and their followers), this pasture will always remain healthy, pure, and unblemished and will
hereafter remain in this sheep stall until the Last Day, no matter how often

56. It is not clear whether Alveldt is referring to Christ or to the pope here.

57. LM: Explanation of the seven sacraments; LM: As Paul says to the Romans, the
first chapter [Rom 1:17]; Matthew in the fourth chapter [Matt 4:4]; John in the third
chapter [John 3:3]; in the Acts of the Apostles in the first chapter [Acts 1:8]; Luke in the
twenty-fourth chapter [Luke 24:29]; John in the sixth chapter [John 6:53–58]; Luke in
the thirteenth chapter [Luke 13:2–4]; John in the fifteenth [chapter] [John 15:16]; Matthew in the nineteenth [chapter] [Matt 19:4–9]; Mark in the seventh [chapter] [Mark
7:24–30]; James in the fifth [chapter] [Jas 5:14–15].

58. The original reads *siben*. The edition in the Bayerische Staatsbibliothek changes
the word to *selen*, which is appropriate.

and how fiercely the wolves and thieves root about, scratch, and dig in it. Yet, they will still not be able to harm this stall, that is, this office of the pope. If it should sometimes have happened that this office had an incapable, evil shepherd, or if it should happen in the future that it would have such a shepherd, the office will remain no less pure and unstained, even as it has also remained untarnished until now, no matter how often it has been attacked vigorously by the polluted heretics. We have [evidence of this] from two true experiences, which no writing that is otherwise right and proven [can contradict].

We know the first one when we read all histories that are right and approved, [namely,] that St. Peter's or the papal chair or the papal office has never desired to tolerate or endure a murderer, a thief, nor a wolf as a pope. I say that a heretic is a murderer, when he kills the little sheep in the faith with false teaching and with the poisoning of the holy sacraments from which the little sheep receive spiritual life, and, moreover, when they [i.e., the sacraments] are taken from them, they are killed. A thief, that is, a secret, subtle, and impious false teacher of the faith, also steals life from the little sheep. However, a wolf is a schismatic, a divider, destroyer, and corrupter of the unity and love of the little sheep and is also not capable of being a shepherd of the sheep, as our Lord himself has warned us concerning these three.[59]

The other experience [is] that there has never been a pope who was so wrong or who lived such an evil life that he harmed or wanted to harm the church with regard to these three matters, [namely,] the faith, scripture, or the seven sacraments. Brother Martin will also never provide proof to the contrary with any writing (even if he himself devised it).

This has also chagrined the devil so often. Therefore, he has awakened such a variety of heretics who were supposed to topple, that is, to kill and to expel this office of St. Peter from this assembly, so that he might then open his shop and trade his precious merchandise all the more profitably. However, because it was made indestructible by God,[60] therefore, this seat has also remained unmoved, as it will be hereafter, no matter how badly the heretics are chagrined. It will surely also not be overturned before Brother Martin Luther, even if (without harm to the godly) the apostate Bohemian

---

59. RM: John in the tenth chapter [John 10:1–18].
60. LM: John in the twenty-first chapter [John 21:15–17].

patrons, such as Jacobellus,[61] Jerome,[62] Hus, and Rockentzan,[63] and all the others, would rise up again, joined him, and allied with him, for the gates of hell shall not be able to do anything against this chair, that is, against this office, etc.

¶Therefore, Brother Martin should, indeed, exit from this dangerous path (which I heartily admonish him to do), for whoever fights against God wins nothing except that he separates himself from God and falls into the power of the devil, which a person (even if he fled into the land of Bohemia—unless he turned around again) may not escape, etc. I have often thought about this chair and power of the pope in my little German book, which I intend to revise and expand eventually, and where I have addressed the papal chair; the papal office; or the papal, spiritual power. My falsifier or interpreter of my writing has distorted this for me and has made the Roman church, external papal power, and papal tyranny out of it, perhaps with the intention of forming [the impression] in the simple people who do not intend to learn Latin that I defend Rome and the evil that happens there and that I allow myself to claim that the Roman chair must necessarily be and remain only and always in Rome. However, Brother Martin Luther has invented this as he has invented many more things regarding me. Everyone who has read my little book must surely perceive this. However, when Brother Martin came to the place in my little book where it is stated that Moses was a consummate figure of Christ and Aaron a figure of Peter, he has shamefully distorted my words and has miserably reprimanded, maligned, and despised me, as is his custom, and has threatened to teach me

61. Alveldt is likely referring to Jacob of Mies (1372–1429), who was educated at the University of Prague, served as a priest in Prague, and joined the reform movement led by Jan Hus. Like Hus, he particularly defended the distribution of both elements in the sacrament of Holy Communion.

62. Jerome of Prague (1379–1416) studied at the University of Prague as well as at the Universities of Paris, Heidelberg, and Oxford. He was introduced to the writings of John Wycliffe in England and was impacted by the English reformer's theology. He traveled throughout Europe and taught at several universities. However, his sympathies with Wycliffe inspired opposition wherever he studied and taught. He also became a follower and supporter of Jan Hus, and when the latter was summoned to appear before the Council of Constance, he also traveled to Constance and was arrested. While imprisoned he became seriously ill and recanted his theological positions as well as his support of Wycliffe and Hus. He remained under suspicion of heresy, however, and was compelled to appear before the council, where he withdrew his recantation and was subsequently condemned as a heretic and burned at the stake in May 1416.

63. Alveldt is likely referring to Jan Rocycana (ca. 1396–1471), who was a Hussite theologian and archbishop of Prague. His appointment was not confirmed by the papacy, although Rocycana attempted to receive papal approval. He enjoyed the support of King Jiři z Poděbrad (or Georg von Podiebrad; 1420–1471), who served as political leader of the Utraquist community in Bohemia from 1458–1471.

logic properly (which I [intend] to write [about] without [seeking] fame, perhaps as soon he teaches me, since it may once upon a time[64] come to a sleight of hand). I would not at all be ashamed of such learning, if I could discover it in him and would also know that his teaching was everywhere sound. However, I absolutely presume that he will not capture me with his logic, for the wise man says that the one who intends to catch birds casts the net in vain in their sight.[65] I now let this go. I do not want to presume that I have great courage or skill, but with strong confidence in God (whose honor I solely seek in this matter and not my own honor) I will not at all be afraid of Brother Martin's theological logic nor tyranny. However, my dear people, in order that I might make it understandable to you what I have written about the figures of Moses and Aaron and for once come to the conclusion of this sermon, you should know that there were three types of priesthood. The first [was] in the law of nature, namely, the priesthood of Melchizedek, which was then a consummate figure of the priesthood of Christ in the New Testament. Therefore, St. Paul said that God the Father has sworn that Christ will remain a priest eternally after the order and manner of Melchizedek, for the same Melchizedek was, after all, a king of peace and a priest of the most high God, without father, mother, and lineage.[66]

The other priesthood consisted of two persons, namely Moses and Aaron, who were then the highest priests, as it is written, "Moses and Aaron among his other priests."[67] However, Moses was a consummate figure of Christ in ten ways.

First, since he was a prince and highest priest; also no one was over him but God.

Secondly, since he freed the people of God from the power of Pharaoh, the king of Egypt.

Thirdly, that he fasted forty days and so many nights before he received the covenant of the law from God.[68]

Fourthly, that he was a bridegroom to whom the synagogue, that is, the Jewish people, was married, though not completely married, because he was not the right one who could awaken the children of God to eternal

64. The original reads *eim*. The Bayerische Staatsbibliothek edition reads *eins*. The latter rendering of the text has been translated.

65. RM: In the book of the Proverbs in the first chapter [Prov 1:17].

66. RM: In the book of Genesis in the thirteenth [chapter] [Gen 14:18–20]; To the Hebrews, in the seventh [chapter]; David in the 109th Psalm [Ps 109:4, Vg.; Ps 110:4, EVV].

67. RM: In the ninety-eighth Psalm [Ps 98: 6; Vg.; Ps 99:6, EVV].

68. RM: In the book of Exodus in the twenty-fourth and twentieth [chapters] [Exod 24:18; Exod 20:2–17, 23–26; fasting is not mentioned in either of the chapters cited].

blessedness. For this reason he was commanded by God to remove his shoes as an indication that another would come to whom the people would truly be married. Therefore, Moses's house was supposed to be called the house of bare feet.[69]

Fifthly, Moses is Pharaoh's god in terms of power.[70]

And sixthly, he was like Christ, as God has said through the prophet: "I will raise up a prophet from among your brothers who shall be like you."[71]

Seventh, Moses had a transfigured face, though covered with a veil.[72]

Eight, he was a faithful servant among the people of God.[73]

Ninth, he was a witness of Christ on Mt. Tabor.[74]

Tenth, he had his brother Aaron under his authority in the matters related to the people, like a vicar or deputy.[75]

Whereupon, it should be publicly noted that Moses is a consummate figure of Christ.

First, since Christ is truly the highest prince and priest.

Secondly, [Christ] is the Savior of the whole world from the power of Pharaoh, that is, of the devil.

Thirdly, that Christ fasted forty days and nights before he gave the new covenant.[76]

Fourthly, that he became a true bridegroom of his holy church (as a result of which we [are] children of God).[77]

Fifthly, since he is true God of all creatures.[78]

In the same way, sixthly, that he was and is the supreme [prophet] above all of the prophets.

Seventh, he was miraculously transfigured in body and in clothing, and he revealed to us his holy countenance, since he revealed all truth.[79]

---

69. LM: In the previously mentioned book [Exodus] in the third [chapter] [Exod 3:5]; In the book of the second covenant in the twenty-fifth [chapter] [Deut 25:9–10]; In the book of Ruth in the fourth [chapter] [Ruth 4:1–17].

70. LM: In the book of Exodus in the seventh [chapter] [Exod 7:1].

71. LM: In the book of the other Covenant in the eighteenth [chapter] [Deut 18:18].

72. LM: 2 Corinthians, in the third [chapter] [2 Cor 3:13].

73. LM: To the Hebrews in the third [chapter] [Heb 3:2, 5].

74. LM: Matthew in the seventeenth [chapter] [Matt 17:3–4].

75. LM: In the book of Exodus, in the seventh [chapter] [Exod 7:1–2]; In the book of Leviticus, in the eighth [chapter] [Lev 8].

76. LM: Matthew, in the fourth [chapter] [Matt 4:2].

77. LM: Matthew, in the fifth [chapter] [Matt 5:45].

78. LM: John, in the first [chapter] [John 1:1].

79. LM: Matthew, in the seventeenth [chapter] [Matt 17:2].

Eighth, he is a faithful Son in his house, that is, among his people, and not a servant like Moses was.[80]

Ninth, he was his own faithful witness, as an only-begotten Son who rose from the dead.[81]

Tenth, he also wanted a vicar on earth, as Moses had Aaron, so that all things happened in an orderly manner.[82] Therefore, he said to Peter: "Peter, you shall feed and rule my little sheep, not that I give them to you as your own but that they remain mine and that I remain their chief head. However, I commend these to you so that you should feed and rule them so that no heresy; no error; no poison in the holy faith, scripture, or sacrament (on which the life of the little lambs stands) may appear, etc."

Aaron, the other priest, was also [a figure], but not a consummate figure of Christ.[83] As Paul says, the priesthood of Christ is not according to the order of Aaron but according to the order of Melchizedek. However, since Aaron went to the high altar once a year with the blood of the animals, he was also a true figure of Christ. This Christ, our God and Savior, went to the high heaven with his own blood. I have, then, written nothing against this in my little book (as Brother Martin falsely imposes on me). However, since Aaron was a vicar of God and of Moses and was, therefore, subject to Moses—although he was above all the other priests—he was not a figure of Christ, for Christ is subject to no human being. He is also no human being's vicar, because he is God over all things. And since Aaron was a figure of Peter and of no one else,[84] Aaron [wore] twelve precious stones around his neck as a sign of this, [just] as St. Peter carried the other apostles, and he was the thirteenth, as it is apparent that there were thirteen apostles who were called by Christ. Thirteen rods were also taken into the tabernacle, but only the rod of Aaron brought forth fruit. This, then, signified Peter (who alone was to be the chief among the thirteen apostles). In addition, there were twelve lions on the throne of Solomon. They signify the twelve apostles on the chair of Peter. However, St. Peter, as the thirteenth, was to be the only one to sit on this chair, that is, in the office. This is what Christ commanded Peter to do, saying: "Peter, guard and rule my sheep, etc."

I expect that Brother Martin Luther will not crack open this nut for me. However, the nut that he presented to me in his latest little rebuking book and thought that it would be too hard for me to crack open, I will open

80. LM: To the Hebrews, in the third [chapter] [Heb 3:5–6].

81. RM: In the book of the holy Revelation, in the first [chapter] [Rev 1:5].

82. RM: John, in the twenty-first [chapter] [John 21: 15–17].

83. RM: To the Hebrews, in the ninth chapter [Heb 9:7, 24].

84. RM: In the book of Exodus, in the twenty-eighth [chapter] [Exod 28:17–20].

for him soon with the help of God in such a manner that the kernel will not taste good to him. Since he boasts how he has written other things about the papal office, about which he is not concerned (that I will touch them), he will experience that I will destroy for him the selfsame foundation together with the structure with the help of the eternal truth. And where he[85] has written unjustly and falsely, I want to reveal it openly, whether he is angry or laughs, and show him his error (only the truth must remain eternally). [I will] regard nothing else than God's praise and honor and also the salvation of human beings. AMEN.

Printed in Leipzig by Wolfgang Stöckel after the birth of Christ 1520.[86]

85. The original reads *es*, but the Bayerische Staatsbibliothek edition changes *es* to *er*. The context indicates that the latter reading is intended.

86. The Bayerische Staatsbibliothek edition continues with a discussion of Luther's eucharistic theology. This discussion is not translated, however, because a number of pages are damaged and sections of the text are missing. The edition in the Bayerische Staatsbibliothek is also of the second, revised, and expanded edition of the original sermon. The expanded edition can also be accessed via http://digital.staatsbibliothek-berlin.de.

6

Wolfgang Wulffer

Against the Unholy Rebellion of Martin Luder

—Martin Lohrmann

INTRODUCTION

A NATIVE OF SCHNEEBERG, Saxony, Wolfgang Wulffer entered the University of Leipzig in 1491.[1] Though listed as an assistant priest in Dresden in 1508, he seems to have lived in Leipzig, likely receiving an income from the Dresden church *in absentia* (a common practice of the time). He moved to Dresden in 1513 to serve as a town clerk, and local records indicate that he helped modernize bookkeeping methods there.

Beginning in 1519, Wulffer worked in the residential chapel of Duke George of Saxony. After hosting the Leipzig Disputation between Martin Luther and Johann Eck in 1519, Duke George became a lifelong defender of the Roman church. With his support, theologians in Albertine Saxony such as Hieronymus Emser vigorously opposed Luther and the Lutheran Reformation. Wulffer's first tract against Luther was published at the beginning of 1522. In it he refuted Luther's concept of the "common priesthood," which Luther had developed in *To the Christian Nobility of the German Nation concerning the Reform of the Christian Estate* (1520).

---

1. Biographical information is found in "Wulfer, Wolfgang," in *ADB* 24:269. Additional information about Wulffer appears in WA 8:245–46. Alternate spellings of Wulffer include Wulfer and Wolfer.

Later in 1522, Wulffer published a second tract, *Against the Unholy Rebellion of Martin Luder*.[2] It provided his response to *A Sincere Admonition by Martin Luther to All Christians to Guard against Insurrection and Rebellion* (1522), in which Luther had warned against the violent implementation of Reformation ideas.[3] Wulffer claimed that Luther was indeed guilty of fomenting insurrection, despite Luther's appeals to peaceful protest. His text therefore provides a skeptical Catholic perspective on Luther's early attempts to balance strong evangelical preaching with respect for political institutions and social harmony. Because this tract so closely follows the logic and language of Luther's piece, readers will benefit from reading or reviewing *A Sincere Admonition*.

Wulffer used biblical citations, arguments for the social good, and appeals to tradition to undermine Luther's views and reforms. While willing to express some critiques of the papacy, he generally identified apostles, popes, bishops, and teachers of the Roman church as reliable bearers of the gospel across the centuries. In contrast to such continuity, Wulffer viewed Luther as a radical who would rather tear down the church than tolerate imperfections within it. He also rejected Luther's claim that an individual could speak for God or interpret the faith over against the institutional church, as if the church did not have divine sanction or spiritual understanding in matters of self-governance.

Frequently borrowing Luther's language of "Christ alone" and "faith alone" throughout the tract, Wulffer applied such evangelical phrases to the teaching and preaching of the traditional church. With other early critics of Luther, Wulffer noted that the reformer's emphasis on right faith seemed to have come at the expense of Christian love; it is, however, hard to imagine a situation in which Luther could have demonstrated the right quality or quantity of love to satisfy his adversaries. He also accused Luther of extreme subjectivity in biblical interpretation. For his part, Luther had consistently tried to address the critique of subjectivity by pointing to both scripture and tradition for his positions, though such arguments failed to convince traditional Catholics who viewed him as more willful than faithful.

In the early years of the Reformation, Luther's rhetoric against the papal church escalated in proportion to the hierarchy's rejection of his reforms. As a work of the early 1520s, therefore, Luther's *A Sincere Admonition* uses heightened language to describe the social confusion, end-times judgment, and work of the antichrist that the reformer saw around him.

2. Wolfgang Wulffer, *Wid[er] die unselige auffrure Merten Luders* (Leipzig: [Landsberg], 1522).

3. WA 8:676–87; *LW* 45:57–74.

Even so, Wulffer's response still managed occasionally to overstate Luther's words, providing a good example of the rhetorical impasse that had already arisen between the traditional and reforming parties of the time.

Like Luther, Wulffer was concerned about the Reformation's effects on the "common people," whom he personified as *Herr Omnes* and *Karsthans* (see notes below). Wulffer believed that Luther was guilty of leading the general populace into spiritual error, social upheaval, and violence against priests and monastics. At the same time, his arguments here and in the earlier tract against Luther's "common priesthood" suggest a traditional, limited role for lay people in spiritual life.

Throughout the tract, Wulffer refers to Luther as "Luder." In his earlier tract of 1522, Wulffer used both "Luther" and "Luder" when referring to the reformer. Indeed, "Luder" was the original spelling of Luther's family name. At the same time, the German word "Luder" also carried a negative meaning, as it could refer to a scoundrel or a person of bad morals.[4] Whether Wulffer meant to invoke this meaning or not, his use of "Luder" is retained here because of its consistent use in the text.

Overall, this tract provides a glimpse into the conflicts of the early Reformation. While theological and spiritual divisions were certainly central to these debates, these participants also embodied the diverging religious policies of Ernestine (electoral) Saxony—where Luther lived and worked—and Wulffer's native Albertine (ducal) Saxony. Though addressed to the people of Wittenberg, the tract does not seem to have received much attention outside of Albertine Saxony; no records show that it was printed again in the sixteenth century after its original publication in Leipzig. For that reason, it likely functioned more to strengthen the views of people in Wulffer's home territory than to sway the minds of those in favor of the Reformation. In any case, it raised strong objections to Luther's early Reformation agenda and stands as a valuable witness to the commitments and conflicts of the period.

TRANSLATION

Peace and blessing to you in Wittenberg who live in the fear of God.

Dearest brothers, at the turn of the blessed new year, we sent you a work of Christ Jesus, our God and Lord, as the Father gave him to us for the salvation of humankind from eternal death.[5] In him alone is our salvation.

---

4. Thomas Kaufmann, *A Short Life of Martin Luther* (Eerdmans: Grand Rapids, 2016), 1. See also, "Luder," in Jakob and Wilhelm Grimm, *Deutsches Wörterbuch* (Leipzig: Hirzel, 1885), 6:1231–34; also available online: http://dwb.uni-trier.de/de.

5. This paragraph refers to Wulffer's tract from earlier in the same year, *Wid[er]*

In him alone do we find all peace and truth, overflowing with the treasure of all grace, so that through faith we are armed to resist all rebellions, revolts, and false deceits of the harmful prophets who treat our holy gospel wrongly and treacherously. This leads them to ruin and us to salvation and holiness, for we partially agree with Martin Luder's teaching from the word of Peter: "You are a royal priesthood."[6] We should not sacrilegiously boast that we are all truly priests—as Luder falsely interprets—when he says that because we are all equally baptized, therefore all baptized Christians come out of the water as true priests. This is unchristian. Even worse is the deceptive, harmful, and unfaithful advice he has written to all of us—yet which crawls especially into the ears of the unlearned simple folk—that says they should indeed boast, because they all speak with the true mouth of the Spirit of God.[7] This is how Luder and others try to create a holy rebellion.[8] But they do not say how all are priests, even though not everyone has been commanded to live and work in this Christian office. Neither do they say how everyone supposedly speaks with the mouth of the Spirit of God, when such power has not been given. Yet such is the unholy work that Luder spreads.

May God preserve us all from Luder's wicked ideas, dear brothers in Christ Jesus. There are two kinds of harmful uprisings by bad people on earth: physical and spiritual, the death of the body and of the soul. Luder has written of both. The title and contents of this heretical little book [*A Sincere Admonition by Martin Luther to All Christians to Guard against Insurrection and Rebellion*] awaken these desires, even as it cloaks them. It is written against us Christian believers who are in religious estates, as it calls for help from the secular authorities and the mob.[9] It falsely sets its evil will against the blessed light of Christian truth, which teaches all peace and unity. But Luder explains that we are not worthy of physical safety. Or, if we were

---

de[n] ketzrischen widerspruch, Merten Lutters, vff den spruch Petri, Jr seyt eyn koniglich pristerthumb (Leipzig: [Landsberg], 1522).

6. Luther had commented on the meaning of 1 Pet 2:9 in works such as *To the Christian Nobility of the German Nation* (1520), earning rebukes from writers such as Emser and Wulffer.

7. Speaking with the "mouth of Christ" is a major theme in Luther's 1522 tract, *A Sincere Admonition by Martin Luther to All Christians to Guard against Insurrection and Rebellion*, WA 8:676–87; LW 45:57–74.

8. Wulffer uses the phrase "*ein selig auffrure*" [*sic*] as an equivalent to Luther's "*geystlich auffruhr*" [*sic*], WA 8:683.31 and LW 45:68. LW translates "*geistlich auffruhr*" as "spiritual insurrection," in contrast to armed insurrection. This translation, however, will follow Wulffer's consistent use of the word *selig* by referring to "holy rebellion."

9. Wulffer used the phrase "*er omnes*" ["*Herr Omnes*," literally "Lord Everyone"] to describe popular opinion and mob behavior.

worthy, it would certainly not come to us, because we do not want it.[10] Luder is glad, however, to hear that we are afraid of human bloodlust.[11] But we who have been strengthened in grace are not afraid; we do not lie in faith's sickbed. We will be an unflinching and noble sacrifice to the Lord, should we ourselves become a pleasing aroma to Christ [2 Cor 2:14–16]. For no one can separate the elect from the love of God; that is certain [Rom 8:33–39]. Therefore, we believe in the Lord and die with him, as he died for us, setting our souls alongside those of our brothers. Luder writes not one word of this in this rebellion of his, as we shall hear.

"The blessed light of Christian truth . . . has risen again"[12] among Christian believers. That is true, but not with the help of Luder's raving and writing, as he ignorantly says of himself.[13] This past year of 1521 has brought Christian light to eyes other than Luder's. It has brought the holy rebellions that prosper the faithful, as shown to us in the rebellion of Cain against his brother Abel, Pharaoh against the children of God, the dangerous unholy ones in contrast to their Messiah—our God and Lord Christ Jesus—along with all the Lord's elect disciples. Scripture abundantly reveals the end of these rebellions, which are all the rebellions of devilish people, the same as Luder. As happened to all unfaithful people and as will happen at the Last Day, so will it go for all those who thirst for the blood of God's children in this Lutheran rebellion, which strikes the entire spiritual estate (with or without a sword) in body and soul, word and deed. This judgment fell upon Cain and Lamech in Genesis 4 and applies to all murderers [Gen 4:12 and 23]. And everyone who hates their brother is a murderer (1 John 3[:15]). This blessed Christian light will not be hidden under the bushel basket (Matt 5[:15]).

The holy sacred scriptures that describe the Last Day and the severe judgment of the Lord, which Luder pieced together to clothe his nonsense, are just as much against Luder as against the pope. The even more unspeakably heavy words of the prophets—for instance, Amos 5; Joel 2; and Zephaniah 1—threaten all Christian believers together with the wrath of God and the day of judgment, as the painters illustrate.[14] All the godless and the antichrists will be smashed not with the hand but rather with the mouth of the Spirit of God, just as dust is blown away by the wind and brought

10. WA 8:679; *LW* 45:60–61.

11. WA 8:676; *LW* 45:57.

12. A loose citation of Luther's *A Sincere Admonition . . .* (WA 8:676; *LW* 45:57).

13. WA 8:684; *LW* 45:70.

14. A reference to Luther's own words about artwork portraying the Last Judgment; WA 8:677; *LW* 45:59, including n 6. Amos 5:18–20; Joel 2:1–11; Zeph 1:2–18.

to nothing. Hellfire awaits such antichrists, just as heavy lead is consumed by a hot oven [Jer 6:29 and Ezek 22:18–22]. For judgment has fallen, from which Luder will not escape any more than he can evade God's severity. It is entirely true that those who believe this will not be judged with this wrath, for they will sit with the Lord in judgment, while those who do not believe will not stand before such judgment, for the judgment has already come [John 3:18]. But all must be judged, whether pope or Luder, living or dead, because they have loved rebellion and darkness more than the light (John 3[:19]). Their faith will not help them, as Luder writes, for even if they suffer great injury to body, goods, and soul, they will not be redeemed.

A damnable rebellion has recently started on earth. It refuses to end among the evil children of Belial [2 Cor 6:15, et al]. There is no peace for them, as the prophet says [Isa 48:22], only strife. They drive out the flock of God, the love of neighbor, and peace; they drive in the devil's rebellion and discord. Their hellish pain will increase, even as the heavenly honor and glory of God's elect children increases. And yet, these poisonous tongues think to themselves that God wants to give them a big, comfortable reward, as described in John 16 about those in the world who outwardly have the form of righteousness but inwardly are ravenous wolves in sheep's clothing [John 16:2–3 and Matt 7:15]. They come to judge and condemn your brothers, tempting the mob to do the same. But in your synagogue is Christ alone. He is not here in Luder's rebellion. When you read his work carefully you will find such rebellion disguised under the form of friendliness, loveliness, and sweetness; you will find the old serpent transformed into an angel of light. Because of the Christian truth that we know so well (2 Cor 2[:11]), we should not be surprised that the devil's apostle will see himself as a good servant who will seduce us away from goodness by speaking with the mouth of God's Spirit: "Their rewards will match their deeds" (2 Cor 11[:15]).

In his letter of warning, Luder finds no scripture more useful than this one in which he seductively boasts: "Follow me! Follow me! I am the true mouth of the Spirit of God, and so all of you must boast in this, too, if you want to destroy the pope and the entire papal regime." This is all devilish and unchristian, as holy St. Paul admonishes us in many places in his epistles, saying, "Dear brothers, imitate me, just as I imitate Christ Jesus," [1 Cor 11:1] not like Luder's "follow me, follow me!" The gospel of Matthew, chapter 13[:29–30], forbids tearing out the weeds whose roots are mixed with the Lord's wheat, so that we do not thereby destroy the good wheat. Instead, we should let the weeds grow until the harvest is ready, at which time God's angels will do the harvesting, not Luder and his friends. But our dear Luder wants to tear out the weeds through his own efforts before the proper time. Too high, Luder! The stone you have lifted to throw has fallen on your own head. You have dug the grave that you yourself will fall into (Ps 7[:15–16 and Sir 27:25–26]) and you will be captured by the snare that you have laid.

Luder blasphemes God and the holy mouth of God's Spirit. We will now prove this. Luder teaches in this unholy rebellion nothing except that these new Christians, who boast in themselves with the name of Christian, should speak the way Luder speaks: "My mouth is God's mouth, my teaching is God's teaching, my gospel is God's gospel (not mine), so that it can truly do its work of destroying the entire papal regime," etc.[15] This human fabrication by Luder woefully misleads these new Christians, so that they turn into antichristians. Dear Luder, why should not the traditional Christians also boast in themselves, saying, "My mouth is God's mouth, my gospel is God's gospel, not mine but rather his who sent me" [John 7:16]. Please tell us the difference, so that it alone will receive glory. On the Last Day—which Luder wrongfully and heretically teaches about—the old papists and the new Lutherans ought to boast, because they are all Christians. This is said by all in the great houses of the Lord, the holy Christian church, which alone believes the gospel and preaches Christ, all with the mouth of God and the help of God's Spirit. This Holy Spirit and mouth of God need not tolerate Luder's blasphemies, because it is eternally almighty and glorified in peace. The Lord will use this rebellion for the building up, not the tearing down, of the holy Christian church. The Holy Spirit shows itself where it wants, when it wants, and if it wants (John 3[:8]) against the desires of Luder and all heretics, as it says in 1 Corinthians 14 and 2 Pet 1[:20–21].

Dear brothers, let all with ears to hear listen [Matt 11:15]. Chapter 9 of holy St. Paul's epistle to the Romans describes the "holy rebellion" of the Lord. Luder clothes himself in this passage, as if we do not know Paul and his desire to become "accursed and cut off" for the sake of the Jews, his brothers according to the flesh.[16] Similarly, the holy prophet Moses would have been erased from the book of life, if only to drive the Jews from the law so that our holy Christian faith might enter into their hardened hearts [Rom 9:16–10:4]. God wants to have mercy on them. Such mercy does not only exist concerning the hard-headedness of the Jews alone. For how much more of a "holy rebellion" from the beginning of the world has there been through all patriarchs, all prophets, the Lord Christ Jesus himself in his human nature (Bar 3[:5–8]), all apostles, martyrs, popes, bishops, cardinals,

15. Wulffer again paraphrases Luther's *A Sincere Admonition* . . . (WA 8:683; *LW* 45:67–68).

16. Wulffer returns to Luther's theme of "holy rebellion" or "spiritual insurrection" (in contrast to armed rebellion). However, Wulffer incorrectly connects Luther's work with Rom 9:3–5 at this point.

priests, and monks, along with all the doctors of the Christian church. Yet Luder identifies all of these with the swarming vermin of the papal regime.[17] Up to today, all of these people have taught this holy work, that faith alone is holy. This, however, comes from God's will and inscrutable counsel (Rom 9–11), in which God wants all to be holy, for God does not desire the death of sinners (Ezek 33[:15–16]). One can plainly see that everyone has been spreading this message for well over a thousand years. Yet our Luder thinks he can accomplish far more—overturning the entire papacy—in three years.[18] No, no. Luder will not change anything as long as he is no proper son of God, born of the Father. Even if Luder had a thousand bodies to give to the fires of hell, nevertheless, he would still not separate one pious papist from the heart of a pious Christian.[19]

Yes, it is indeed true, that a holy Christian life stands in faith and love alone. St. James says in chapter 2[:18]: "Show me your faith apart from love."[20] You pious St. Luder, we Christian believers say, "Show us your faith with your love, in your Christian faith and papal love." One might be able to deceive a blind person, but the children of the light of Christian truth will clearly see that Luder's faith without love is full of rebellion and blasphemy against God. This holy Christian faith of ours was taught to us in the holy gospel of Christ Jesus, through which we have come to recognize and believe our heavenly Father, his only-begotten Son, and the Holy Spirit. This faith, which called us in eternity, shows us that ungodly human rebellion and damnable misbelief can appear under the pleasing form of a Christian faith.

Karsthans[21] is much smarter than Luder. This is because Karsthans doesn't laud his own proud faith. He also does not make himself a true mouth of God's spirit, saying that his teaching is not his own but rather is the teaching that his father gave him, as Luther and his father say. Even so, Karsthans threatens to beat us into a heap using spears and clubs. Dear

17. Wulffer over-paraphrases a list that Luther used to describe the papal church, WA 8:683, LW 45:68.

18. In A Sincere Admonition . . ., Luther described how much dramatic activity had taken place through his preaching in a single year and imagined what might happen in two more; WA 8:684; LW 45:68–69.

19. A reference to A Sincere Admonition . . . (WA 8:677; LW 45:59): "If I had ten bodies and could acquire so much favor with God that he would chasten them with the gentle lash of bodily death or insurrection, I would from the bottom of my heart most gladly offer them all in behalf of this wretched crew."

20. Wulffer substitutes "love" for "works" in his citation of Jas 2:18.

21. Meaning "the man with a hoe," Karsthans was a name given to personify the peasantry or commoners. It is similar to Herr Omnes, mentioned above. See LW 45:57n1.

Karsthans, go beat up an untouched field. Otherwise you might meet Luder and the pope, which will grieve no one more than yourself. On this point, though, Karsthans has grown unreasonable, thinking to be effective by using both his aggression and the books of God. But this would be wrong, because might does not make right.[22] And just as much as Karsthans's bundle of straw can help the sun to shine at midday (which is impossible), so much will Luder do the Lord's work through his holy commotion, which he thinks he will accomplish in three years. They are both nothing: Karsthans is nothing, Luther is nothing. Karsthans and Luther are one thing, but Christ Jesus alone is the true proper son of God and the promised Messiah, who drives out those empty speeches, enters into the hearts of God-fearing children, and gives power to become children of God to all who believe in him [John 1:12].

Luder has no Christian faith and, therefore, no Christian love. If Luder had all faith (which we do not believe), he would still not have love, much less all Christian love. That should accuse him in his own conscience. With his writing and raving, Luder has turned Christian faith and Christian love, being damned and being blessed, upside down, and much more besides. This is another form of rebellion that Luder would not escape, should we all act like he does without any kind of brotherly or Christian love. Both of the following things, however, are blessed: to ignore human rebellion and to do penance for our sinful life. For it is always true that Christ Jesus alone, the proper son of God in heaven and on earth, was given the power to kill and make alive, to cut down and to save, to cast into hell and to raise up again, to put belief in his holy faith into humans hearts and to drive all sins out [1 Sam 2:6]. In Christ Jesus alone is it commanded that we believe, keep his divine law, and pray for his truly holy rebellion. Through these things, one recognizes the children of God from among the children of the devil.

With our impure mouths, we want to spread the pleasing aroma of the Lord, though we are all impure sinners. Unfortunately, all our ignorance, blindness, falsehood, hypocrisy, lying, cheating, pride, blasphemy, adultery, murder, foolishness, gluttony, knavery, greed, and many other unholy sins, shames, and vices—in short, all evil—has been revealed and uncovered to the Jews, heathens, and the entire world. It is getting inexplicably out of hand, how all flesh wanders in darkness in these last evil days. If all this is true, as many are prophesying,[23] why should we pay attention to one evil among many and start a rebellion over it, storing God's wrath for ourselves

---

22. Wulffer invokes a proverb: "*Wer schlecht [schlägt], der ist unrecht.*"

23. Prophetic literature predicting the great sinfulness of the nearing end times had been common since the end of the fifteenth century.

(Rom 2[:4–5]) and rejoicing that we who are nothing truly are the mouth of the Spirit of God? Dear brothers, what kind of bargain can we make between God and the devil, between light and darkness, between the mouth of God and the mouth of the devil? So it is with the mouth of sinners, which we all are without exception. No one—including you, Luder—speaks with the mouth of God. You may not want to be a papist. Nevertheless, even if you prize your innocence, it will not justify you (1 Cor 4[:4–5]).[24] If you are without sin, then throw the first stone at the pope (John 8[:7]). Scripture testifies when it says that if we think we have no sin, we deceive ourselves, and whoever is guilty of one sin is guilty of all of them (Jas 2[:10]).[25]

Now, dear brothers, although Luder is not without sin before the terrifying, angry face of God, he nevertheless pushes his gospel, certain that he is a mouth of God's Spirit. Boasting before the entire world, he is confident that he has done more to dismantle the papacy with his godly mouth than any emperor, king, or duke has ever done with the sword.[26] None of this will help Luder, when he inevitably stands in judgment, as said above. Whether he wants it or not, the reward of his guilt will be his. How we hope that you all stay in Wittenberg, because nothing will be forgiven concerning this holy man! In Acts 10[:34], Rom 2[:11], and Jas 2[1:9], the scriptures tell us that God is no respecter of persons. Everyone has to take their part in the dance, getting the partner they deserve. As we sow here on earth, so shall we reap, whether in the flesh or in the spirit, as Gal 6[:7–8] says. The Lord's providence remains inscrutable.

Oh, what a damnable rebellion Luder's rebellion is in contrast to the holy rebellion of the Lord. The Lord's rebellion compares to Luder's rebellion just as you can tell the difference between Christ Jesus and his adversary, Satan. For the Lord's rebellion is not Luder's rebellion any more than God's mouth is Luder's mouth. St. Paul saw things that would not be proper to describe (2 Cor 12[:2–4]). Such improper and unchristian things to say include the notion that Luder's mouth is Christ's mouth. It is even less proper to write that all Lutheran mouths are mouths of Christ or that the entire body of Christ is an idle mouth with no head, no eyes, no ears, or feet. Compared to St. Paul's teaching, Luder's teaching is an idle mouth (1 Cor 12[:12–26] and Eph 4[:16]).

---

24. In *A Sincere Admonition* . . ., Luther had already complained that his opponents expected perfection from him and his colleagues: "We are not supposed to reproach them with the fact that among them there is hardly anything good; but if even a single one of us is not wholly spiritual and a perfect angel, our entire cause is supposed to be wrong" (WA 8:681; *LW* 45:65).

25. Loosely paraphrasing 1 John 1:8; Jas 2:10.

26. WA 8:683; *LW* 45:67.

As you read in Luder's heretical little book, Peter and Paul, pope, bishop, cardinal, monks, nuns, and Christians of all secular estates should be equally supplanted by the proud boasting and holy heretical rebellion of the heretic Luder, who applies all godly honor to himself. With beautiful evangelical words he presses onward, saying: "Now everyone—whether it be I or another—who speaks the word of Christ may boldly assert that their mouth is the mouth of Christ. I for my part am certain that my word is not mine, but the word of Christ; my mouth, therefore, must also be the mouth of him whose word it speaks."[27] Matthew 24[:4–5, 23–24] describes this boasting of the Christian antichrist, who would say: "Here is Christ, my mouth is Christ, my speech is Christ, my work is Christ." But when the Lord comes and judges, they will not want to boast in themselves anymore, saying: "I am not your mouth; I have not spoken your word; I have not done great miracles in your name. Such works would not have been possible, except through the mouth of your spirit" (Matt 7[:22] and Luke 13[:26]). It is truly a different kind of person who says: "I do not want to know Luder. He wants to play his game for two years. And if after two years Luder has turned the swarming vermin of the papal regime to dust and gone up to heaven to bring his Father's kingdom, I still will not thank him." As if we should be thankful for the destruction of the holy papacy. Such a destroyer sits on the seat of pestilence. Such idols are the devil's accomplices. For even if an angel from heaven were sent to us to preach a gospel other than that which St. Peter, Paul, pope, bishop, cardinal, priest, monk, and all Christian doctrines have preached, we would not believe such a one (Gal 1[:8]). Believing Luder's mouth would be the same.

Storms, rumors, persecutions, and pains are what Luder and his friends can expect from the mouth of God, because he is the pickaxe and gentle lash of the Lord, through whom God is giving us a home, as a benevolent father does for his beloved children, if we do penance here on our journey (Heb 12[:6–7]). The kingdom of heaven and the day of the Lord are drawing near. Therefore, we should subdue our evil hidden will and let reason guide us, as is in our power (Gen 4[:7]; Isa 1[:16–20]; Sir 15[:11–20]). All of this is with the help and grace of God, without whom we could not confess Christ for our salvation (1 Cor 12[:3–6] and 2 Cor 2[:14–17]).

Therefore, Luder: uproot, push, and destroy. Call all your friends to the gates of hell so that they help you drive and destroy all human law from the hearts of Christian believers. Just take care, Luder, that you do not uproot God's law along with the rest. Drive out pope, bishop, cardinal, priest, monk, nun, and all the swarming vermin of the papal regime. But watch out

27. WA 8:683; *LW* 45:67.

that you do not drive out Jesus Christ's pope, bishop, cardinal, priest, monk, nun, and the entire swarming vermin of God's regime. For these same ones teach, preach, write, and share that our Christian life stands in faith and Christian love alone, just as all popes, bishops, cardinals, priests, and monks have preached from the beginning until now. Take care, Luder, that you do not uproot all faith and all Christian love. Do not take part in such alien sins. Your ideas may be good, but your judgments and verdicts betray you, just as the Jews' good ideas led to false verdicts (Rom 10[:2–3]). This is how all Christian heretics are deceived, when they agitate our holy Christian church with its promises and commands of Christ. Everything right and true has been promised and commanded: the holy promise of eternal life and our keeping of the divine commands. This is true and right, as all elect children have been chosen; otherwise all would have been condemned to damnation. Everyone must confess that nothing happens unjustly, for God alone is the just judge, who does not treat anyone unjustly (Rom 2[:2–16]).

To drive home this severe judgment and wrath of God in order to drive out sins from those who are weak in faith—while letting the papal regime remain undisturbed by those who have perfect faith—is pleasing in the eyes of God, the angels in heaven, and the spirit of peace on earth. We should not pray with the sinful prayer, which Luder heretically and seductively teaches, that fire should fall from heaven and consume all papists and antichrists.[28] This is not the mouth of the Spirit of Christ (Matt 9) or of any children of Christ. Christ Jesus is the one who blesses (Matt 1[:21]), who came to bless and not to condemn. Members of his body should do the same, killing no one with their rebellions. They give all judgment to the Lord, for they love this divine love, which alone overcomes all things (1 Cor 13[:1–8, 13]) and comes from the same Spirit. It is unbelievable that all papists, of whom we write, are children of Belial. It is just as unbelievable that all Lutherans, of whom Luder writes, are all children of Christ. But this is true: that all children of God are children of Christ—not children of papists or of Lutherans—when they all pray to one God. No one but God alone can separate the sheep from the goats (Matt 25[:32]).

Nevertheless, all heretics dare to separate the evil ones from the good. They do this against our Christian light and truth, as we read in history even to our own times. Here the holy papal regime is often afflicted, tossed around, with enemies pressing themselves upon Peter's little boat, as can potentially happen according to the will of God. But it neither should nor must crash upon the rocks, even if all devilish antichrists were to destroy

---

28. Wulffer paraphrases *A Sincere Admonition* . . . (WA 8:682; *LW* 45:66): "You should in all humility pray against the papal regime as Ps 10[:12–15] does."

and annihilate both the papal and Lutheran regimes. We see this in the example of the Jews, whose regime began to act wickedly against God our Lord, yet whom the mouth and Spirit of God has not destroyed, to this very day. Were there in fact among the Jews still an idolatrous, devilish antichrist and enemy of God, even such a Jewish antichristian regime should and must remain undestroyed by the mouth of Luder and his spirit, as St. Paul wrote to the Romans in chapter 11[:26–28]. For a remnant of the Jews remains blessed, whom the Lord keeps for himself and who have not bent the knee to the idol Baal. [Rom 11:4] This was written for the comfort of us Christian believers as much as for the Jews. Luder has no need to destroy the entire spiritual and papal regime, because a remnant of Christian believers will persevere, whom the Lord alone knows, at his final return. The flesh, too, of such believers will also be holy, as Paul writes. Therefore, let us not sleep, lest we be led into Luder's rebellion and into deep, endless blindness.

Deliver us, God, from this devilish blindness and from the evil will, nature, heart, rebellion, and revolt of Luder, his friends, and all evil ones. Lead us not into the temptations of the devilish spirit, who from the beginning has delighted in revealing all the world's sins, shames, and vices. Such a spirit wants your *gloria* for itself, so that God in heaven and all supernal heavenly courts are despised, defamed, dishonored, and slandered more and more among God's people on earth, and so that one member bites, gnaws, claws, and devours another, until they swallow each other alive, rushing headlong into hellfire (Gal 5[:13–15] and Ps 124[:3–5, Vg.; 125:3–5, EVV]). There this evil worm and rebellion will never die, and its hellfire will not be quenched (Isa 66[:24; also Mark 9:48]). In that place is nothing but weeping and wailing and the gnashing of teeth, as the Lord warned many times in the gospel [e.g., Matt 8:12; Luke 13:28]. Luder's unholy rebellion teaches all these things. Who now wants to follow his advice and help him spread this message? The use of his sinful mouth and poisoned tongue works rebellion not only against pious Christians and beloved friends of God on earth but even more against God in heaven. Therefore, dearest brothers, let us and all who love and fear your God pray that—God willing—you might be safe from Luder's rebellion and all human rebellions, taking our well-intentioned sincere brotherly admonition to heart.[29] Do not sacrilegiously boast in yourselves, saying that you are the mouth of God, when you speak, write, or preach such sin, shame, and vice to your brothers. Instead—in brotherly unity and in faith, hope, and true love—make your hearts ready

---

29. With the phrase "sincere admonition" [*getraw vormanung*], Wulffer plays on the title of Luther's tract.

for the Lord's blessed coming. To this end, may the grace of God help us all. Let everyone say, "Amen."

Printed in Leipzig in the year 1522.

7

Augustin Alveldt
Against the Wittenberg Idol Martin Luther
—GEOFFREY DIPPLE

INTRODUCTION

AGAINST THE WITTENBERG IDOL *Martin Luther* (*Wyder den Wittenbergischen Abtgot Martin Luther*) was published in a single edition in 1524 without indication of either publisher or place of publication, although it was likely printed in Dresden at a press under the control of Luther's opponent Hieronymus Emser.[1] It was one of several responses to Luther's *Against the New Idol and Old Devil, which shall be Translated in Meissen*, a reaction to the canonization on May 31, 1524 of Blessed Benno of Meissen, a late eleventh and early twelfth-century bishop who had supported the papacy in the German Investiture Controversy. Luther had rushed to get his response into print before the formal translation of Menno's bones to the Meissen cathedral in mid-June. We know that Emser had a copy of Luther's work by June 8, and so it must have been to the press by the beginning of that month.

---

1. Heribert Smolinsky, *Augustin von Alveldt und Hieronymus Emser: Eine Untersuchung zur Kontroverstheologie der frühen Reformationszeit im Herzogtum Sachsen*, RGST 122 (Münster: Aschendorff, 1983), 425. Alveldt's pamphlet also exists in one modern critical edition: Augustin von Alfeld, OFM, *Wyder den Wittenbergischen Abgot Martin Luther*, edited by Käthe Büschgens, CCath 11 (Münster: Aschendorff, 1926). The Büschgens edition is based on the copy in the Görres-Gymnasium in Koblenz. This, like the Kessler copy, has an apparent misprint at sig. Djr, suggesting that there were two impressions of the 1524 printing.

Alveldt was not alone in his defense of the bishop's canonization; Emser chimed in as did the Cistercian Abbot of Altzelle, Paul Bachmann (Amnicola).[2] However, in important ways Alveldt stood out among Luther's opponents on this issue and others. Likely about the same age as Luther, he, too, was a member of a mendicant order, the Franciscans. Also like Luther, he held positions of authority within his order. There is no evidence that he had a humanist training, but he was a fluent Latinist, conversant with Greek and Hebrew, and familiar with the ancient classics and a number of humanist writings. He was also one of the most prolific of Luther's opponents, writing in total seventeen works that responded directly or indirectly to criticisms and claims by the reformers. Many of these works were written in the vernacular in a popular style reminiscent of Luther's, which suggests that he shared the Wittenberg reformer's strategy of trying to reach the widest possible readership. He was the only preacher among the most prolific Catholic controversialists and the only one to publish sermons. Like Luther, in many of his pamphlets he based his arguments exclusively on scripture.[3]

Alveldt's involvement in Reformation polemics began in 1520 with his defense of papal authority, *On the Apostolic See*, which provoked a heated exchange between the reformers and the defenders of the old church, to which Alveldt contributed two more works: *A Poultice, Newly Best Prepared* and *A Devout Collection*. However, Luther himself remained aloof from these polemics, until Alveldt contributed to the debate a vernacular reworking of *On the Apostolic See* (*A Very Fruitful and Useful Little Book*) with a more popular slant, to which he responded with *On the Papacy in Rome*. Alveldt responded in turn to this work with *A Sermon against Martin Luther*.[4]

Noteworthy among Alveldt's other writings were his works on the sacraments. In July 1520 he published his *Tractate Concerning Communion in*

2. Alfeld, *Wyder den Wittenbergischen Abgot*, 12–13; Smolinsky, *Alveldt und Emser*, 144, 289–93; WA 15:170–73.

3. On Alveldt's place among Catholic controversialists during the early years of the Reformation, see David V. N. Bagchi, *Luther's Earliest Opponents: Catholic Controversialists, 1518–1525* (Minneapolis: Fortress, 1991), esp. 198, 206, 267. Possibly the best recent summary of Alveldt's life in German is Smolinsky, *Alveldt und Emser*, 18–24. For a dated account in English, see Henry G. Ganss, "Alveldt or Alveldianus," in *The Catholic Encyclopedia* (New York: Encyclopedia Press, 1913).

4. The best overviews and analyses in German of Alveldt's place in the exchanges between the Wittenbergers and their opponents on the authority of the papacy are Smolinsky, *Alveldt und Emser*, 50–87 and Johannes Schlageter, *Die sächsischen Franziskaner und ihre theologische Auseinandersetzung mit der frühen deutschen Reformation* (Münster: Aschendorff, 2012), 46–68. For valuable comments in English on Alveldt's contributions to the dispute over papal authority, see Scott H. Hendrix, *Luther and the Papacy: Stages in a Reformation Controversy* (Philadelphia: Fortress, 1981), 101–103; Bagchi, *Luther's Earliest Opponents*, 50–52.

Both Kinds, which, again, did not call forth a direct response from Luther, but references to Alveldt in the prelude to *Babylonian Captivity of the Church* indicate that Luther was answering him at least in part in that work.[5] Alveldt responded in turn to Luther's work with *On the Marital State against Brother Martin Luther*, which appeared in German in late 1520 or early 1521, and *A Sermon on Sacramental Confession*, which appeared in Latin and German editions in late 1520.[6] Other works, published and unpublished, answered criticisms by the reformers of the religious life, the veneration of the Virgin Mary, and traditional burial practices.[7]

Note on translation: The original text of *Against the Wittenberg Idol Martin Luther* includes in its margins scriptural references supporting claims made by Alveldt. These I have included in parentheses at relevant places in this translation. Alveldt's biblical citations are not always completely accurate—in particular it appears that the printer did not have the type for the number 2 and substituted the Tyrian et. Furthermore, he refers to the titles of biblical books in the Vulgate, which do not always correspond to the titles in many of today's Bibles. Therefore, where necessary, I have provided corrected or updated citations in square brackets within the parentheses. I have also included the pagination/signatures of the original printed version of this work in parentheses in the text. Finally, Alveldt seemed to employ the German term *"Erhebung"* sometimes to designate the solemn translation of the saints' bones and sometimes as a synonym for canonization to designate the elevation of an individual to the sainthood. I have rendered this term in English as "translation" or "elevation" as suggested by the context.

TRANSLATION

Against the Wittenberg Idol Martin Luther
    Augustin Alveldt
    Guardian in Halle in Saxony
    Proverbs 16 [:27–28]
    The foolish man causes evil,
    and fire burns on his lips.

---

5. See *LW* 36:6–7, 12–17, 23–27.

6. For a complete discussion of the exchanges between Luther and Alveldt on the sacraments and analysis of the pamphlets involved, see Smolinsky, *Alveldt und Emser*, 105–43. A brief assessment in English of Alveldt's place among Luther's opponents in the controversy leading to the writing of *Babylonian Captivity of the Church* is available in Bagchi, *Luther's Earliest Opponents*, 121–22.

7. For the details of these works and the contexts in which they were written, see Smolinsky, *Alveldt und Emser*, 78–105, 151–66, 190–208, 403.

A perverse man incites war,
and a babbler divides the princes
Anno XXIIII

[Ajv] I, Brother Augustin of Alveldt, offer and wish the holy church, that is, all Christian people gathered in the unity of the true Christian faith and not scattered, disordered, and divided with M. Luther, peace, grace, and blessedness in Christ Jesus, our God and Savior, Amen.

Now have come (certainly we may speak here with King Hezekiah) (4 Reg 19 [2 Kgs 19:3]) the days of tribulation, of blaming and slandering God. Now are come to pass the words of the kingly prophet, when he says (Ps 54 [36:1–4]): "The wicked man has spoken, in that he sins within himself; for the fear of God is not before his eyes, and he deceives himself in his own sight, so that he neither discovers nor detests his own wickedness. The words of his mouth are simply wickedness and blasphemy. He does not wish to perceive anything good to do. Wickedness he devises in his cell, he stands in all evil ways, but he does not hate evil."

For he is the seven-headed beast that rises from the sea, over whose heads every (Apoc. 13 [Rev 13]) vicious, slanderous name is written, and as was revealed to St. John, that opened its mouth in blasphemy, slander, and vilification of the name of God, his holy church, and all those who live in heaven.

But how might one actually challenge, limit, and call to account this dreadful beast, this run-away monk, this pimp [*Ruffian*] and con-man [*Lotter*] of the Holy Spirit [Aijr], who so often has sinned in himself, acted wickedly, blasphemed, forbade good to be done, did and thought up villainy and wickedness in his dwelling, stood in all evil ways, defended and loved all wickedness, and conversely, annulled and censured all virtues. How he has blasphemed, defamed, and abused his [God's] holy church and scorned the beloved saints, of that all his venomous books are so full that he could hardly squeeze a little truth in between. He falsified the holy, godly scriptures in many places; polluted the holy sacraments of the church; reviled the most blessed queen and virgin Mary, along with all the saints on high; from the sacrament of baptism he made a knave's bath so that in some cases the peasants baptize their dogs and say: "Name the child," and baptize them in the name of (to the disparagement of) the most holy Trinity.

The holy chrism (which according to the words of Paul is a sign of the coming of the Holy Spirit) (Rom 8)[8] he calls oil-dolatry [ölgötzerey],[9] just

8. Alveldt likely has in mind here Thomas Aquinas's reference to "the first fruits of the Spirit" in Rom 8:23 in his discussion of the chrism. See Thomas Aquinas, *Summa Theologica* 3.72.2.

9. WA 6:407, 19–25. See also Timothy J. Wengert, "The Priesthood of All Believers

like a completely brutish person who thinks, as St. Paul says (1 Cor 2[:14]), that everything done in the church is folly.

The most venerable sacrament of the altar he calls a sign of the sacrament, that is, bread and wine, so that he brings it into such disrepute and misunderstanding that his wicked rabble even celebrated the mass with beer in Nordhausen.[10] Shame on you for your dishonorable heresy, which is even worse than Pikhartism.[11]

The sacrament of confession and penance he has so diminished that [Aijv] among his rabble it is no longer observed except on account of worldly shame and fear.

Out of the sacrament of marriage he has made—as the devil's master of the hunt—a vain mockery and chase; priests, monks, and nuns all become kith and kin, and as a result, from the priestly office he created a devil's net.[12] And so, with his hounds and preachers, the run-away monks, he can drive the poor souls headlong [fry in den hals] to the devil. Thus he blasphemes God in his holy church and the sacraments by mocking the grace of the Holy Spirit, which, as Mark says (Mark 3[:29]), can never come to his aid (because he is the devil's own and desires no grace).

Since Luther has now condemned, reproached, and cast scorn on the congregation of the holy Christian church (which according to the teaching of St. Paul is one congregation, one church, and one body in which also one spirit is lord, which holds its members together in peace and unity) (Rom 12[:4–5]; 1 Cor 12[:12–13]; Eph 4[:4–6, 15–16] and 5[:23–30]), including its sacraments, so he must have another church and in it another head and other members, which according to the nature of its spirit is quarrelsome, discordant, and irrational. Therefore, this same enemy of virtue and concord condemns God's beloved friends and saints, who have passed on from the true Christian church and are now with God. And he attempts to raise up a new church and also to populate it with new saints, such as the Wycliffites

---

and Other Pious Myths," (Valparaiso, IN: Valparaiso University, 2006). Online: https://scholar.valpo.edu/ils_papers/117.

10. I have not been able to find any account of this event.

11. During the course of the fifteenth century, heretics from northern France, including Picardy, moved to Bohemia, and in some circles the term "Pikhart" was used to malign the Hussites. See Thomas Fudge, "Incest and Lust in Luther's Marriage: Theology and Morality in Reformation Polemics," *SCJ* 34 (2003), 335.105. Clearly, Alveldt is using the term in a generic way to designate all heretics and idolaters.

12. Alveldt's meaning is not completely clear at this point. The German reads, "*ein eyttel gespöt und hundes jachet pfaffen, munchen und nonnen, gespten und gefreundten gemein und also aus dem priesterlichen stand des teuffels netz gemacht.*" Because priests, monks, and nuns were considered brothers and sisters in Christ, their marriage to each was decried as incest by Catholic polemicists. See Fudge, "Incest and Lust," 319, 322–23.

and Hussites and those recently burned in the Low Countries.[13] And for this reason the elevation of holy Bishop Benno so grievously afflicted him that he wrote against it not only as a Pikhartian heretic, but also as a raging, raving madman [Aiijr] (is he otherwise worthy of being called human?).

But you will learn shortly the difference between the body of Christ and Luther's church, and afterward each person will decide with which he wants to remain, because they are completely opposed to each other. What one praises, the other condemns; one tries to resist the flesh to remain in true obedience and to perform virtuous, Christian, and good works; the other gives free rein to the flesh, wishes to be obedient to no one, and in sum, to do nothing good.

The One Church or Congregation

This is the church or congregation, that is, a spiritual body of Christ, of which the lamb Christ is the head, yesterday, today, and in eternity (as Paul writes) (Heb 13[:11–16]; Col 1[:17–18]). In this body and its members, he has been killed since the beginning of the world (Rev 13[:8]). The first member in this church or congregation, in which the lamb was killed, was Abel, who was struck down because of his pure sacrifice (Gen 4[:8]); next Seth, the first to call on God's name (Gen 4[:25–26]; 5[:8, 22–23]);[14] Enoch, who walked with God and afterward was taken up to God and never seen on the earth again; Noah, who preserved the world in the ark and then restored its bounty; Shem, who served God in the tabernacle; Melchizedek, the high priest of God; Job, the righteous; Joshua, Caleb, and Phinehas,[15] who avenged the dishonor done to God; Miriam, the sister of Moses; and Rahab,[16] who willingly housed the strangers; thereafter, holy Abraham, who through his strong faith left the land of his father for a foreign one and was willing to sacrifice his own most beloved son to please God; Isaac, the just; Jacob, the innocent; and [Aiijv] the other beloved patriarchs.

In the course of time, came elect Moses with his brother Aaron, under whom almighty God gave to this his church a fitting, immaculate law and

13. Two Augustinian friars from Antwerp, Henri Voes and Jan van Esch, were burned in Brussels on July 1, 1523 for refusing to recant their "Lutheran" attitudes. For Luther's comments about them in *Against the New Idol and Old Devil*, see WA 15:184.

14. According to Gen 4:26, Seth's son Enoch was the first to call on God's name.

15. Caleb was one of the spies sent into the land of Canaan (Num 13–14). Phinehas was the nephew of Aaron (Num 25:7–8, 11–13).

16. Rahab, a woman of Jericho, housed and protected the spies sent into the city by Joshua (Josh 2).

appropriate testament to observe (Exod 20), until the promised and great prophet Christ himself visited us on earth.

For this church Moses raised up at God's command a tabernacle (Exod 4[:40]) (in which day and night divine service was to be observed). After that Samuel assembled a group of monks or spiritual men (who should praise God) in Bethel (1 Roma 10 [1 Sam 10:3–4]).[17] Similarly, in Gilgal Elisha served God with one hundred monks and received alms from the people (4 Roma 4[2 Kgs 4:38]).

In this church David instituted, maintained, and increased from day to day the divine service with prayer, hymns of praise, organs, and rejoicing (2 Para 24 [1 Chr 24]); Solomon built the most beautiful temple (3 Reg 9 [1 Kgs 9]); Jehoshaphat and Hezekiah (2 Para 19 [2 Chr 19]) diligently roused the people in service to God and again purified the temple; Josiah restored it (4 Reg 22 [2 Kgs 22:3–6]); and, after it was destroyed, Zerubbabel, Esdras [Ezra], and Nehemiah rebuilt it. Also, the Maccabees struggled so nobly, shed their blood, and finally died for the sake of the temple and God's service and law. In the same way, the holy prophets have so variously, diligently, and earnestly taught, commanded, and counseled holy penitence, fasting, prayer, almsgiving, and other good works for the church, as one finds in many places in Isaiah, Jeremiah, Ezekiel, and the twelve prophets. And in the same church Solomon taught virtue, discipline, humility, righteousness, temperance, [Aiiijr] earnestness, and fear of God in all his books.

This church or congregation has never left any depravity, vice, wickedness, or knavery go unpunished. But when it has remained silent and (as one says) peeked through the fingers, then God (who is the head of this church) has fiercely and grievously punished it, as is clear in the contents of the entire Old Testament. But when that same head, Christ our savior, came down to us and visited us, then he rebuilt anew, purified, and commanded the holy twelve apostles and seventy-two disciples that they should assemble it from the four corners of the earth and increase in it the wheat and the chosen (Matt 10[:1–4]; Luke 10[:1]). To this church he also gave and dedicated the Holy Spirit to rule it and to teach it everything necessary, to make statutes to command and forbid, and to remain with it, even to the end of the world (John 16[:13–15]; Matt 28[:19–20]). He increased it such that in one day it grew by around 8,000 people, among whom none retained his own possessions (Acts 2[:41–47] and 4[:4, 32–37]);[18] all served God in the temple day and night; and all lived from their common goods

---

17. "Roma" (Romans) is a misprint of "Regi" (Kings).

18. Alveldt appears to be adding together the numbers of new adherents to the early Christian movement contained in Acts 2:41; 4:4.

and alms (1 Cor 16[:1]; 2 Cor 8[:1–4]). Paul and Barnabas cared for them, gathered and then sent them alms from Macedonia, Galatia, and Corinth (Gal 2[:10]), as Paul, Peter, and John had promised, and preserved them during the famine under Claudius (Acts 13[11:28–30]); in those days the whole church was nothing but monks and nuns, not according to their dress but according to their lives.

Christ commanded Peter to protect this church from the wolves [Aiiijv], thieves, and murderers, that is, from those who tear asunder love and unity, the falsifiers of faith, the thieves of honor, and the murderers of souls (John 10[:8–12]; 14[15:18–20]; 16[:2–4]; 21[:15ff]). This church the wolves, thieves, and murderers have furiously assailed so often from its beginning until now. However, because it was built on the rock that is Christ, they could raise nothing against it (Matt 6[16:18–19]; 1 Cor 10[:4]). Although the devil raised up thirteen universal persecutions, twenty-one *schismata* or divisions, and 300 heresies against it to this point (Matt 16[:18]), he was able to accomplish nothing, because the gates of hell can do nothing against it.

This church also has an obvious name, which neither flesh nor the world nor the devil can take from it, namely Catholic, that is: manifestly universal; for it is free of divisions among its members and united throughout the whole world.[19] It is also called apostolic, because it alone has the seat or office of an apostle, in which even now a constant representative of Christ and St. Peter should be sitting (Luke 22[:31–32]). This seat alone has remained whole. But the other seats of the apostles have fallen through the devil's sieve; for Christ prayed for Peter that his faith would not be separated by the devil and never again be found lacking. And, therefore, there is no other apostle's office (except the office of Peter) in the entire world stronger in its inheritance. On this seat no pope has sat who could have done damage to this church or congregation in faith or nourishment of the soul (even if he led an evil life and therefore was harmful to himself alone) (Rom 1).[20]

This church and congregation (in which Christ is the head and in which the Holy Spirit resides, because it is a body and a spirit) alone has examined, tested, confirmed, and accepted the four evangelists (Eph 4[:4ff]), similarly the holy four doctors,[21] and other writings that together we call the Bible, and [Bjr] proclaimed that faith be given to these alone, and

---

19. Here, again, Alveldt's meaning is obscure. The German reads, "*dann sie ist in yren gelidern yres dings frey und eintrechtig uber die gantzen welt.*"

20. Alveldt's reference here is not clear.

21. St. Gregory the Great, St. Ambrose, St. Augustine, and St. Jerome.

besides, that other gospels and books, written by Nicodemus and others,[22] be rejected. But whoever strives, speaks, or writes against it and for this reason is punished or admonished twice and still does not amend his ways, is then thrown out of or flees this church (Titus 3[:10]) and is regarded as a heretic. And it should not be otherwise than that (Exod 22[:20]); they should be rooted out with the sword, fire, or water just as Moses, Phinehas, Elijah, and Peter have done, under the new law just as under the old (Exod 33[34:13–15?]; Num 25[:5, 7–8, 11ff]; 3 Kings 13[1 Kgs 18:40]; Acts 3[5:1–10]); for Christ came not to abolish the law but to fulfill it (Matt 5[:17]), and the same God who gave the old law also established the new law. For this reason, Peter through the Holy Ghost pulled up the tares Ananias and Sapphira, who did not introduce as much evil into the world as Wycliffe and Luther have, from among the wheat, that is, out of the Christian congregation. Although some, claiming to be evangelical, cry and write in Hebrew, Greek, Latin, and German that according to the gospel one should not root the tares out from the wheat but let them grow until the harvest, they remain silent about the fact that at that time the tares should be bound together and thrown into the fire, and the wheat should be gathered up into barns. But these same simpletons do not consider that Christ here has not forbidden at all that the tares be rooted out. Instead, as St. Paul says [1 Cor 11:19], it is necessary that the heresies arise so that the steadfast are revealed; so, in order to distinguish the wheat, he wants to let the tares grow up with it a while [Matt 13:24–30], [Bjv] and first at the last judgment to separate all the goats from the sheep and thus throw the wicked into the eternal fire and lead the God-fearing to eternal blessedness (1 Tim 5[:20]).[23] It is no wonder that the wicked wish to remain unpunished (which, however, Paul does not want), but doubtless it would be much better that they be punished here than that it wait until the hereafter.

This church has now celebrated the holy sacraments for over 1,400 years, highly revered true poverty, chastity, and obedience (all of which Luther now wants to destroy), and diligently practiced fasting, praying, giving alms, going to church, praising God, and other good works. It has remained steadfast in true penitence, in correct belief, in burning love, and sturdy hope. And still today, God willing, it will continue standing and none will challenge it, except those who do not belong to this church.

This church or congregation has through the councils, of which more than thirty were held, first by the apostles and afterwards their successors,

22. The *Gospel of Nicodemus*, also referred to as *The Acts of Pilate*, was an apocryphal gospel attributed to Jesus's associate Nicodemus, mentioned in the Gospel of John.

23. Cf. 2 Tim 2:14–4:18.

legislated, ordained, commanded, and forbade (Acts 1[:13–26]; 6[:2–6]; 15; 7[21:17]) how things are to be observed in matters concerning the holy Christian faith, challenges to holy scripture, the most revered sacraments, good morals, love, unity, and vice; and these things it ordained and arranged in such a laudable and seemly way that one must obviously recognize that this occurred and was brought about not by human temerity but through the grace of the Holy Spirit.

On the Other Church or Congregation

Now there is another church or congregation, completely opposed and contrary to the first, whose head and king, the devil (Job 41),[24] [Bijr] is not only a liar but a father of lies (John 8[:44]), through whose hatred death has come into the whole world. He also has his own members and successors, (Wis 7[2: 24]) as we will learn later.

Holy David calls this church an *ecclesia malignantium* (a congregation of the wicked) (Ps 25[:5, Vg.; 26:5, EVV]) that is, the church of blasphemers and the ungodly and evil rogues. But St. John calls it the synagogue of Satan, that is, the devil's congregation, through which the fire of lewdness and impiety burns (Rev 7[2:9]).

In this church the devil has ruled and maintained order with his members since the beginning of the world (Sir 16),[25] and he has gathered in and held those same members in such a state that he left them neither peace nor rest. They must lie and deceive, scold and curse, quarrel and squabble such that even Solomon complained about them, saying: "They cannot sleep unless they have first done wrong (Prov 4[:16]), and they have no rest until they have deceived or brought someone down." "They leave the light and wander the path of darkness. They delight in sin and glory in wickedness" (Prov 2[:13–14]).

In this church or congregation is Cain, the murderer; Lamech, the lewd; Ham, the mocker; Nimrod, the despoiler; and all their successors in evil (Gen 4[:8, 19]; 9[:22–27]; 11[10:8–10]).

At the same time this church held its first council in Babylon, where they wanted to build a tower up to heaven and regain what their head, Lucifer, had previously lost (Isa 14[:13–14]). God the almighty demolished

---

24. Job 41, which describes Leviathan, might be meant here. See "Leviathan," in *Oxford Dictionary of the Christian Church*, edited by F. L. Cross and E. A. Livingstone, 3rd rev. ed. (London: Oxford University Press, 2005).

25. Presumably, Alveldt is referring to the lists of the wicked mentioned in this chapter.

the council and scattered the participants [*conciliabeln*] and damned knaves throughout the world. But straightaway, he raised up an evil church [Bijv] in Sodom, Gomorrah, Zeboiim, Admah, and Zoar (doing nothing good and everything evil), which the Lord consumed entirely with hellish fire (Gen 19[:24]).[26] However, at the same time, (as he still does and has always done) he spared and blessed pious Lot and his daughters, and thus something good in the midst of evil. But afterwards the devil raised up and established in his church a wicked rabble, for example the 23,000 who prayed to the calf and indulged in other villainy (Exod 23[:32]), whom immediately thereafter Moses had strangled at God's command. Still the devil filled his church more and more with wicked knaves and inspired their three leaders—Dathan, Abiram, and Korah—against Moses and Aaron, the leaders of God's church (Num 16[:1–35]). These, too, drew a great crowd to themselves and (like Luther now) taught that the whole people of Israel were priests. But the earth opened up (Ps 103[105:17, Vg.; 106:17, EVV]) and swallowed these leaders along with their followers and sent them to the depths of hell, to their supreme head. But how this church of the wicked thereafter grew and caused much mischief and bloodshed is described by turns in the nineteenth chapter of the book of Judicum [Judges 21]. This continued until the archvillain Jeroboam came, who undertook to overthrow completely God's church (as Luther does now) (3 Kings 12[1 Kgs 12:2]) and on behalf of the devil built two churches, one in Dan and one in Bethel, made all people priests, and permitted all evil (3 Kings [1 Kgs 16:31–32]). In this he was helped most diligently by two knavish and evil harlots, Jezebel and Maacha Priapissa [2 Para 15[2 Chr 15:16]). The first established [Biijr] the Pikhartian pit, where 400 Baalish and 400 Pikhartian priests feasted at their table.[27] The second increased and strengthened the devilish Priapist sect, and that so strongly that Elijah claimed that beside himself there remained none steadfast in God's church (3 Kings 19[1 Kgs 19:10, 14]). For, (as is now clear in Lutheran areas) when the altars of the temples were smashed, the divine service overthrown, and the servants and prophets of God murdered, he claimed that the whole house of Israel had fallen. For that reason,

26. In Gen 14:8 the kings of Zeboiim, Admah, and Zoar are identified as the allies of the kings of Sodom and Gomorrah.

27. Jezebel, the wife of King Ahab, encouraged her husband to abandon the worship of Yahweh for the worship of Baal and Asherah. To this end she organized guilds of prophets of Baal and Asherah and persecuted the prophets of Israel. There are several people named Maacah in the Bible. Here the reference is to the daughter of Absalom, wife of Rehoboam, mother of Abijah, and grandmother of Asa (1 Kgs 15:1–14; 2 Chr 11:20–22; 15:16). The reference in 2 Chr 15:16 to the abominable image Maacah had made for Asherah likely called to mind Priapus, a minor fertility god in Greek mythology, sometimes identified with the Moabite god Baal-Peor.

God the Lord consoled him, announcing and showing that there remained loyal to him still 7,000 men, who had not yet bent their knees before Baal[28] (Luther's forerunner) (Num 1[:45–46]). Although the number 7,000 seems insignificant when measured against six times 100,000, still it was a sign that God will always preserve and bless the good in the midst of the evil. These other heretics, both men and women, followed: Athaliah, Ahab,[29] Ahaz,[30] Antiochus,[31] Annas, Caiaphas, Herod, and Pilate, each with his or her own rabble. Also, at the same time, the devil awakened still another sect with the name Sadducees (Matt 22[:23]; Acts 23[:8]). These wanted to acknowledge no angels, no soul, and no life after this one. Nor did they tolerate any worldly authority, rather they wanted to live freely and they believed no scripture except the Five Books of Moses.

In this church belongs also Judas the traitor, the reviler of God and murderer on the left side of Christ, the liar Ananias and his wife, and the cursed knave Simon Magus.

When the devil noted that after the work of saving God's children wrought by the holy apostles, his church was greatly weakened and, on the other hand, the church of God was greatly strengthened, [Biijv] he was moved to furious envy toward God's church and became extremely angry, and as St. John has shown (Apoc 12[Rev 12]), he sowed evil seeds—that is, dangerous heresies—among the seeds of the holy gospel that Christ and his apostles had scattered, from which the lambs of Christ became diseased and finally were ruined (Matt 13[:24–25]). Christ himself has lamented and Paul has indicated how the false prophets were established in conformity with their head, of which we have been warned recently by holy scripture (2 Cor 11[:13–15]).

But the holy apostles restrained and suppressed these evil seeds to such a degree (Matt 24[:11, 24–26]; Acts 20[:28–31]; 1 John 2[:1ff]) that the weeds were not able to grow fully, and the wheat among them could grow and multiply. Thereafter, with God's permission the devil awoke in his church raging tyrants, like Dacianus,[32] Nero, Decius,[33] Diocletian, and

28. The text reads "Balaam," but clearly "Baal" is meant.

29. Athaliah is usually considered to be the daughter of King Ahab and Queen Jezebel of Israel and the wife of King Jehorum of Judah (2 Kgs 8; 2 Chr 21–23).

30. King of Judah from 736–716 BCE (2 Kgs 16; Isa 7).

31. Presumably Antiochus IV Epiphanes, Seleucid emperor from 175–164 BCE. He is referred to in Dan 11:21–32.

32. This name appears in a number of the histories of the saints, usually associated with their persecutors.

33. Trajan Decius, Roman emperor from 249 to 251 CE. With an edict in 250 demanding that all residents of the empire sacrifice to the Roman gods, he initiated what

others who martyred and sent to heaven the beloved apostles and other beloved friends of God and members of Christ's church. Then, as eternal God
took to himself these same apostles and members, the devil also gave to his
church new leaders and apostles like Maxentius, the ruthless;[34] Cerinthus;[35]
Ebion and Marcion, the slanderers and defamers of God's mother and the
queen of mercy;[36] Arius, the denier of Christ's divinity and his true sacred
body and blood; Donatus, the falsifier of baptism; Acesius, the condemner of
holy penance;[37] Basilides, Dolcino, and Muhammad, the persecutors of the
married estate;[38] Anastasius, the condemner of spiritual authority;[39] Aerius,
the condemner of fasting;[40] Julianus, the run-away monk and Pikhartian
knave;[41] [Biiijr] Jovinian, the persecutor of chastity;[42] and Felicianus, the
profaner and burner of holy pictures;[43] Nestorius, Monicus,[44] Appollinaris,[45]
Eutices,[46] and many more, who all together doubted and erred concerning

became known as the Decian persecution.

34. Roman emperor (r. 306–312 CE) who opposed Constantine at the Battle of
Milvian Bridge.

35. Gnostic heretic who flourished c. 100 CE.

36. The Ebionites were an early Jewish-Christian sect that accepted Jesus as Messiah
but denied his divinity. Marcion was a second-century CE heretic who rejected the Old
Testament and endorsed a docetic Christology.

37. A fourth-century Novatianist bishop of Constantinople, who maintained that
sins committed after baptism could not be forgiven.

38. Basilides was a second-century Gnostic who actually revered marriage. Fra Dolcino of Novara was a late thirteenth and early fourteenth-century heretic who rejected
marriage along with private property. Muhammad is likely included in this list because
of his endorsement of polygamy.

39. Anastasius I Dicorus, Eastern Roman emperor from 491–518 CE. He was a
miaphysite Christian and in 512 deposed the patriarch of Chalcedon so that he could
replace him with a Monophysite.

40. Aerius of Pontus, fourth century CE, rejected prescribed fasts.

41. To whom Alveldt is referring here is unclear, perhaps the Roman emperor Julian
the Apostate (r. 361–363 CE).

42. A fourth-century critic of Christian asceticism who was condemned as a heretic
by synods in Rome and Milan in 393 CE.

43. Likely Felix, the Bishop of Urgel in Spain (d. 818), who was prosecuted for
Adoptionism, but he was also associated with iconoclasm by Eck in his *De non tollendis
Christi et sanctorum imaginibus contra haeresim Faelicianum sub Carolo magno damna-
tum* (1522). It is quite possible that Alveldt was dependent on Eck here.

44. Peter Mongo, one of the leaders of the Monophysite party in Alexandria in the
late fifth century CE.

45. Apollinaris, a fourth-century CE bishop of Laodicea who denied the existence
of a rational soul in Christ.

46. Eutyches, a fourth-century heresiarch credited with founding Monophysitism.

the most holy Trinity and the humanity of Christ, and also with their errors have sent a great crowd from their church to their head, the devil, in the depths of hell. The four doctors and other holy doctors of the Christian church have so fiercely and valiantly contended, written, and fought against these errors and heretics that there are more books than there are days in the year, with which, by the grace of God, they have cut them down and rooted them all out. That is, until the arrival of the arch-knave Wycliffe (who not that long ago arose in England), from whose books afterwards hatched the Bohemian goose,[47] which has flown not much further than over its own land (at least openly) and otherwise [whose heresy] has been extinguished by the holy Christian church, except for what glowed among the ashes in a few perverted hearts, which the wind from Aquilon[48] has recently revived. But first now, as the time of tribulation nears, the devil himself has come and mounted on a false monk (that is) on Martin Luther. This Luther is the devil's saddle, with which he saddles the antichrist, and when he has ridden them into the ground, he will throw both horse and saddle into the hellish fire.

This Lotter[49] is not just a simple author of villainies, evils, and heresies, but also (without introducing to him now at the time of the devil what he has forgotten from the ancients) a renewer of all earlier evil and wickedness [Biiijv] and now the devil's vicar and a chief in his church.

What he now holds for leaders, members, and saints in this same church are those named above, who now receive their eternal reward in the place where they did their work. But what sort of members are now in the devil's church militant is not to be written about. Almighty God can even in an instant make a severed limb into a living limb and from a sinner again a righteous person. Therefore, I will not write about them, and I place my hope entirely in God that they themselves will acknowledge this, and through God's attraction they will flee from the wolves into the true sheepfold of St. Peter, that almighty God will gracefully help them and awaken Luther (to whom I do not begrudge this).

But, with that I come to the blasphemous little book in which Luther recently raged more than wrote (God forgive him) against the translation or canonization of the holy father and bishop Benno and other beloved saints of God. So, you should take note what was revealed above about how the devil's church has been ever since its very beginning dedicated with all of its members and diametrically opposed to God's church and its members. For

47. The Czech reformer Jan Hus.

48. On the north wind, as a bringer of evil, see Prov 25:23; Sir 43:20–21.

49. A play on Luther's name and the term *Lotterbube* ("a vagrant or blackguard").

the same reason Luther also fights against it. For as long as he has neither head nor members from his church in heaven, he wants to throw the saints of God's church out of heaven—I believe if he were able, he would throw God himself out—although he boasts about his martyrs in heaven, especially Hus and the heretics burned in Brussels.[50] [Cjr] But I am concerned that if they died in their heresy, they now have joined their head in the depths of hell for eternity. And besides, there are also certainly still more from Luther's rabble who have been hanged or broken on the wheel, who perhaps might also be martyrs in his church. Nonetheless, he does not have confessors in his church, and also few virgins, especially virgins of conscience, because all his members fight strenuously against these two things, just as he has written strenuously against them, which one perhaps has discovered even less in him. He wants to have a few widows in his church, but usually the meddlesome kind, of which Paul writes in 1 Tim 5[:13].

The doctors of his church are: Arius, Wycliffe, Hus, and others I have listed above, and the cattle are equal to their stall and the herd their pasture. Luther has such respectable saints in his church, whom he raises up happily, while he wants to tread the saints of God under foot. Therefore, it also vexes him greatly that the holy Christian church honors the beloved saints so, that it celebrates their feasts, translates and canonizes their bodies and bones, who, however, as Saint Paul says, were members of Christ and temples of the Holy Spirit while they were on earth (1 Cor 6[:15–20]); these he condemns, scorns, and mocks, and elevates against them members of his own church. These are knaves and vixens, run-away monks and nuns, wanton, drunken, and lascivious priests, adulterers and degraders of virgins. These he wishes to make saints, while they are still in this life, and not tolerate that the holy father and bishop Benno (whose holy life has been tested and accepted by the church) should be elevated and counted among the [Cjv] number of the living, as the holy Christian church has done for a long time in commendable practice. Did not Abraham purchase a piece of land in order to bury his beloved wife Sarah, (Gen 23) where Adam and Eve had been buried? Did not Abraham, Isaac, and Jacob especially arrange to be buried there? And Joseph at his end made his brothers swear that they would take up his bones out of Egypt to the same place (Gen 50[:25]), which then holy Moses took up with him out of Egypt and faithfully carried away, as the brothers had sworn (Exod 13[:19])?

King Josiah had the graves of the Pikhartian prophets opened up, their bones taken out and burned to powder (4 Kings 23[2 Kgs 23:16–18]). But the grave of the prophet who had chastised Jeroboam, the heretics' friend,

50. See WA 15:184.

for his evil ways he left untouched (as we now care for the bones of the saints) and allowed his bones to lie there and be preserved honorably. But how holy scripture praises, exalts, and honors those who lived virtuously and committed to holiness we have described for us in the forty-fourth to the fiftieth chapters of Ecclesiasticus.

Perhaps Luther also wishes to dig up his saints and like the beloved patriarchs have them taken into another land and elevated. But he is unable to bring this about, so he wishes to have the ashes gathered and made into wheel and gallows dust, which he can then exhibit as his relics; but he can't do this with his two martyrs, whom he passes off as saints in his scandalous booklet[51] (perhaps because the ashes are too long gone). But maybe he might still find on the gallows the run-away monk who was hanged outside Mühlhausen this past winter,[52] [Cijr] and otherwise he can also regard as saints and put in his calendar the many wanton priests, run-away monks and nuns, who this year suffered a foolish death here and there or otherwise died; for in such a church belong such saints that one does not dig up and translate from churches and churchyards (like our saints), but rather must seek and scrape together under the gallows and wheels; just like those from his rabble who frequently say that they would be just as happy, if they were buried under the gallows as in a consecrated churchyard. Perhaps some will get this wish. But the church or congregation is like its burial.

But now, Luther, I want to lay against you how treacherously and often you have slandered and injured with your insolent lies holy Bishop Benno and the holy church in this your libelous little book.

First, you begin by lying that the pope and his rabble do not wish to suffer that the gospel be proclaimed.[53] If you mean by gospel what you and your apostles have proclaimed up to now, according to which they permit all manner of villainy and evil, which they themselves have pursued—that is, what they have begun to do and to teach—that I will concede, but otherwise not (Acts 1[:1]).

Second, you lie that the popes raise up few saints, and those they have canonized are papal and not Christian saints.[54] Here you hang high on your lies; for who other than the pope has established and introduced all the festivals for the beloved saints, aside from your congregation of saints like

51. WA 15:184.
52. It is unclear to whom Alveldt is referring here.
53. WA 15:183.
54. WA 15: 184.

Hus, Wycliffe, Jacobellus,[55] Jerome of Prague,[56] Rochezan,[57] [Cijv] and the likes? For these you might make feasts of Bacchus and Venus, and celebrate these with your run-away monks and nuns.

Third, you lie that through the translation of saints' bodies the Christian people turn away from God's grace,[58] cling to stone and wood, and from this become lazy, gluttonous, and idle fat pigs in the chapters and monasteries. What further lies do you dream up, my Luther? But what does the cross mean other than the little word *"crux"* and the expression *"crux Christi"* than Christ? Can the expression *"crux Christi"* not hurt me (if I read it in scripture and am thereby reverential and thankful to Christ), so little also can a crucifix carved from wood hurt me, if I do not read scripture, but I am moved by it to remember the sufferings of Christ and to thankfulness. Similarly, I can be moved just as well by thinking on the carved and painted pictures and stories of the beloved saints, the grace they received from God, and that they acted and suffered according to his will, as I can be reminded from scripture. And thereby I am made thankful to God (as this serves us all as an example and model of goodness) and so sin much less just as if I read the same in scripture. But since you like to write big books about your saints (you want to put in them bare-face lies as is your habit), so you have no material that does not bring you shame, and therefore, I would rather be a fattened pig (as you call it) among godly people who serve and honor God day and night than live among your rabble, who are full days and nights and in between [Ciijr] even less temperate and wallow like pigs in their lasciviousness. Those who decamped and were among us, are now (God be praised) almost all departed from the monasteries and chapters, and therefore out of the Christian church and into your pigsties and Pikhartian pits; indeed, the devout stand before you and the devil.

Fourth, you lie,[59] [just as you do] about what Pope Adrian VI did, concerning what the Council of Constance did when they burned your holy martyr Hus and, on the other hand, [you claim] elevated blessed Thomas Aquinas. Indeed, this is clearly a lie (although with you lying is an easy thing), for St. Thomas, as is abundantly clear, was elevated long before the heretic Hus was burned.[60] You do this because you cannot smuggle your

55. Jacob of Mies, a Czech reformer and colleague of Hus.

56. A friend and colleague of Hus, he, too, was condemned at the Council of Constance and ultimately executed.

57. Jan Rokycana, a fifteenth-century Hussite theologian.

58. WA 15:183.

59. WA 15:184.

60. Here, again, Alveldt's meaning is not completely clear, but this seems the best interpretation of his intent. St. Thomas was canonized in 1323 by Pope John XXII not

saints in any other way. But our church has nothing to do with your saints. Put them in your *Cisio-Janus*.[61] We don't want to dirty our hands with that.

Fifth, you lie even against yourself when you say[62] that the gospel must be truly observed. And that is true, if it refers to not just being heard but also observed with works. How often have you, together with all your apostles, written and preached that one should observe it alone in faith and do no good works? And you lie besides,[63] without scripture, witness, or proof (which I also in no way grant to you without evidence) that St. Benno acted openly against the holy gospel, and if he had ever done that in his whole life, you have not proven thereby that he had not confessed or not done penance. But if it were necessary, the opposite could very easily be proven. [Ciijv]

Sixth, you lie so unashamedly when you say that Adrian VI's bull made beloved Benno a god[64] *eo, quod vocat eum divinum hominem*; because God himself said: "I have said to you, you are gods" (John 10[:34]; Ps 81[:2, Vg.; 82:6, EVV]). Similarly, he said to Moses: "I have made you a god over Pharaoh"—thus I now say: "Pfui, would that God had given you your due and punished you! Shame on you, you evil Luther!"

Seventh, you lie[65] that the pope has established a new article of faith in that he has proclaimed Benno to be holy. Ach, you sly fool, do you even know what faith is, what the community of saints is, what the members of Christ are in body and spirit (Eph 4[:4]; 1 Cor 12[: esp. 12 and 13])? It is no wonder that you are obdurate in this and in other things, since you do not have the spirit of Christ but rather the spirit of your church. Therefore, for you everything with which the church is engaged is folly, as St. Paul says (1 Cor 2[:14]): "*Quia animalis homo, id est qui spiritum Christi non habet, non percipit que Dei sunt, sed videntur sibi stulticia.*"

Eighth, you lie[66] cunningly that the pope only pretended to pray and in that mocked God's prayer, since his bulls contain the sentence: "And we have prayed to God that we do not err in these things"—and you seek to confirm your lies thus: since the pope confidently acknowledged the holiness of Benno on the basis of his signs, why then did he pray to God that he not err? Luther, listen, here the devil discredits himself in you. From what sign (tell me) does one know that the baptizer of Christ is in heaven other

---

at the Council of Constance (1414–1418).

61. A tear-off calendar.

62. WA 15:187.

63. WA 15:186.

64. WA 15:187–88.

65. WA 15:191.

66. WA 15:191.

than from his justification and his holy life, since he did no miracles? [Ciiijr]
Nevertheless, the pope could, if he wished to establish another festival for
him to honor God and the holy church, certainly, ask God the Lord that he
did not err in doing that. But for you everything good is contrary.

Ninth, you lie maliciously[67] as a malignant falsifier of scripture that
the holy scripture says little or even absolutely nothing about the saints in
heaven but speaks rather about the saints here on earth. My dear fellow, but
what does Paul write in Eph 4[:8]? Does he not write that Christ released
the devil's captives and led them to heaven with him? But tell me, you run-
away monk, what kind of saints are these, if scripture says nothing about
saints! Have you read nothing of this in scripture? Then read Ecclesiasticus
44 and all of the Revelation of John! But I know well that you have said
that Ecclesiasticus is not a canonical book and that Revelation is a dream
just like the fourth book of Esdras [2 Esdras]. But I do not dispute with
a Jew, whose canon does not include Ecclesiasticus, but with a perverted
Christian, against whom the scripture accepted by the church is sufficient.
Do you want to regard Revelation as a dream? Then, by the same token,
you must dismiss all the prophets like Ezekiel, Daniel, Jeremiah, Zechariah,
and Hosea, who saw such miraculous visions, and like John who spoke in
strange images and figures. Go, take a close look at yourself and learn to
recognize your blindness!

Tenth, you lie fraudulently[68] when you want to claim that the Psalm,
"Praise God in his saints" [Ps 150:1], refers to temples of stone and wood.
Thus St. Paul has said that everything that has occurred here, has occurred
in a figure and sign [1 Cor 10:6, 11], [Ciiijv] and that men exist not for
the sake of the temple, but more the temple was built for the sake of men,
who are the temple of the Holy Spirit (1 Cor 6[:19])—and that everything
recorded occurs for our betterment (Rom 13[15:4]): Scripture is here to be
understood as speaking more about the spiritual than the physical temple,
and the Hebrew in this place, where you force it to support your side, is
more suitably translated into German in this way. For one has in Hebrew
there "bekadeschu." Now the word "kadesch" means not only holiness or
holy temple but also in many places in scripture a holy person, as for example in Psalm 33[:10, Vg.; 34:9, EVV]: "Timete Dominum, omnes sancti eius!"
Similarly, you have "kadoschaff," that is, "his saints," in Ps 77[:41, Vg.; 78:41,
EVV], "Et sanctum Israel"; in Psalm 105[:16, Vg.; 106:16, EVV], "Et Aaron
sanctum Domini," where there is always the word "kadesch," and therefore,

67. WA 15:192.
68. WA 15:195.

our translation is correct. Likewise, the holy fathers correctly and truthfully interpret this word as "saints."

Eleventh, you lie temptingly[69] that when Christ said that one will pray neither here nor in Jerusalem (John 4[:21]), he did away with all physical locations for prayer. That you are here lying once more is evident from the fact that Christ, after he said this, himself went into the temple and there prayed (John 8[:2]); furthermore, the first Christian church diligently praised and called on God the Lord in the temple (Acts 2[:46, especially]); Peter went into the temple with John at Nones[70] (Acts 3[:1]); and Paul made his offering in the temple (Acts 21[:26]) and taught the Corinthians that they should not disdain the temple (1 Cor 3:16–17). But perhaps there is no need for God's temple in your church, because your congregation comes together seldom or never to serve God or do something good. You can accomplish evil [Djr] in any place, and especially in the corners and dark Pikhartian pits. Our temple has now stood for 1,400 years, and it will certainly continue to stand before you and the devil.

These are Luther's eleven lies fabricated against the Christian church and the holy Bishop Benno. Indeed, a good printer could set three times eleven and still not encompass all his lies in it.[71] With what other abusive words and names he has slandered the holy man of God, I will leave to God the Lord, according to the teaching of Paul (Rom 12[:19]); he will certainly answer and also punish it in time.

I would like to know who has sent out this shameless slanderer of saints and also commissioned him to write, scold, and teach. Paul says that no one should preach unless he is sent (Rom 10[:15]). Then, who sent him? I can truly find no one who sent him other than the spirit that led Judas out of the congregation of Christ and among the wrathful Jews and evil knaves to betray Christ (John 3[13:27])—in this Luther wishes to sell and betray the same spiritual body of Christ, that is, the churches of the world, to the devil and the flesh, just as Judas did to Christ, after he was led out of the congregation of the holy Christian church (Rom 12[:4–5]; 1 John 2[:18–19]). Therefore, Judas is nothing more than the figure of Luther, and he [Luther] has nothing more to do than to hang himself.

Luther has searched here and there for a long time and (as he writes) could find nothing other than Moses's grave and the bronze snake.[72] Look

69. WA 15:196.

70. The fifth canonical hour.

71. "Three times eleven": our copy, and the one used by Büschgens, reads d ey o, but other copies read drey o. o is the medieval roman numeral for 11.

72. WA 15:184.

further, you blind leader of the blind! In all of this you sought nothing
other than a bird call. Could you not find the grave of Joseph *et ossium
eius laudem*, [Djv] the translation of his bones (Sir 23[49:15]), similarly, the
grave of the prophet whom Josiah saved (4 Kings 23[2 Kgs 23:17–18]) and
afterwards the grave and bones of Elisha who raised up the dead man? All
of these your blind eyes have not seen or—because they do not serve you
in your wickedness—perhaps did not wish to see. But where will you find
the graves of Brother Johann and Brother Heinrich, the two Augustinian
monks, your two martyrs who were burned at Brussels? That I don't know.
But you complain extensively that they were killed and not regarded as martyrs. Don't let that gnaw at your heart; for if they were true martyrs, then
rejoice that you have two patron saints in your synagogue, but if they are
(as one says) wicked knaves, then why lament them so much? If you claim,
however, that Adrian VI is for this reason a murderer[73] and, if he does not
repent this, is damned, then you must equally damn St. Peter, [who killed]
Ananias and Sapphira [Acts 5:1–10] and holy Elijah who killed around 800
Pikhartian priests [1 Kgs 18], and similarly damn other beloved saints even
more.

You accuse the beloved holy father and bishop Benno[74] of submit-
ting to Pope Gregory VII for help against the tyrannical Emperor Henry
[IV] (who undertook, as you would now like to see, to take temporal goods
from the church with illegitimate and ungodly force), and you condemn the
same pope together with Bishop Benno (because for this reason he deposed
and then placed the emperor under the ban, in which state he then died).
Furthermore, you do not regard Benno as a saint, because this occurred
on account of temporal goods.[75] Ach, how diligently you seek to vilify the
saints and prelates of the Christian church, [Dijr] none of whom, indeed,
you spare. Should holy Benno be damned, because he sought to protect his
prelates and equally his church, the plundering of which you would have
supported? Then what about Moses, Abraham and David, Phinehas, Elijah,
and St. Peter, who also for the sake of temporal goods spilled blood and for
that not only banned, but even condemned the wicked to death? Just read
the tenth chapter of the Gospel of Mark [vv. 29–30], not superficially but
with attentive diligence! Then you will find that the Christian church not
only may have temporal goods but should have them.

You, enemy of the saints, you scratch together another matter against
the holy Benno in that you want to remove his name, which you do not

73. WA 15:184.
74. WA 15:185–86.
75. WA 15:186.

presume to take from the book of the living but from the hearts of devout Christians (which you could not carry out with lies) and accuse the holy man[76] of wishing to murder the archduke of Meissen [William I, Margrave of Meissen] for a slap in the face and thus acting against the gospel (which teaches the opposite). Shame on you, Luther, what you so diligently teach others you don't do yourself. Tell me: who killed the archduke? Did God do it? Then why do you disparage God's vengeance, since it is written (Rom 12[:19]): "Vengeance is mine, I will repay"? Did the devil do it? Then rejoice that you have a patron saint and martyr in your Pikhartian church! I maintain that he who murdered the first-born in Egypt and killed Ananias and Sapphira also struck down the archduke. Just as little as the angel of God, Moses, and St. Peter are shedders of blood, just so little also is Bishop Benno a murderer, [Dijv] but you are a useless babbler who never has his fill of scoffing—but that is no big thing, because a useless man can take no honor from a devout man with his scoffing.

On this you seek high and low and want to bring something important to market; you take Paul and Deuteronomy as witnesses[77] that miracles are very deceptive, and one should not believe that such things are important. Tell on, where have Paul and Moses (whom you have drawn here by the hair) written such words? For, if that were true, then neither Paul nor Moses nor any of the apostles believed in miracles. Perhaps you agree with and share the opinions of the Jews that the miracles of Christ, our beloved God and Lord, also happened by the devil's power and that the Christian faith (which also has been verified by signs) is a deception. Shame on you in your lies, you useless monk. You slander further God's[78] vengeance by claiming that Archbishop Wilhelm[79] unjustly lost an eye for the sake of temporal goods; and because Bishop Benno and the Provost of Meissen prayed for that, it happened through the devil. Master Luther, my dear fellow, here you belong with the Jews who said that Christ drove out devils in the name of Beelzebub (Matt 12[:24]). I am absolutely convinced that the same spirit that blasphemed against Christ through the Jews has here spoken through you. If you did not have the words "temporal goods" (which you use so often to excite envy), with what would you slander the holy church? And yet you know that the proper use of temporal goods is not forbidden to the church. Tell on, when Joshua had Achan stoned for the sake of temporal goods, did he do wrong (Josh 7[:24–25])? What was it that Ananias and

76. WA 15:187.
77. WA 15:188.
78. WA 15:188–89.
79. William I, Margrave of Meissen.

Sapphira hid from the [Diijr] church and did not surrender [Acts 5]? Was it not temporal goods? How is it, then, that you come forward like a rabid dog on a chain, claiming that the holy patriarchs have only punished for the sake of God's word?[80] Are you not ashamed just once to lie? Don't you mean that Archduke Wilhelm[81] lost his eye, more because he wanted to restrict the divine service (which is the true word of God), *cui servire regnare est*,[82] than because of temporal goods? Who is blinder than you so that you regard as unimportant[83] [the fact] that holy Benno crossed over the Elbe with dry feet, because it is possible for the devil, too, to do that. As I understand it, it is your opinion that he was able to do this through the power of the devil. Then you could also say that Christ, and also St. Peter, walked on water with the same help [Matt 14:25–29]. That is no surprise, because the name of the devil is more common for you than the name of God, and for this reason nothing pleases you more than to blaspheme and abuse. If there were a devout Christian vein in you, you could certainly write that this occurred through God rather than through the devil.

Further, you dismiss the book *Dialogorum Sancti Gregorii*.[84] That is no wonder, for some heretics have also dismissed the Gospels of John and Luke. Should we then also dismiss it, just because your rabble won't have it? *Dixit insipiens in corde suo: non est deus*;[85] but the foolish man has said there is no God. Should one immediately believe, then, that there is no God, because a fool has said so?

You also assert, besides,[86] that were Bishop Benno holy, one should prove that. Then tell us, there is a common rumor that you are possessed by three devils, [Diijv] can you also prove that this is not true? I cannot really say, but since nothing good comes out of you, I fear there is nothing good in you.

You grumble furiously against the glorious preparations for the translation of holy Benno and insist that the same should be given to the poor.[87] From this I perceive completely that Judas, the thief and betrayer (John 12[:3–6]) (whom I believed to have died in a noose) still lives in you, who grumbled devilishly about the expensive ointment that the Magdalene

80. WA 15:189.
81. William I, Margrave of Meissen.
82. To serve him is to rule.
83. WA 15:189–90.
84. *The Dialogues* of Gregory the Great.
85. "The fool says in his heart, 'There is no God.'" See Ps 13:1, Vg.; 14:1, EVV.
86. WA 15:190.
87. WA 15:193.

poured out on the Lord—but he did this (as the evangelist says) not for the sake of the poor, but because he was a thief. I do not know whether you are a thief, but I do know well that it is rumored that you are a defender and protector of the monstrance thief, the chalice thief, the treasure thief, the money thief, and the document thief. Hence an old parable that a penny is like the thief, and this one also: you carry water on a pole. Oh, dear Luther, if you and your rabble wanted to give to the poor, you could certainly give service and honor to God without challenge or hindrance. They say, however, that you have given far more to the maids whom you procure for their virginity than you have distributed to the poor. I find this hard to believe, because it would be an especially knavish trick.

You wish further[88] that no one be regarded as holy (through whom God has already worked miracles and who has also lived a holy life), unless one can prove conclusively that they were saved and remained with God. But how will you prove [Diiijr] that Peter or Paul, the apostles, patriarchs, prophets, or martyrs were saved in the end? Shame on you for your foolish allegations and your blasphemous abuse. You want the same and take Paul (1 Cor 4[:5]) to support[89] the claim that one should not judge or regard anyone as holy before the last judgment.

But how frightfully the spirit rages within you. Before you wanted the saints to be only on earth and have none in heaven, and you wanted to prove that with the words of Paul.[90] Now you want to have none on earth and want to prove this with Paul. You want, and you don't want; you disagree with yourself and your own spirit. You want to regard as holy none of the saints the pope has elevated, and yet you recognize beloved Elizabeth and Francis,[91] whom the pope canonized and translated. See now what a mad, fickle man you are! Who can take you at your word, or how does one answer you in this? Indeed, nothing other than: it is so; or it is, it is not—and thus one answers the fool in his folly (Prov 6[:26:5]).

And so to come to an end at this time, I hold you to your teaching as being completely against, *generalia contra*, how one should praise, honor, and call on God in his saints, and on this you have written so abundantly contrarily. But your drivel is so completely run through with lies, and so contradictory, and therefore so obscure, that one could very easily run aground and never come again to the true light. On this stand all your foundations. It is well known that the holy Christian church now for 1,300 years

---

88. WA 15:193–94.
89. WA 15:194.
90. WA 15:192.
91. WA 15:194–95.

has not honored and praised the saints as God, also has not called on them [Diiijv] other than: Holy Mary, pray to God for us! Holy Peter, pray to God for us! and so on. So now, if even a damned person can pray to God for his brothers that they not be damned (Luke 16[:22, 27–28]), how is it, then, that the beloved saints should not pray to God, our creator, redeemer, and savior, for us? To him be praise and honor forever and ever. Amen.

8

Johannes Cochlaeus

The Seven-Headed Luther

—Ralph Keen

INTRODUCTION

THE OBVERSE OF CLAIMS that Catholic teaching is coherent and comprehensive is the certain belief that the absence of these qualities is a defining mark of heresy. By 1529 there was over a decade's worth of writing by Luther and others that could, it was assumed, be marshalled as proof that Wittenberg theology was a fragmented amalgamation of contradictory propositions. Among the earliest Catholic controversialists to seize on the apparent inconsistencies in Luther's various works, Johannes Cochlaeus (1479–1552) was probably the most vociferous; and in *Seven-Headed Luther* he gave new form to the polemical task of exposing inconsistencies.

The dialogue form was a well-worn mechanism for refuting questionable religious ideas. Often there would be an imaginary conversation between a representative of the position being critiqued and a defender of the established order. Frequently the heretical spokesperson would be portrayed as young or confused or ignorant, in the end yielding to the superior erudition and reasoning of the proponent of orthodoxy. Elenchic dialogues are found in the Patristic corpus, and comprehensive refutations, line-by-line or paragraph-by-paragraph, are found in the works of many Reformation-era Catholic controversialists.

Cochlaeus's text is a conversation among seven different Luthers, seven personalities that he finds in Luther's works. Each "Luther" advocates for a particular part of the Reformation program: the Doctor, the pedant; Martinus, who strays from the topic in his writings; Luther, an enemy of the church, with the name suggestive of liar (Lüger) and rascal (Luder); and so forth (see the list of seven and the significance of each in the opening of the pamphlet body). The seven actively disagree with each other, pointing out inconsistencies and each asserting the authority of his own position. Each interlocutor's position is consistent, and each persuasive in its own way: the fact that everything said is the words of one person is what is meant to undermine Luther.

The concept for *Seven-Headed Luther* was a natural development of Cochlaeus's polemical campaign against the reformers. Well-versed in everything Luther wrote, both in Latin and German (while frequently asserting that none of it was worth reading), Cochlaeus had composed dozens of pamphlets refuting Luther's positions and denouncing his alleged impiety and immorality. Luther in turn attacked Cochlaeus along with other controversialists like Hieronymus Emser (1477–1527) and Johann Eck (1486–1543). Of the Catholic polemicists of that generation, Cochlaeus was the most influential over time: his 1549 *Life* of Luther shaped Catholic views of the reformer until the modern era.[1]

Why seven heads, if proof of inconsistency is sufficient to prove heresy? The image of a seven-headed creature is found in Rev 13:1, the beast rising from the sea with seven heads, ten horns, and ten diadems: the beast whose name is Blasphemy. In the Latin edition, a letter by Johann Hasenberg (Jan Horák, d. 1551) to Ernst von Schleinitz (1482–1548), canon of Meissen Cathedral, asserts that there is no more fearsome monster than the seven-headed beast.[2] As early as 1523 Cochlaeus was applying mythological beasts to Luther's work, calling him a "cowled minotaur" for his teaching about the sacraments.[3]

A secular priest, educated at Cologne and Ferrara and ordained in Rome, Cochlaeus had been a canon at St. Victor in the diocese of Mainz before joining the service of Duke George of Saxony, cousin of Luther's prince Frederick the Wise and at the time arguably the most determined opponent of the Reformation. He was in Dresden in January 1529, when the

1. Adolf Herte, *Die Lutherkommentare des Johannes Cochlaeus*, RGST 33 (Münster: Aschendorff, 1935).

2. Johannes Cochlaeus, *Septiceps Lutherus* (Leipzig: Schumann, 1529), sig. P2.

3. Johannes Cochlaeus, *Adversus cucullatum minotaurum wittenbergensem: De sacramentorum gratia iterum (1523)*, ed. Joseph Schweizer, CCath 3 (Münster: Aschendorff, 1920).

Latin original of *Seven-Headed Luther* appeared, dedicated to Duke John of Saxony, Frederick's younger brother and a promoter of the Reformation. In the preface to the reader, Cochlaeus states that the devil is the father of all dissension, including the discord among Luther's "seven heads in one cowl."[4] To the duke he declares that nothing is more important to him than presenting Luther: someone who has revived condemned teachings and disrupted territories (sig. (3v). "May God open your heart and eyes, so that, in the ancient piety and religion, you may see and discern the deception and malice, and perversity of this proud apostate" (sig. (4).

What follows is the first translation into English, or any other language to our knowledge, of *Sieben Kopfe Martin Luthers / von acht hohen sachen des Christlichen glaubens*, which was issued in 1529 without the printer's identification but was most likely published by Valentin Schumann, printer of the Latin *Septiceps*. A different version by the same title was published, most likely in Augsburg by Ulrich Morhart. A longer version of the Latin *Septiceps* appeared in 1564 in Paris, printed by Nicolas Chesneau.

The German version, completed on the first of April, 1529 and addressed to the city councilors of Lubeck (a city that would adopt the Reformation in 1531 under the guidance of Johannes Bugenhagen) is shorter than the forty-five chapters of the *Septiceps*, but serves the same purpose of exposing the inconsistencies in Luther's writings. Meant for a broader readership, the eight chapters of this version dispense with subtle arguments to concentrate on matters affecting lay life and practice: On Christian Doctrine, On Proclaiming the Gospel, On the Ten Commandments, On the Fear of God, On Good Works, On Prayer to God, On Feast Days, and On the Merit of the Saints. In each chapter the seven "Luthers" debate one another (the two exceptions are chapters four and seven, in which respectively Barabbas and Ecclesiast are omitted). In both Latin and German versions Luther appears at his most iconoclastic and incoherent, with the boldest and most bluntly contradictory statements kept closely together. Every statement by each of the seven "Luthers" is a direct quotation or translation from Luther's works. That is to say, with the exception of connective phrases like "dear brother" and the summary paragraphs by Cochlaeus at the end of each chapter, this colloquium is 100 percent Luther.

It may escape notice at first, but each "Luther" is consistent and coherent. In drawing together his collage of quotations, Cochlaeus drew from works in which Luther articulates a sound argument. Thus the Ecclesiast's statements are found in a single 1522 sermon cycle, the Visitor's[5] from

4. Johannes Cochlaeus, *Septiceps Lutherus* (Leipzig: Schumann, 1529), sigs. 2–2v.

5. "Visitor" in this translation of Cochlaeus's work is used for Luther's church

the 1528 *Instruction for Visitors*, the Enthusiast from the 1520 *Assertion of All Articles* (against the papal bull condemning those articles) and the 1525 *Instruction on how Christians Should Regard Moses*. Two notable exceptions are "Luther" himself, whose statements are drawn mainly from the *Babylonian Captivity* (1520) but interspersed with passages from all over his writings, and "Martinus," whose words are drawn from various works, including several collections of "Resolutions," expanded discrete theses rather than unified treatises. Few of the polemicists knew so much of Luther so well, and Cochlaeus most likely had compiled notes of the points at which Luther diverted in one text from something he had said in another.

In contrast to the typical elenchic dialogue, in which the views of the brash upstart are refuted by the wiser defender of orthodoxy, there is no clear victor in *Seven-Headed Luther*. Luther stands refuted amidst the confusion of his own contradictory statements, reduced to a shambles by Cochlaeus in his exhortations to the councilors of Lubeck.

This is the first translation of *Seven-Headed Luther* into English, and we know of none into any other language. Cochlaeus's sentences, due to the fluidity of vernacular punctuation rules, occasionally run on, and these have been broken up for the sake of clarity.

TRANSLATION

Seven Heads of Martin Luther: On the Eight Principal Points of Christian Faith

By Dr. Johannes Cochlaeus

To the Honorable and Distinguished, prudent and wise Burgermasters and Council of the City of Lubeck: I, Johannes Cochlaeus, Doctor, etc., wish you the grace of God for good peace and Christian unity.

Honorable, prudent, wise, gracious, dear Sirs:

Last year I assembled several chapters from a German booklet of Martin Luther entitled, *Instructions for Visitors,* in a seven-headed dialogue in Latin. I did it to show pious people, whose honor, bravery, virtue, and the salvation of their souls is dear, how inconstant and contradictory the monk is in his teaching. He himself recognizes that he is creating a new Christian church and striking down the old, which has withstood the test for over 1,500 years, and to crush it with such arrogance and mischief that he not only scorns, demolishes, and dishonors the doctors of holy scripture and illustrious universities like Paris, Louvain, Cologne, Leipzig, and the like, but

---

inspectors (*Visitator*, German), who visited parishes to ensure that they were functioning well. See Gerald Strauss, "Visitations," in *OER* 4:238–43.

also the holiness of the papacy, the Imperial majesty, and other high estates (which according to scripture he should honor and obey), and defiantly insulted and obscenely slandered, and touted his own teaching so much as nothing other than the clear gospel of Christ. He has also discarded, and with much falseness slandered, all the holy doctors who have written over the past thousand years, as well as their teachings and the holiness of their lives and miracles, which they have sealed with their blood. In addition, he has criticized several books of the Old and New Testaments and tossed them aside as worthless books, and he has set them aside so that the poor common people are in error and their devotion, love, hope, and faith are miserably weakened and disrupted—so that he himself must recognize that the devil is wrathful and puts all at sixes and sevens—and creates so much confusion that almost nobody knows what to believe. However much he blames the enthusiasts and rabble-rousers, still the greatest guilt is his own, since he has created enthusiasts and rabble-rousers out of fine, learned people with his fickle and self-contradictory writings. They lead the poor people astray and cause them to doubt, whether Luther likes it or not. Indeed, he himself waffles and says, "In sum, the devil is too sharp and powerful for us. He obstructs and hinders everywhere: when we are in scripture, he creates so much ambiguity and quibbling in it that we become tired and stupid about it. He raises so much discord and factionalism about scripture that you are not going to know where scripture, faith, Christ, or you yourself are." This is Luther's word and admission. Would it not have been better, if he had never started than speaking so shamefully and unrestrainedly about the German nation and saying that the devil was too wise and powerful? He has often boasted that he had battled and beaten the devil and had some salt with him once or twice. But unfortunately one has found, in many great cities where his teaching is openly preached, how much misfortune, misery, and division the devil has created through this monk and other apostates of his. Almighty God has, by means of your faithful leadership until now, protected your city with special grace (may God continue to do so), so that now, among Christian kings and princes and the people, Cologne and Lubeck enjoy special praise and honor among all other realms and trading cities on account of your steadfast faith. For that reason I, a poor and puny little sheep of Christ, have been compelled to urge you to remain steadfast to the end in the old, universal Christianity and not allow new evangelists in your city. For that reason you may want to take and consider this little extract. Given at Dresden, April 1, 1529.

The Seven Heads

Although they all speak from one mouth and in the books of a single monk, still this division is to be noted, namely:

Doctor speaks decisively in the first books.

Martinus follows soon after, rather verbosely in his writings.

Luther spreads heresy loosely as an enemy of the church.

Ecclesiastes, the preacher, out of whose thirty-six sermons Cochlaeus drew 500 erroneous articles.

Enthusiast, who is coarse and unstable, as Luther accuses other enthusiasts of being.

Barabbas like his type is rebellious against the princes and especially all the spiritual authorities.

Visitor who wants to improve and arrange all the above, who must keep returning, as the others became more coarse and unchristian.

On Christian Doctrine. Chapter 1

VISITOR. Now we find in the doctrine, among other things, principally this error, that although one should preach much on the faith whereby we are made righteous, it is not sufficiently indicated how one is to arrive at this faith. And almost all of Christian doctrine flows from this, and without it no one knows what faith is or means. For Christ says in the last chapter of Luke that one should preach in his name repentance and forgiveness of sins, but many are now speaking only of forgiveness of sins and saying little or nothing of penance. And without penance there is no forgiveness of sin. Forgiveness of sins cannot take place without repentance.

ENTHUSIAST. Oh what a new type of papist I'm hearing—even more than a papist, since according to the papists, a child received forgiveness of sins without penance through baptism. But you place a work, penance, before faith and before forgiveness of sins—which no papist demands from a child. But we say that neither the work of penance nor the sacrament justifies, but faith alone. Scripture states (Rom 1[:17]; Hab 2[:4]; Heb 10[:38]) that the righteous lives from faith. It does not say that the righteous person lives from the sacraments or works of penance.

LUTHER. See, Visitor, that the pomp of works and human teachings deceives you, that you make an abuse of divine truth and your faith, since you must begin with faith in the sacraments without any works to be blessed; but the works follow the faith.

VISITOR. One should take great pains to teach nothing before faith except repentance (a doctrine that proceeds from and out of faith), so that our opponents cannot accuse us of contradicting our earlier teaching. Nonetheless, it is to be observed that repentance and law belong to the common belief that one must already believe, namely that God is one who threatens, commands, and terrifies, and so on. So, for the common simple folk, such articles of the faith can remain under the names of repentance, commandments, laws, fear etc. These are to be understood differently from the faith of Christ, which the Apostle calls 'justifying faith,' that is, the faith which makes righteous and destroys sin, which the faith of commandments and repentance cannot do. This is how the common folk fall into error over the word 'faith' and raise useless questions about it.

BARABBAS. Now you are bringing back a two-fold faith (like the papists and Thomists). Watch out that that we do not say to you, as we did to Catharinus, that you are a real Thomist: a godless and more monstrous murderer of holy scripture.

LUTHER. You say, Visitor, something different from what you first taught us in the Psalter, where we said that faith was the head, the life, and the strength of all other works, and that no work was good unless it was done in faith. But now faith might not be; it might be a continuous and unmistakable delusion in which a person is aware above all else that one is pleasing to God and has a gracious and forgiving God in all that one does or deals with. A gracious God in good works and a forgiving one in evil ones: what kind of faith is that if not a delusion?

ECCLESIASTES. These new papists are doing nothing different from the old papists, who do not want to suffer; that I believe and say that faith in Christ does all things and makes them right. With this statement I overthrow the monkey-game of the whole world, while it performs works.

LUTHER. You obviously do not know, Visitor, how much that has irritated Cochlaeus, so that this word "alone" set next to "faith" (which neither Paul nor any other part of scripture does), which some of us feel or say, it would be an outrage and unchristian to insert such a word and declare my error. But I have shown my reason and excuse myself.

ECCLESIASTES. I have also said at times that faith alone is not sufficient for God, since there must also be payment for our redemption, while the Turks and Jews also believe in God, but they believe without means and payment.

LUTHER. But you've often said that where faith is, no sin can harm, and that faith alone is our transaction with God and that works do not enter into it. Also, Paul and all of scripture drive us to faith, so that one deals with God only through faith.

MARTINUS. But I have said, and I still say, that we must have contrition and pain, confession and good works, indeed that we must let our faith in the sacraments be the most outstanding good in seeking the grace of God.

DOCTOR. Our Lord and Master Jesus Christ, when he said, "Do penance etc.," meant that all our life should be a penance. But he does not just want inner penance, because the inward is nothing; it works outwardly in many ways of mortifying the flesh. Thus it follows that these three forms of satisfaction (fasting, prayers, and almsgiving) are the penances enjoined by the gospels. For fasting in itself contains every mortification of the flesh. Prayer involves every exercise of the soul in contemplation, reading, listening, and prayer. Almsgiving is service and goodwill to the neighbor; thus one serves oneself in fasting, the Lord God in prayer, and the neighbor in alms. Through the first he conquers desire and appetites of the flesh and lives moderately and chastely. Through the second he conquers the pride of this life and lives faithfully. Through the third, he conquers the desire and concupiscence of the eyes, and lives piously in this world.

ECCLESIASTES. That is about monks and nuns and other papists who want to become blessed by doing good works. But I say to you that the way is narrow, if you want to come through it and press on through the rock, you must become poor. If you want to be burdened with works like pilgrims to the shrine of St. James, laden down with scallop shells, you will not pass through. That is why you must become small and lean and set aside the burden of works. Otherwise you will not come through.

DOCTOR. If that were true, we would have done wrong to the indulgence preachers, since we said that the people were better off making satisfaction on their own than by buying indulgences, since an indulgence is nothing other than the neglect of good works by which satisfaction is made.

ENTHUSIAST. But we discarded this concept already in the *Babylonian Captivity*, since we asked all booksellers and readers to burn all our books about indulgences, and before that said that indulgences were the mischief of Romanist flatterers.

VISITOR. When you discarded everything and preached forgiveness of sins without penance, it follows that the people imagine that they have already received forgiveness of sins and are thus certain and fearless. This is an error and sin greater than all others before this time. And we should be concerned that (as Christ says at Matt 12[:45]) the last will be more troublesome than the first.

ENTHUSIAST. No wonder we call you a new papist and say you've given up the ghost! You drive Christians from faith and from freedom back to the old drudgery of confession, fear, and works so that you leave no room for believing in Christ and bring forth an insatiable bloodsucker that tells the people, "Bring, bring, and conduct business with your sin."

J. COCHLAEUS

Here you see, honorable wise ones, how solid a foundation the poor man has in his teaching about faith, repentance, and good works. I have often and heartily pointed out to him that he builds all his teaching on this false foundation of faith alone making one righteous and blessed—which is found nowhere in scripture. Your Excellencies may see how well he answered it in my Latin booklet *Against the Wittenberg Minotaur*—to which he has not further replied. But how could he seriously defend his obnoxiousness among the learned? He has long been condemned as an open heretic among us Christians; and his enthusiasts can also condemn him with his own words when he says, "Such disunity cannot and must not be from the Holy Spirit; it is instead from loathsome Satan, etc." Such disunity comes not from one person (if we can say that about one with seven heads) but from Zwingli, Oecolampadius, and many others who have no common statement or sentiment about the sacrament (which I have also shown in another booklet about Luther's seven dizzy heads). Now it is much more shameful that one person writes and teaches so often in contradiction to himself that the seven characters cannot write or teach harmoniously. But true children of the Christian church all harmoniously have one understanding of the sacrament and other matters of Christian faith, wherever they are throughout all of Christendom, because they have only one Holy Spirit that Christ promised and gave them for teaching all truth. But the heretics have the spirit of many enthusiasts, and it makes them disunited and errant as they plunge into scandal and depravity with pride and disobedience. God willing, they will be gone.

On Proclaiming the Gospel. Chapter 2

VISITOR. We have instructed and warned that the pastors are to preach the whole gospel, as is their duty, and not just one part without the rest. For God says (Deut 4[:2]) that one should not add anything to this word or take anything from it. But these, since they do not preach repentance, tear away a big part of scripture, while speaking about eating meat and similarly minor items.

ENTHUSIAST. What did the papists give you, such that you even challenge us in the gospel in which we have a particular reputation? I am certain that Christ who is the master of my teaching, called me an evangelist and holds me to be one, and will bear his witness on the Day of Judgment that it is not my but his pure gospel.

BARABBAS. When we scorn God's word, it demands punishment. And he will punish us too, though he delay a hundred years. But he will not wait that long. And the more clearly the word is being preached, the greater will be the punishment. I fear that the cost will be all Germany, for God cannot let this knavery go unpunished. He will not long tolerate it, for the gospel has never been so clearly preached since the apostles' time. Thus it matters for Germany as I fear it will be destroyed.

ECCLESIASTES. I notice, Visitor, that you have lost the spirit and are pretending to the papists and worldly princes to attack our gospel; but the world wants neither to hear nor suffer such teaching, because the gospel is a hateful thing to preach.

VISITOR. Not so, dear brother. We have warned the pastors that they should carefully and frequently instruct the people about confession, to have regret and pain over their sin and fear of God's judgment.

ENTHUSIAST. Warn our enemies the papists also. You know well how hard we have attacked them for teaching not faith but the doing of works. Christians should most of all be attentive to divine approval. They say, "Whoever believes and is baptized will be saved." What is more outrageous than saying that salvation depends on everyone doing works, making vows, and following human teachings. In that we should practice our faith and never doubt that we are saved after being baptized.

ECCLESIASTES. This gospel of yours, if it is correct, means that we have wrongly included the pope, the bishops, monks, and priests in the ban, since they have not preached the faith but rather good works, and so all Germany has not had the correct gospel until now.

VISITOR. Say what you will, one should not ignore that great and necessary item, confession.

LUTHER. See that you do not make a Moses out of Christ, Visitor, or a law or manual out of the gospel. That has already happened, and you can hear it in various prefaces of St. Jerome. For the gospel actually does not want our works (in fact it condemns such works) but only faith in Christ, who alone has conquered sin, death, and hell for us.

ECCLESIASTES. Our Visitor sounds like Luke in his Gospel, when he talks about works as the way to righteousness, like the tax collector seeking forgiveness of sins and righteousness through prayer and beating his chest.

LUTHER. First you must know that we have to dismiss the idea that there are four Gospels and no more than four. But John's Gospel is the sole, precious and true chief Gospel and far, far to be preferred above the other three and held higher. So do St. Paul and St. Peter in their letters far surpass the three Gospels of Matthew, Mark, and Luke.

ENTHUSIAST. What are you saying, Luther? Do you want to be one of the heavenly prophets who say that you must listen to the voice of God? That has nothing to do with scripture. Bible, Boor, Babble.

LUTHER. If I am not a prophet, I am still certain for myself that the word of God is with me and not the papists.

ENTHUSIAST. But I know that we, who have and know the gospel, no matter what poor sinners we are, have the right spirit or, as Paul says, the first fruits of the spirit, if not the fullness of the spirit.

ECCLESIASTES. But who are the false prophets of our time?

LUTHER. You are asking that? Do not you know how many books I have written against them? Against Karlstadt, Müntzer, Zwingli, and other enemies of the sacrament, and against the Anabaptists, who previously were my best companions, my brothers, my children, my golden friends, and who knew nothing bold either from Christ or the gospel that Luther had not already written.

ECCLESIASTES. Then no one can know who has the spirit. But in sum, briefly, it is the pope and his whole retinue who all teach what is against God.

MARTINUS. That is too bluntly put, dear brother. You know that ten years ago I wrote quite differently to Pope Leo, specifically that I wished to hear his voice as the voice of Christ speaking through him. He may take or discard my writing; for that reason I have also submitted to him all that I am and have.

ENTHUSIAST. But it is a stupid submission, since you appealed from him shortly afterward, as from a godless one, heretic, tyrant, and antichrist.

MARTINUS. I did that not on my own initiative but by the counsel and inclination of those who seek not peace and quiet but unrest and novelties, but then I wrote to him and made this offer: though I had not spoken of him entirely well or honorably, I would in no way praise myself for it, and that there was also nothing I would rather do than to recall such scandal and evil.

DOCTOR. Dear brother, such honor, praise, shaming, quarreling, or contradicting is not at all evangelical. Whoever lives strictly evangelically fulfils the commandment willingly and gladly, and the works of the gospel are not called "external" but rather come from within, which is why they are even called "the works of God," for they are works of grace and the spirit. Christ speaks of this (Matt 5[:20]): "Unless your righteousness is better than that of the scribes and Pharisees, you will not enter the kingdom of heaven."

J. COCHLAEUS

What can Your Excellencies see or do here about the gospel? You want everything from Luther's teachings and new sects and groups to be considered evangelical, while you live in no way according to the gospel, as the Doctor above states. You do not preach the gospel correctly, as the Visitor complains. While Luther wants to have more than four evangelists, the Enthusiast also wants to be one. Luther also [wants to be] a prophet. The Ecclesiast does not want St. Luke's Gospel to be that important, because it has so much about good works. But Barabbas wants all of Germany to embrace his rebellious gospel (which he regards as clearer than what the apostles preached). But whatever good has been done until now can be found in the preface to Emser's New Testament, clearly explained with steadfast and lucid truth. May God give grace so that the princes and leaders of the German nation may honestly and carefully see themselves in the same faith they had before, before this Barabbas's menacing and bloodthirsty prophecy, which harms all of Germany, is fulfilled.

On the Ten Commandments. Chapter 3

VISITOR. The pastors should preach the Ten Commandments often and thoroughly, explaining and invoking them—and not just the demand, but also how God will punish those who do not obey. God regularly does punish people in this life, and these examples are written, and one should present them to the people.

ENTHUSIAST. You are really one of us enthusiasts, if you read and exalt Moses and present the people with how Moses governed the people with commandments. You want to be wise and smart and know more than what is contained in the gospel, minimizing faith and introducing something new.

DOCTOR. Do not dismiss Moses, dear brother, since in the Ten Commandments are encompassed all the salutary laws.

ENTHUSIAST. Dear Doctor, we do not want to have Moses as a ruler or lawgiver any more, and God does not want that either. Moses is an intermediary for the Jewish people, to whom alone he has given the law. One has to shut the mouths of the rabble-rousers: when they say, "Thus spake Moses," you should reply, "Moses means nothing to us."

LUTHER. Consider what you are doing, Enthusiast: if you discard Moses, you have to accept the pope in order to preserve the distinction between blood relations and your kin's family, as God explains in Lev 18[:6–18].

ENTHUSIAST. If I accept Moses in one commandment, then I have to accept all. Thus, it follows that if I recognize Moses as a master, I have to let myself be circumcised, wash my clothes according to the Jewish manner, and eat and drink in that way, dress accordingly, and all the rest.

LUTHER. Why did we translate the five Books of Moses into German? Did our peasants and stable boys already know well that the word of God endures forever? How can you dismiss it?

ENTHUSIAST. Our rabble-rousers rush forward and to everything that they read in Moses they say, "No one can deny that there God is speaking, therefore we must observe it." Then the rabble falls on it, saying, "Whoa! If God has said it, who will speak against it?" And they herd around it like pigs at a trough. But God's word here, God's word there, I must know and take seriously to whom the word of God is being spoken. You are still a long way from being the people to whom God spoke.

LUTHER. Do not you know, Enthusiast, how sternly we attacked some of the papists, who answered that Paul wrote about both kinds in the sacrament, but only to the Corinthians and not to the whole church? Thus we say, "What depraved or mad thing could that be?" Thus we say that it is far, far from us to hold that there is one letter in all of Paul that does not apply to the whole church. And one can easily say the same of any other book in the Bible.

ENTHUSIAST. There are two types of statements in scripture: the first does not apply to me or concern me at all; the other does apply to me, and on that word that does apply to me I can boldly stake all and rely upon it as a firm rock. But if it does not concern me, I should stand still. The rabble-rousers go about introducing something new and saying that one must also obey the Old Testament. They also raised a sweat among the peasants, harming their wives and children.

LUTHER. You should at least not discard the Fifth Book of Moses, since it contains a really masterful explanation of the Ten Commandments; nothing else in life is so completely and correctly ordered.

ENTHUSIAST. I shall tell you again: the Ten Commandments were not given to us, but only to the Jews, because God says in the Second Book of Moses [Exod 20:2], "I am the Lord your God who brought you out of the land of Egypt, out of servitude." Now he has not brought *us* out of Egypt, but only the Jews. Also, Paul and the New Testament abrogate the Sabbath, leading us to see that the Sabbath was given to the Jews alone and that it was a strict command to them.

DOCTOR. You see in my sermons on the Ten Commandments that the Sabbath is given as a figure (as Paul says, in Col 2[:17]), as a foreshadowing of things to come.

MARTINUS. It is certain, Enthusiast, that the highest, greatest, and chief commandment in the Decalogue is the first and that it encompasses works like faith, hope, charity, fear of God, and what God is. Does not that apply to us?

ECCLESIASTES. I really cannot agree with you, Enthusiast, because if the Ten Commandments do not apply to us, we have complained unreasonably against the pope and the sophists about placing themselves and their statements before us in place of God's Ten Commandments.

ENTHUSIAST. Dear brother, stop bothering me with Moses, since if I accept one part of Moses, I am responsible for all, as Paul says (Gal 5[:3]). But no smidgeon of Moses applies to us.

BARABBAS. I have written the same about the thieving peasants, namely that it does not help them at all that they say that according to Genesis 1–2 all things are free and shared and that we are all equally baptized, since Moses does not apply in the New Testament.

ENTHUSIAST. We understand it differently, as we create sects and mobs and spew among the people, into the common horde, saying without distinction, "God's word! God's word!" It is called that, my dear fellow, when it is directed at you.

LUTHER. But how often have you joined us in going after the pope and his laws with Deut 4[:2], "You should not add anything to my word, which I say to you, or take anything away"?

ENTHUSIAST. There are more refined people and many great preachers, who cannot preach about Moses, being witless, frenzied, ranting, and raving, chattering to the people, "God's word! God's word!" while they lead the poor people astray and throw them into their graves.

J. COCHLAEUS

Where does the word of God reside that Luther's following has until now praised so highly and often? I have no pity on the willful monk who has for so long invoked the word of God against the pope and councils, and who now makes fun of it saying, "God's word here, God's word there." Turks and Tartars never speak or write as mockingly about the word of God or the Ten Commandments, as this Enthusiast here does. There have been certain heretics, like Marcionites and Manichaeans, who discard the Old Testament completely, who never wrote so disdainfully and haughtily about the word of God. This Enthusiast goes farther than they do and says whatever he wants. Who gave him the power to control, minimize, and discard Moses and the word of God? When he likes it, it applies, and when he does not, it does not. Lucifer himself is not as arrogant and haughty toward the word of God as this monk. "It does not apply here." In his book on marriage he wants to show, from the Third Book of Moses [Lev 18], that having your sister's child is godly and Christian and that he wants his brother's or sister's daughter. As to what laws the Old Testament binds us or does not bind us as Christians, the councils and holy fathers and doctors have determined and concluded this matter clearly enough that we can break this monk's mockery on the wheel. Your Excellencies will surely know how highly this monk esteems the word of God in his letter against Worms, since he says he trusts neither the whole empire nor a future council—and now tosses it audaciously into the muck.

On the Fear of God. Chapter 4

VISITOR. The pastors should punish certain extreme forms of depravity like divorce, drunkenness, envy, and hate and show how God himself punished them. Thus he can show that there is no doubt that he will punish them much more harshly after this life, should they not improve. Thus he would stimulate and encourage the people in fearing God, confession, and contrition, and that bold and fearless life will be punished. Thus Paul says (Rom 3[:20]), "Through the law comes only knowledge of sin," and knowing sin is nothing other than genuine contrition.

ENTHUSIAST. I have shown above at length that the law does not apply, only the gospel.

LUTHER. The Law of Moses does not promise forgiveness of sin or eternal things, only temporal goods like the land of Canaan.

MARTINUS. You know that the gospel commands us also to repentance, the beginning of which is contrition. For God was so intent on making persons righteous that he first damned them, and because he wanted to build them up, he broke them, and to heal them he weakened them, and to give them eternal life he killed them, as he says in 1 Kings 2[:6–7, Vulg.; 1 Sam 2:6–7, EVV] and Deut 32[:39]. But he does that when he crushes and humbles persons and makes them recognize their sins and tremble, so that the poor sinner says [Ps 38:3], "There is no strength in my bones when confronted with my sins."

LUTHER. Martinus, you do not know how rich a Christian or a baptized person is when he cannot lose his salvation, no matter how much he sins or does not want to believe, since no sin can damn him, but only lack of faith. But contrition and confession for sin, and satisfaction afterward, and all other extra practices and care for others will leave you quickly and make you unhappy, when you forget godly truth and acceptance, which happened to you at baptism.

MARTINUS. But I know one who endured the pain of purgatory on earth, which, though it lasted only a short time, was so great and gruesome that no one could speak or write about it, and no one believe it who had not experienced it. At that time God appeared horribly wrathful, and with him all creation. There is no escape or consolation, inner or outer: only accusation and culpability.

ECCLESIASTES. In the monasteries and universities we must listen and study what a hard judge Christ is, whereas in fact he is nothing but a mediator between God and humans.

DOCTOR. Contrition, which one has upon reflection, reckoning, and suffering, when contemplating one's sins in bitterness of the soul and moderating the weight, number, and impurity of sins: this contrition makes one a hypocrite, indeed an even greater sinner.

ENTHUSIAST. I consider it an unfortunate doctrine, teaching people to be contrite over their sins after contemplating suffering and payment.

VISITOR. The people should be carefully warned that saving faith is impossible without sincere and honest contrition and fear of God, as is written in Ps 110 [Vulg.; 111:10, EVV] and Eccl 1[:14], "Fear of God is the beginning of wisdom." And Isaiah says at the end, "To whom does God look, except to a frightened and contrite heart?" [Isa 66:2] Where there is no contrition, there is a feigned faith.

ENTHUSIAST. We have a better teaching: repentance does not start with contrition and suffering over one's sins but with love of righteousness.

VISITOR. True faith should bring consolation and peace with God. Such consolation and peace are not felt where remorse and terror are, as Christ says (Matt 11[:5]): preaching is for the poor.

J. COCHLAEUS

Here Your Excellencies can easily gather that it was much better when we first recognized the monk's error concerning obedience to the pope and the Christian church. The pope indicated several articles in a bull, of which the sixth was what the Doctor said above. We have seen this in him for a long time, until the people have fallen so far from consideration and fear of God that now, as a Visitor, he must call his people away from his former teachings back to contrition and pain, penance and confession of sins, and fear of God. For many of his followers have not confessed in many years or truly done penance for their sins, consoling themselves only with faith. But that by itself is dead without works accompanying it (Jas 2[:17, 26]).

On Good Works. Chapter 5

VISITOR. The third part of the Christian life is doing good works such as chastity, loving and helping your neighbor, not lying, not deceiving, not stealing, not murdering, not being eager for revenge, not asserting your own authority, and the like. The Ten Commandments should be preached again with diligence, because all good works are included in them.

ECCLESIASTES. Our highly-learned doctors do that, when they try to overrule the Holy Spirit and say that good works belong to faith and that faith is not sufficient for blessedness. But that is not true, because faith alone without works makes us blessed, as the word of God states clearly, and works do not help us at all toward righteousness or salvation.

DOCTOR. I have often preached and discarded the false illusion, saying that we should with all care have contrition and pain over our sins, confess, and do good works. For faith in the sacrament remains the foremost good and inheritance by which we reach the grace of God and then do many good works.

ECCLESIASTES. That obviously renders all our acts worthless, so that we must have Christ alone. For where faith is, sin will do no harm, for it makes us one with Christ.

MARTINUS. But I say that all works, no matter how good they are and how appealingly they shine, count for nothing, if they do not flow from grace. Not completely worthless, because God rewards good works that take place outside of God's grace in this life with prosperity, honor, strength, power, happiness, friendship, skill, prominence, etc. But none of that achieves eternal life.

ECCLESIASTES. Are you saying that good works that do occur in God's grace merit eternal life?

MARTINUS. That is easily understood from that.

ECCLESIASTES. But you are quite wrong, dear Martin, since even our best work, which we imagine brings grace, help, and consolation from God, is reckoned to us as sin, as the Prophet says in Ps 108[Vulg.; 109:7b, EVV]: "Let his prayer be counted as sin."

DOCTOR. But you are even more wrong, dear Ecclesiastes, because we know that what is written endures regarding the useless tree that bears no fruit. I have taught the people better by telling them that they should be sober on feast days and spend the time in prayer and good works, for that is how God and his kingdom are honored. And while the brotherhood should be a particular collection of [those doing] good works, it has bothered me that it has become a money-making operation.

LUTHER. In how many books have I shown than a person sins in doing good works?

ENTHUSIAST. I have shown likewise that the righteous person sins in all good works.

VISITOR. This is lofty talk that the novice laypeople cannot understand. People should teach their children to go to the school benches.

BARABBAS. I have decided to stop my ears and let the blind, ungrateful creatures, who seek in me nothing but causes of offense, smother in their own vexation until they had to rot.

ENTHUSIAST. I want to say something else. When the pope said to me that a good work done the best it can is a venial sin, I refuted it and modified it: a good work done the best it can is a venial sin only because of God's mercy. It is actually a mortal sin according to the judgment of God.

VISITOR. That opinion sounds particularly wicked, since we call good works not only those that benefit the neighbor but also are commanded by God. Thus they are pleasing to God, and God does not like those who do not do them.

ENTHUSIAST. Whoever condemns my statement or article condemns the verse in Isa 64[:6] also: "We have all become unclean, and all our righteousness is like a foul stinking rag." Also the verse Eccl 7[:20]: "There is no righteous person on earth, who does good deeds and yet does not sin."

ECCLESIASTES. The more you sin, the more God will pour grace upon you. When you do not want to groom yourself like a cat with good works so that God will accept you, you will achieve nothing. For scripture praises God for casting sin aside and casting it into the sea.

VISITOR. If you want to oppose us so arrogantly, we shall not fail to seek help and counsel from our gracious rulers.

BARABBAS. The princes only want to lead with the sword, grabbing God by the beard, who in turn will smack them in the mouth.

J. COCHLAEUS

Your Graces see here how the enemy of the human race has misused the seven heads of this wretched monk and confused him with so many contradictions to the eternal shame of the German nation and the irredeemable loss and disgrace of souls. The ancient and crafty serpent knows well that the human is created by God to praise God through good works and earn benefits for eternal life, and that God will reward each one according to his works (Ps 61[Vulg.; 62:12, EVV]; Rom 2[:6–8]; and 1 Cor 3[:8, 14]). He knows also that a tree that does not bring forth fruit should be cut down and thrown into the fire (Matt 3[:10] and 7[:19]). Thus he fights all these years against good works by means of this wondrous instrument. And as a result, many of us Germans live every day like beasts: without thought, without fear of God, without veneration of the holy sacrament, without any care and practice of good works—simply in the appetites of the body and freedom of the flesh, exactly as if Christ had not openly said (John 5[:29]): "those who have done good, to the resurrection of life, and those who have done evil, to the resurrection of condemnation." And Paul [wrote] (Col 1[:10]): "that ye might walk worthy of the Lord unto all pleasing, being fruitful in every good work."

On Prayer to God. Chapter 6

VISITOR. The pastors and preachers should often encourage the people to pray, because that is the fulfillment of the commandment. Prayer is seeking God's help in all afflictions. And they should teach the people what prayer is and how one should pray. First, they should teach that God has commanded prayer. Thus just as it is a great sin to murder, so is it a sin not to pray to or desire God.

ECCLESIASTES. But we have already said that praying is also a sin, as it states in Ps 108[Vulg.; 109:7, EVV]: "and his prayer should become a sin."

ENTHUSIAST. We have similarly shown from scripture that a good work, even if done at its best, is sin.

BARABBAS. The sixth duty of priests is praying for others; but Christ has given the Lord's Prayer to all us Christians, so the papist priesthood is an outright lie propagated from outside God's church, because what they most want priests to be is those who pray for the laity. There is your Dagon and the only god of your paunch.

MARTINUS. You are too coarse, Barabbas. The priests and religious celebrate Mass every day, pray every hour, and exert themselves with the word of God in their studies, reading, and hearing. For this reason they have more freedom than others and are supported by tithes so they are not bound to work.

BARABBAS. Dear Martin, see that while they alone want to be the ones who pray for the people, they have become, thanks to the marvelous counsel of God, nothing other than pictures of praying people. For whoever is in the whole collection of colleges, monasteries, and benefices prays. They probably have the words of the prayers on their lips and think they have the collection of songs like David. But he knows it is a cacophony of song and knows it when it says, "This people honor me with their lips, but their heart is far from me." [Isa 29:13; Matt 15:8; Mark 7:6]

MARTINUS. When priests and the religious sing and read, and when people pray as the result of a penance imposed or a vow made, out of sheer obedience, their obedience is almost at its best in this and close to other works of bodily obedience. For there is so much unspoken grace in the word of God that even when spoken just with the mouth and without thought (in the spirit of obedience), it is a fruitful prayer, and it brings woe to the devil.

BARABBAS. Let Christ be the judge, as he says that God is a spirit and whoever prays to him must pray in spirit. From that it follows that the pope and his papists have their own priesthood and rite for praying; but they are neither priests nor praying people, but rather masks and images of priests and praying people.

MARTINUS. But it helps you to contemplate and pray properly, if you hear the words and thus understand the reason for them. No one should give preference to his heart to want to pray without the word; unless he is well trained in the spirit and has experience of casting away foreign thoughts. I do not dismiss oral prayer or the words, and no one should dismiss it but instead accept it with much thanks as a special and great gift of God.

ENTHUSIAST. You know well, Martin, that we have told about the sixth of the twelve faces of the Roman antichrist, which is in and is sent into the churches, where the daily offices are either bellowed or murmured with great effort, but in such a way that they are never said in prayerful spirit.

BARABBAS. Thus this undeniable sentence stands: in the New Testament there can be no visible priests who are different from the laity.

MARTINUS. But Christ teaches us to pray for all spiritual prelates, especially for those who should give us God's word, but if it has not been given, then we should ask God that we be made worthy to receive it through them.

ECCLESIASTES. It is foolish that we would want to give precedence to the work and faith of others and say that nuns, monks, and priests, with their songs that they practice at night in the monastery, might help others and share their treasury [of merit].

MARTINUS. From the law of love, everyone is commanded to be responsible for everyone else. And the apostle says to bear the burden of another, and thus will you fulfill the law of Christ. Thus both higher and lower prelates are able to establish confraternities, in which the brothers are in community with each other and share their concerns and works. The same applies to monasteries, orders, hospitals, and parish churches. But that cannot be true if the works of one cannot make satisfaction, provide help, or praise God for another.

VISITOR. God is so generous that he not only wants to help those who seek him but has also commanded us to pray at Luke 18[:1–8] and many other places, which the pastors should make clear to the people. Secondly, they should show them that God has also told us that he hears us (Matt 7[:7]; Luke 11[:8]), "Ask and it will be given to you." We should rely on such words and not doubt that God hears our petition, as Christ says at Mark 11[:24].

DOCTOR. Prayer is a special exercise of faith, which makes prayer so pleasing that either the prayer is answered or something better is given. For as James says [1:6], "Whoever asks for something from God should not be doubtful in faith, but whoever doubts will never believe that he received something from God."

LUTHER. God has never done anything with people (and still does not) except through the word of promise, and in return we can do nothing else with God except through faith in the word of promise. God neither notices nor rewards works.

VISITOR. The prayer of the sinner or hypocrite who does not repent over his sin and hypocrisy is indeed not heard. For it is said of those in Psalm 18[:41], "They call upon the Lord, but there is no help, for he answers them not." But those who have remorse and believe that God and Christ forgive: their sin and hypocrisy will not be allowed to harm them.

LUTHER. Free will is a fictitious thing and a name without an object, for it has no power of its own to think anything, good or evil. Rather all things happen from absolute necessity, as Wycliffe's article, condemned at Constance, rightly teaches. What are we praying to God for, since he himself works and does good and bad in us?

VISITOR. You are wrong and far too impudent, Luther, for a person has free will in his own power to do or leave off doing external works, impelled either by law or punishment. Pastors should also instruct the people that one should desire something temporal or eternal from God; indeed they should encourage each to bring their need before God.

J. COCHLAEUS

Has there ever been, I would wager, one night in which everyone had the manifold and contradictory dreams that this monk enthuses about regarding prayer, or a poet so versatile in his fabrications as this Enthusiast is in such a serious matter, necessary for the salvation of the soul? Indeed no fables and old wives' tales are so strongly and so often contradictory as this seven-headed dialogue about lofty and godly things. I am certain that there is no simple woman more inconstant, no scoundrel more frivolous, no false prophet more dishonest, no enthusiast more changeable than this new evangelist appears to be. I also hold that no Turk or Tartar has blasphemed God so blatantly as Luther here does, when he says that no person has in their own power the ability to do good or evil, but rather that God does everything in us, good and bad. In fact no master would willingly have tolerated some knave speaking dishonestly or equivocally in a message. If someone wants to be a doctor, an apostle and evangelist of the Germans, constantly tolerating and permitting the all the change and vagueness that he shows in his published books, like a drunken blockhead or a suckling who can neither go nor stand still. When were the common folk more astray or doubtful in almost all matters of the sacraments of our holy faith than they are now? It is no wonder, since so many enthusiasts are tolerated, and Luther wavers so often from one view to the other and then openly wants people to burn his earlier books. If that is actually evangelical or from the Holy Spirit, then everyone can think and consider however they feel.

On Feast Days. Chapter 7

VISITOR. The third commandment demands that the Sabbath be kept holy.

ENTHUSIAST. But we have shown above with many reasons and from this commandment that Moses and his commandments do not apply to us, only the Jews.

VISITOR. If God has not commanded us to observe external ceremonies the same way as the Jews, that we should do no manual labor on that day, still there should be some observance, so that we hear and teach God's word and the people can come together at specific times.

ENTHUSIAST. But we have shown among the twelve appearances of the antichrist that the ninth indicates the uselessness and unfairness of feast days, since every day can be one of working or celebrating.

BARABBAS. If you have, Visitor, any scriptural text for feast days that show where you may and may not, then you know how much we have used scripture to show that human laws and traditions do not bind us.

VISITOR. The pastors should also not quarrel over whether one feast should take place and the other not; rather, each should maintain his customs in peace, as long as they do not do away with all ceremonies.

BARABBAS. Why not all, since you do not have a single scriptural warrant? Because we are not merely not responsible for observing them, but rather, for the sake of our salvation, we should do away with them altogether, as Paul tells us (Rom 16[Rom 14]; 1 Cor 10; Gal 3–5; Col 2; etc.) and all the prophets have taught us to shun all human teachings and traditions.

MARTINUS. However much the physical ceremonies that we let remain as our handiwork and effort, for which we come to church, go to Mass, hear God's word, and lead others to Christianity is not commanded to us by God, as the apostle says (Col 2[:16–17]), still it is necessary and ordered within Christianity for the sake of the incomplete Christians and workers that the young also come to God's word.

BARABBAS. But I say that, for the sake of such human traditions, all bishops, abbots, seminaries, and monasteries should be overthrown, even driven out and expelled from the land.

LUTHER. Eight years ago I suggested that all feasts should be abolished and only Sunday observed. But if someone wanted to observe a feast to Our Lady and the major saints, they should all be on Sunday, or held only on Mass mornings, so that the rest of the day could be a work day. And one should pay no heed, whether the pope declares it a feast or grant a dispensation or holiday.

MARTINUS. Not so, Luther, because the other work of God's fourth commandment is to honor and obey the divine mother the holy Christian church, the spiritual power, whatever she gives, binds, declares, orders, forbids, releases, and that we should govern ourselves by. And just as we honor, fear, and love our earthly parents, so should we allow our spiritual authorities to have the right over all things that do not go against the first three commandments.

BARABBAS. What are you saying, you hypocrite? Are you saying this on the same page where you contradict yourself and say that there are still a few feast days and celebrations that are better done away with? Do not you instead say above that it would be good to have fewer holy days? David teaches us throughout Psalm 118[Vulg.; 119, EVV] that we should hide from human laws and traditions and flee from them as the greatest misery on earth.

MARTINUS. You do not see, Barabbas, how watchful Christ is in the churches, who does not permit even those who wish to err to do so, so that we do not plunge ourselves into error.

BARABBAS. A blessed conscience knows and does not doubt that the church demands or orders nothing without or beyond the word of God. Whoever dares to do otherwise is not of the church but makes himself a separate church.

DOCTOR. How long are you going to quarrel among yourselves? I want to tell you the real meaning. The church keeps feast days for the sake of God's word for those who are incomplete, in whom the old Adam is not yet mortified; for them it is necessary that they observe specific offices, holy days, vigils, fasts, works, prayers, disciplines, and the like so that they may thus come to fullness of the inner person. One should observe saints' days in five parts, as we find in the decretals, namely hearing Mass, hearing the sermon, praying, sacrificing, and being contrite for sins. And in all of these one should not follow one's own judgment or fantasy or devotion, but rather the teaching and instruction of the church, and subject one's own sense to the service of Christ. For it is written: "He who trusts his own heart is a fool." [Prov 28:26] The church cannot err, but it is possible that someone errs in his thoughts.

J. COCHLAEUS

Whoever is not moved and aroused by the Lutheran faction in this chapter, in trembling and shaking, should recognize whom he follows and how strongly he has sinned against the church for the past ten years, as he has clearly and completely ignored God and is following a wayward sense. It must be a blind irrationality to prefer following this frivolous, inconstant, and disobedient monk (who lives in open sin, reproaches and slanders all, and has never performed a miracle) to following the highest authorities, the pope and emperor, the councils, and all of Christendom that has held power for 1,500 years now to command and forbid. But who has given power to this monk to institute or prohibit feast days? He is neither pope nor bishop and has no universal authority to institute or forbid. As he has for the past few years confessed in saying, I am not so shameless and arrogant that I want to be numbered among the learned men of the holy Church, much less among those with authority to establish such matters or condemn them. God willing, I will be worthy some day to be considered the least and most insignificant member of the church.

On the Merit of the Saints. Chapter 8

VISITOR. It is also not necessary for anyone to dispute subtly about merit and whether God grants it for our works. It is enough to teach that God demands and rewards such works, although he has promised it apart from our merit.

ENTHUSIAST. Where are you creeping to with merit and rewards for good works? You know perfectly well how strongly we proved from scripture that the righteous person sins mortally according to God's judgment in all good works.

VISITOR. So much screeching that good works avail nothing. It would be so much better, if we urged people to do good works and stopped with the nasty disputations.

ECCLESIASTES. Nature does not need us to do good works for the sake of piety or righteousness; instead, it wants to merit or avoid something. But that is false and a sin before God. And Paul asserts (Rom 3[:10]) from Ps 13[Vulg.; 14:1, EVV] that no person is righteous before God.

MARTINUS. If you had proper faith, nothing might be in you or befall you that is not completely pleasing to God, for it must all be good and meritorious. For Paul says this at Rom 8[:28]: "We know that all things serve the holy ones of God."

ECCLESIASTES. We should not be pious in order to merit or avoid something. All such persons are day laborers and bargainers for things, not acting like sons and heirs.

MARTINUS. Have not you yourself taught that there is more merit in giving a poor person one gulden, than in giving a hundred to the saints?

LUTHER. But I taught something better: that all our works mean nothing to God or are all alike, because God asks for nothing in terms of works and does not need them, but he does need his words to be regarded properly by us.

ECCLESIASTES. Who seeks nothing more than to be godly seeks and finds God himself; but the one who seeks reward and flees punishment never finds God, for he makes the reward his God. For whatever the reason one does something, that is their God.

DOCTOR. Dear brother, you should know that God has given us commandments so that we can acquire merit through them. Because where there is no obedience, there is no merit. Where there is no commandment, there is no obedience. And since there is no command to buy indulgences for souls, it is better to stick to what is certain and to meritorious works, so that one may achieve it through good works, than to buy indulgences.

BARABBAS. You are speaking here against Christian freedom, for people should not be enslaved in their consciences, either with laws or with commandments.

DOCTOR. You are way off, Barabbas, since going from what is permitted toward what is commanded is to be more sure: for obedience is certain and freedom is fallible.

MARTINUS. You are right, dear Doctor, because God's commandment is incomparably more worthy of obedience than that which is permitted by humans, since there is merit in obeying the commandment but not in the permission.

ECCLESIASTES. You say a lot about merit but you do not consider that you are discarding God's mercy and pushing us toward wanting to seek God's righteousness with good works—which is most of all to be avoided.

MARTINUS. But I made the case against Dr. Eck that the merits of Christ are a treasury of the church and that we are helped by the merits of the saints. That is certain.

ECCLESIASTES. You did that wrong, Martinus, because there is only one mediator between God and humanity (as Paul says in 1 Tim 2[:5]), Jesus Christ, through whose merit alone we and all the saints are blessed. Thus I would not give a dime for St. Peter's merit, that he could help me, because he could not even help himself. But all that he had, he had from God through faith in Christ.

DOCTOR. That is a blatant blasphemy, because all the saints may do all things, and God has given as much to you through them, if you believe or accept that you have received it. For what are the beloved saints other than drops of dew or drops in the hair and head of the bridegroom (Song 5[:2]).

ECCLESIASTES. Be the merits of the saints what they may, I say for myself that if I saw the heavens open, and that I could earn admission with a single straw, I would not pay it. For I would never say, "Look, I earned this!"

BARABBAS. But I have said that the time of the peasants' uprising was so remarkable that a prince might merit heaven with a bloodbath more than another might with prayer.

ECCLESIASTES. But you did not speak correctly, for God gives us heaven for nothing, not because of our works.

J. COCHLAEUS

From this chapter Your Excellencies may easily recognize how wretchedly this monk has led us astray for all these years on the matter of the merit and rewards for good works that pious persons and the dear saints have done. What has he gotten right? Really nothing good, since the Visitor now himself acknowledges that a youth was never more sacrilegious than what we now see (he says), how disobedient and how disrespectful of his elders he is. For that reason, doubtless many plagues, wars, rebellions, and other evils have come into the world. This he himself admits. But what is the cause other than his disobedient, rebellious, and contradictory writing? Who has been more scornful toward all the virtues and good works? Who has ignored the schools and all education more than he with all those blasphemous books against learning and the universities? Here Your Excellencies see what his coarse Ecclesiastes said about good works and the merits of the dear saints, although I have given just a small portion of the coarse material that he has preached in his sermons against learning and good works. What need is there for us to write many books against him when his own three heads—Visitor, Martinus, and Doctor—themselves reject such lame obscenities and crude loutishness and see them as error? But even when all seven heads blow on the same horn, what is enough for us against them all is the clear word of Christ (Matt 20[:8]): "Call the worker and give him his pay." Mark 9[:41]: "Whoever gives you a cup of cold water in my name while you are of Christ, truly I say to you, he will not be without his reward." And Luke 10[:7]: "The worker is worthy of his pay." Paul too says (1 Cor 3[:8]), "Each will receive his reward according to his work." And chapter 9[:17]: "When I do this willingly, I have a reward, etc."

EPILOGUE

Honorable, esteemed, and wise Gentlemen: I do not want to burden or trouble you any further now with this seven-headed monk. You easily find in these eight chapters that it is not the Holy Spirit (which is one with God) but the evil spirit of Satan—indeed the whole legion of evil spirits—that has spoken and written for the past ten years through this monk, as his Imperial Majesty has openly demonstrated with faithful warning in the Edict of Worms. Many, thus warned, avoided the monk's grasp. And many learned and honorable persons have been revolted by his inconsistent and contradictory writings, like those I have often pointed out and attacked over the years. But it has never been so clearly stated as it is in this dialogue, the like of which has never been heard or seen as long as Christianity has existed. I say that not to my fame but to Luther's shame and to warn the common people so that your praiseworthy city and honorable people may, with this friendly instruction and admonition, remain faithful to universal Christianity to the end. For it becomes clearer and clearer every day that the sacrilege and arrogance of this monk will come to a bad end. And a native Wittenberg resident once told me that Luther himself has often said from the pulpit that if he had not started it, he would not be continuing with it now. He also says that many people in Wittenberg secretly want Luther to be like a wolf and head into the woods, and also that the peasants around Wittenberg often curse his inconstancy. So he has not so far been able, for all his many books and sermons, to win over even his own town of Wittenberg completely to his way, with any steadfast fashion or purpose. Rather he wavers and falters these days from one path to another, so that the common man and the poor simple people have no idea where he is going. In fact the monk writes and prattles on constantly, as long as he thinks he can, although he well knows and recognizes that his favor and following ebb away daily. New sects rise up against him, but also many of his own following have had misgivings about his scandalous and blasphemous pamphlet about secret letters, which he wrote against Duke George of Saxony, without any basis or sincere purpose, as frivolously as possible and with definite lies and blasphemy. Now he trots along like a blind old horse and does not know where he is going to be at the end. Now he writes in two sermons that we are sinners against the Holy Spirit, since we condemn and attack his teaching, whereas it is obvious that there is no greater blasphemy and sacrilege than he himself shows in his seven heads. He also wants people to leave their fathers, mothers, brothers, children, and sisters and join him, while he himself attaches to almost nothing and then heartily rebukes it. It is well-earned reward for his changeable arrogance that like a new messiah he compares his teachings to Christ's, as if they were not his, but God's—which is actually not the most outrageous blasphemy that he heretically and openly condemns God's teachings and sets himself up as a new Christ, as if we had to receive a new law from him (as the Jews had to receive a new law from Christ). He knows perfectly well that Christ remains with his church to the end of the world and has warned us against such false prophets (Matt 7[:15]). And even if we had written nothing against him, still we would know the rotten fruit that has come from his new gospel in all the sects and rebellions, such that Germany had not endured in the previous 700 years. May God protect you, Honorable Councilors, and the honorable assembly of the praiseworthy city of Lubeck.

Your humble servant, Dr. Johannes Cochlaeus

9

Konrad Wimpina and Others
Against Martin Luther's Confession
—DEWEY WEISS KRAMER

INTRODUCTION

THE TITLE OF A "new" *Confession*[1] by Luther, which appeared in the spring of 1530, contained an unusually specific phrase: "composed for the upcoming diet," referring to the Diet of Augsburg, mandated for June 1530 by Emperor Charles V. This was the gathering at which the German princes, principalities, and imperial cities would have to explain and defend the changes in religious teaching and observances occurring within their spheres of jurisdiction, a gathering that could decide on *either* the recognition *or* the continued condemnation of the reformers. A document, penned by the most popular German author of the time, specifically aimed at influencing the participants of the upcoming diet, necessitated swift, clear, and compelling action by defenders of the Catholic side. This pamphlet, *Against Martin Luther's Confession, newly composed for the Diet of Augsburg in Seventeen Articles, Interpreted Succinctly and in a Christian Manner* (hereafter, *Against Martin Luther's Confession*) was the result. It deals with both the theological and political maneuverings around the Diet of Augsburg as well as the diet's results. For both Luther's *Confession* and the Catholics' *Against Martin*

1. Adopting the language of Wimpina's *Against Martin Luther's Confession, newly composed for the Diet of Augsburg in Seventeen Articles, Interpreted Succinctly and in a Christian Manner*, the designation "*Confession*" will be used to refer to the Schwabach Articles.

169

Luther's Confession would serve as drafts for two of the crucial ensuing documents: the Lutheran *Confessio Augustana* or *Augsburg Confession* (a foundational statement of belief for the Lutheran Church) and the Catholic *Confutatio Augustana* or refutation of the Augsburg Confession.[2]

Against Martin Luther's Confession as Detailed Response to Luther's Confession

Against Martin Luther's Confession is a Catholic reaction to a supposed Luther-authored *Confession*. That publication, however, was actually the Schwabach Articles, which had been composed in the autumn of 1529 (but not published) to satisfy the Lutheran reformers' twofold need for an articulation of a common belief and a basis for a political alliance. Although the title ascribed authorship to Luther, he did not claim it as his, stating that he had "merely helped" to draft it.[3]

In response to Charles's insistence at the April 1529 Diet of Speyer that the princely and municipal adherents of Luther's reform comply with the Edict of Worms of 1521 (prohibiting Lutheran teaching and reform throughout the Holy Roman Empire), the princes supporting the reform drew up a declaration of faith (Latin, *protestatio*) and proposed forming a defensive league against the Catholics. Luther and Melanchthon had opposed the formation of this defensive alliance, unless such a federation's members would agree on a common confession of faith that would address the conflict between Zwingli's and Luther's interpretations of the Lord's Supper. The Schwabach Articles was a set of seventeen articles, drafted in late summer 1529 by Wittenberg theologians, which became foundational for further Lutheran efforts at articulations of their belief, serving the Wittenbergers in the discussion with Zwingli and the Swiss Cantons at the Colloquy of Marburg in October 1–4, 1529.[4] They were also used in the ongoing need for a united front, when in late winter 1530 the emperor called for the imperial estates to gather in Augsburg in late spring to explain the changes they were making in their churches. Elector John commissioned his theologians to draft an answer for that diet. The Torgau Articles, drawing also on

---

2. See Vinzenz Pfnür, "Confutation," in *OER* 1:408–10.

3. "Vorbemerkung," *Flugschriften gegen die Reformation (1525–1530)*, edited by Adolf Laube and Ulman Weiss (Berlin: Akademie Verlag, 2000), 2:1247; *Sources and Contexts of the Book of Concord*, edited by Robert Kolb and James A. Nestingen; translated by William R. Russell (Minneapolis: Fortress, 2001), 83–87.

4. "The Marburg Articles," in *Sources and Contexts of the Book of Concord*, translated by William R. Russell, 88–92.

the two former drafts, was the result.[5] All three of these efforts would then serve Melanchthon in his preparation of the *Augsburg Confession*, which would in turn serve as the foundational definition of Lutheranism. Since Melanchthon's aim in Wittenberg's presentation to the diet was to address the *catholicity* of the reformers' teachings as well as the abuses of the Catholic Church, Luther's typical polemical tone is largely absent.

Just as the *Confession* is linked to the Lutherans' preparation for the Diet of Augsburg, its Catholic response is as well. Although ostensibly addressed to one of the most powerful and influential of the Catholic princes, Joachim I, Elector of Brandenburg, the document was clearly commissioned by him. It was crafted swiftly by a quartet of Joachim's seasoned and talented theologians, who had all been deeply involved in the struggle with Luther's ideas from their very beginning.[6] Published in early summer 1530, it caught the public's attention, as had the *Confession,* and it also was quickly reprinted. The seventeen articles of the *Confession* are taken up one by one in the Catholic response and so dictate both the structure and contents of the latter.

In keeping both with the Lutheran *Confession's* interest in the possibility of compromise and with Wimpina's usual, moderate mode of argumentation, *Against Martin Luther's Confession* is itself refreshingly non-polemical in tone. Nevertheless, the contentious topics were still discernible, lurking beneath the surface in both works. The Lutheran *Confession* achieved a conciliatory tone by omitting important ideas that the reformers proclaimed elsewhere but including ideas that had been looked upon favorably by "the other side" (as Luther refers to his Catholic opponent in Article V). Wimpina and his team recognized the dangers posed by the *Confession*—its reluctance to be too critical of traditional beliefs and its apparent affirmation of Catholic truths—and responded by rejecting *any* positive evaluation of the new teaching. The Elector Joachim shared these sentiments and so formed his commission. The lengthy introduction of the *Against Martin Luther's Confession* articulates the main reason for dismissing the positive aspects of the *Confession*: the man Martin Luther himself. His actions and words and their consequences showed him to be an arch-heretic and provoker of unrest that must discourage anyone from taking anything he said seriously. Nonetheless, Joachim's theologians addressed the *Confession's* points skillfully, revealing the dangers to the old faith within seemingly positive statements.

---

5. *Sources and Contexts of the Book of Concord*, 93–104.

6. Cf. nn. 2–5 in the translation of Wimpina's pamphlet for information on *Against Martin Luther's Confession's* four authors.

The Catholic authors of *Against Martin Luther's Confession* make extensive use of scriptural proof texts (thereby employing the power of Luther's own *sola scriptura* to confront and oppose his innovations) but also assert the authority of tradition.

A Curious Reappearance of Against Martin Luther's Confession, newly composed for the Diet of Augsburg in Seventeen Articles, Interpreted Succinctly and in a Christian Manner

The struggle between Catholic Church and Protestants, documented in succinct form in *Against Martin Luther's Confession,* continued for the next 500 years, and the concerns of both sides that were expressed in this same document reappeared in the mid-nineteenth century. Dr. Karl August Wildenhahn (1805–1868)[7] was a Lutheran pastor who also wrote numerous novels focused on the persons and events of the immediate Reformation era, among them *The Augsburg Diet: A History in Life Pictures.*[8] For this work, Wildenhahn incorporated the *Against Martin Luther's Confession* text, as a record of Catholic maneuverings before the diet. Entitling the chapter "A Meeting of Romish Divines," he set Wimpina, Mensing, Redorffer, and Elgersma in Elector Joachim's princely quarters and let them engage among themselves, presenting the seventeen articles, often almost *verbatim,* in lively dramatic form. Wildenhahn is present as omniscient Lutheran observer. Catholic outcries of amazement at Luther's heretical actions and ideas interact with the authorial Lutheran's equal amazement at the blindness of the reformer's Old Church opponents. This observer then concludes the chapter by judging the exchange an example of the foolish difficulties the Roman Catholic Church had caused the reformers.

But the history of *Against Martin Luther's Confession* goes on, as part of another sort of Lutheran "reformation." In 1880 John Gottlieb Morris (1803–1895)[9] published his translation of Wildenhahn's *History*, a time in which the Lutheran Church in America was involved in an internal struggle between liberals, who sought to align their church with mainstream American Protestantism, and traditionalist German immigrants, who wanted to

---

7. Karl August Wildenhahn (1805–1868) earned a PhD in theology from the University of Leipzig, worked with Ludwig Tieck in Dresden, and was pastor, school inspector, and author of popular stories and novels.

8. Easton, PA: Riegel; Philadelphia: J. F. Smith, 1882.

9. John Gottlieb Morris (1803–1895), Lutheran minister who played an influential role in the evolution of the Lutheran church in America. He was also an early American entomologist, one of the first to study butterflies and moths.

retain old customs and language. Nor was this the end of *Against Martin Luther's Confession's* presence. For starting around 2013, Morris's translation with its dramatized "Meeting with Popish Divines" has become available as a reprint by several international companies.[10]

TRANSLATION

Konrad Wimpina, Johannes Mensing, Wolfgang Redorffer, Rupert Elgersma:
  Against Martin Luther's Confession, composed for the Diet of Augsburg in 17 Articles
  To the most illustrious, noble and high-born Prince and Lord, Lord Joachim, Margrave of Brandenburg;[11] Elector and Arch-Chamberlain of the Holy Roman Empire; of Stettin, Pomerania, of the residents of Cassuben and of the Wends, Duke; Burggrave of Nuremberg and Prince of Rugen. We, Konrad Wimpina[12], Johannes Mensing[13], Wolfgang Redorffer[14], Doc-

10. I obtained an attractive and inexpensive copy from: Facsimile Publisher, 12 Pragai Market, Ashok Vihar, Ph-2, Delhi- 110052, India.

11. Joachim I, Elector of Brandenburg (Joachim I Nestor; 1499–1535), Prince-Elector of the Margraviate of Brandenburg (1499–1535), the fifth member of the House of Hohenzollern, brother of Prince-Archbishop-Elector Albrecht of Mainz, in whose diocese Johann Tetzel was so energetically preaching the St. Peter's indulgence, the action that caused Martin Luther to post his ninety-five theses. Joachim had helped his brother to get the dioceses of Magdeburg, of Halberstadt, and in 1514 the Prince-Archbishopric-Electorate of Mainz, which then provided the Hohenzollerns with two of the seven electoral votes in imperial elections.

Joachim was a vigorous adherent of Roman Catholic orthodoxy. He was also a patron of learning and established the Viadrina University of Frankfurt (Oder) in 1506, the first principal university of the Margraviate of Brandenburg. Joachim procured the notable theologian Konrad Wimpina as founding rector, the primary author of *Against*. As one further instance of the interconnections of the persons and ideas involved with this pamphlet, Johann Tetzel obtained his doctorate in 1518 from the Viadrina that Joachim had founded.

12. Konrad Wimpina (ca. 1465–1531), ordained 1500, doctorate in theology from University of Leipzig 1503, engaged by Elector Joachim in 1505 to play a major part in the founding of the University of Frankfurt on the Oder, served twenty-five years as its rector and dean of the theology faculty, setting the university's conservative and scholastic predilections in contrast to Europe's more advanced humanist circle, and strongly opposed by Wittenberg colleagues.

13. Johannes Mensing (1477–1547), Dominican, matriculated at the University of Wittenberg in 1515, doctorate in theology in Frankfurt on the Oder 1518, professor in Frankfurt 1529, advisor to Elector Joachim for theological and ecclesial affairs, author of numerous polemical tracts.

14. Wolfgang Redorffer (1514–1559), Provost of Stendal, theological advisor to Elector Joachim, participant in the Diet of Augsburg and in the preparation of the *Confutatio* of August 3, 1530, author of numerous polemical tracts.

tors, and Rupert Elgersma,[15] Licenciate, etc. offer to you our prayers to God together with our zealous and most diligent services, prepared above all as your most humble and obedient servants.

Most gracious Elector and Lord, it is not unreasonable to wonder how and for what reason Luther has now written a particular *Confession* of his erroneous beliefs presented in seventeen articles, since only a short while earlier he had had a similar confession of his beliefs published.[16] In that *Confession* he boasted that he would persevere in those beliefs to his death. And yet in this most recent *Confession* he has omitted much of what he has earlier formulated and confessed. In addition, several hundred articles that are in part unchristian and heretical and in part inflammatory and misleading are found now and then in his previously published books. Yet in both the earlier one and in this second *Confession* he has referred to such things with hardly a word; in fact, he has passed over them in total silence. If he perhaps wanted to believe that by not repeating these things here, that they would be forgotten and thus no further guilt will be ascribed to him, he would be very mistaken. For as long as he gives cause with his writings and teachings for so much blasphemy, the plunder of spiritual property, the leading astray of many chaste hearts into sinful lust, the breaking of oaths and vows, rebellion, murder, along with many more diverse, unchristian actions, and even though he should now repent of and recant the same, as indeed in the way of all heretics he (apparently) would not do; or further, if the articles confessed here were blameless, as however they all are not, nonetheless so many evil deeds of which he has been the cause, the instigator, the originator, and the rabble-rouser, must not by rights remain unpunished. For this reason no one dare esteem or concern oneself very much with these articles of this, his newly reiterated *Confession*, since his earlier errors and public transgressions are far more important than all of these here and are intended, as they say, to surpass them.

And so as we then heard that these particular seventeen articles of this reiterated and new *Confession* had been sent to Your Electoral Grace here in Augsburg in a form suggesting, perhaps, that everything contained therein is good, Christian and blameless, we are also certain without any doubt that, as a praise-worthy Christian elector, not only as a result of innate Christian virtue received and inherited from your highly praise-worthy grandparents

15. Rupert Elgersma, Dominican theological advisor to Elector Joachim, participant in the Diet of Augsburg and in the drafting of the *Confutatio*.

16. The reference is to the Schwabach Articles, which are here attributed to Luther alone but were in fact likely the collaborative effort of several theologians from Wittenberg and are reflected in the Marburg Articles and in the Augsburg Confession. See Helmar Junghans, "Augsburg Confession," in *OER* 1:96.

and ancestors, but also [because you are][17] highly enlightened, especially by solidly founded Christian teaching, and thus so firmly grounded, such teachings as well as similar unfounded articles cannot influence in the least, much less mislead Your Electoral Grace.

Because nonetheless these assertive arguments of Luther's have been regarded among some persons as quite good and correct, as though nothing of substance might be brought against them, we have summarized as briefly as possible a particular and a Christian meaning, as it is to be understood, in several articles, so that every devout Christian may now know how to understand them according to the law and ordinances of the universal Christian church, free from any danger or doubt.

We humbly implore that it might please your Electoral Grace to accept with your wonted benevolence this document, the result of our efforts and loyalty, written with the full extent of our abilities, diligence, and devotion, and dedicated to your Electoral Grace, submitted in all eager readiness to serve.

Article I

Schwabach:[18] *Article I quotes from the Athanasian Creed[19] regarding the Trinitarian nature of God, supported scripturally by John 1 and Matthew 28.*

It would have been completely unnecessary for Martin Luther to repeat so diligently and elegantly this confession in Article I, because everything, and far more than is summarized by him in this article, has been proclaimed, determined, and repeated often previously for many centuries and by many councils. Further, it is prayed, read, and sung far and wide daily in the Athanasian Creed at the office of Prime as well as in the Mass and at other times by priests as well as regularly by all devout Christians.

17. Words and phrases in brackets are the translator's additions.

18. The summary of each Schwabach article relies on the translation by William R. Russell in *Sources and Contexts of the Book of Concord*, 83–87.

19. The Athanasian Creed is a statement of belief focused on Trinitarian doctrine and Christology, used since the sixth century. It differs from the Nicene-Constantinopolitan and Apostles' Creeds in the inclusion of anathemas of those who disagree with it. It is considered part of Lutheran confessions in the *Book of Concord*.

Article II

Schwabach: *Article II continues reference to the creed, with focus on the Son. Only the Son of God became human. The article refutes various heresies concerning the nature of Christ.*

This article is even less necessary to repeat than the former one, for [the Incarnation of the Son of God] has now not been contested in the universal Christian church for centuries. The errors that were evident among the heretics named in the article and many other errors have all been condemned and extinguished through God's help and the judgment of the church fathers in many councils. For Luther to repeat it at this time would not have been necessary.

Article III

Schwabach: *Article III continues reference to the creed, focusing on Jesus as true God and true man. It emphasizes the whole divine-human nature of Christ, plus his suffering as the effective means of our salvation.*

This article, like the one that the Christian church prays, and especially as understood in the form of the Creed, that the only begotten Son of God, our Lord Jesus Christ, born of the Virgin Mary, suffered under Pontius Pilate, crucified and died, etc. has also not been called into question. So its restatement now by Luther was unnecessary. The more profound meaning of these words [of the Creed] is more properly to be explained in academic terminology than in everyday speech.

It can be seen, however, why Luther has drawn these three above-proclaimed articles into his *Confession* and placed them at the beginning, for with them he intends to disguise his other numerous errors (which are also not included here) and would like to introduce the errors that follow as all the more plausible.

Article IV

Schwabach: *Original Sin is a real sin that condemns all persons and separates them from God, had not Christ intervened. His suffering made satisfaction for sin and destroyed it.*

Original Sin is a real, genuine sin and not merely a flaw or a weakness. Further, it is the kind of sin that condemns all persons descended from Adam and separates them from God eternally. This should be understood as applying only before baptism, for after baptism there is no condemnation for those who now live in Christ Jesus (Rom 8[:1]). This Christ, through his bitter suffering, at work in the sacrament of holy baptism, washes away all sins. To be sure, the inclination and the temptation to sin remain after baptism—called in Latin *"fomes peccati"* and by Paul *"lex in membris"* [cf. Rom 7:23]—as a weakness to be dealt with by humankind. Psalm 52 [Vg.; Ps 53, EVV] and Romans 5 should be understood in this way.

Article V

Schwabach: *All persons are sinners and subject to sin, death, and the devil, totally unable of themselves to prepare themselves to obtain righteousness. The sole path thereto is belief in the Son of God. This belief is our righteousness.*

We admit that all human beings are sinners before baptism, and also those who commit mortal sin after baptism are sinners subject to sin, death, and the devil as well, as Luther acknowledges in this article. And that such sinners cannot free themselves therefrom by their own powers or their own works and become once again righteous or holy; indeed, they cannot even prepare themselves and are not fit for righteousness in and of themselves or able to begin everything by themselves. For we know as Paul says, that we are not capable on our own of doing anything good as though by our own intention. [2 Cor 3:5]

But that the sinner, through unceasing divine gracious help and mercy, which the almighty God denies to no one, as he says through John in Revelation [3:20], "I stand at the door and knock. If anyone lets me in, I will enter into him etc.,"[20] should not be able to prepare himself to receive further grace by means of which he might have good works and merit, neither Luther nor anyone else will prove, as written clearly in Prov 16[:9], "It is the task of the human being to prepare his soul," and in Sir 2[:17], "Those who fear God will prepare their hearts and in the sight of his face will they sanctify their soul."

From this it is evident that also the sinner, being protected by divine gracious help, may prepare himself for more grace and righteousness and ultimately for salvation, through good works by the power of that same divine help. This is clearly indicated by the text from Acts 10[:4] concerning Cornelius, to whom the angel spoke, "Your prayers and your alms have been remembered by God," by which he has come to the full knowledge of Christ's righteousness and ultimate salvation.

---

20. Unless otherwise noted, all biblical citations are my own translation from the German.

From this it follows that there is not only the one single way to righteousness and to redemption from sin and death: that one wholly without merit or works believes in the Son of God who has suffered for us, etc. While faith is necessary in all these matters, yet no passage of scripture extols faith alone in such a way that it alone is salvific. Especially that faith that works through love (Gal 5[:6]) is also the same faith that justifies, as Paul says in Rom 10[:10], "With the heart one believes, etc." Further, then, that faith that does not act through love is of no use, as the same Paul proclaims in 1 Cor 13[:13]. To speak precisely regarding this, works are actually more accorded to love than to faith, for faith can indeed exist along with many flagrant sins, [but] without love, without merit. Further, John's text that all those who believe in the Son shall not be lost but rather shall have eternal life [John 3:15] should be understood in this manner, as John himself explains where he says in 1 John 2[:4], "Whoever says that he believes in God and does not obey his commandment, is a liar, and the truth is not in him."

Article VI

Schwabach: *Faith is not a human work nor possible to obtain by human power. It is God's gift, given to and effected in us through Christ by the Holy Spirit, as a new, vital essence that always does good toward God (by praising, thanking, praying, preaching, and teaching) and toward neighbor (by loving, serving, helping, offering counsel, giving, and suffering all kinds of evil until death).*

We agree that faith is not a human work nor possible to obtain by our power. Rather, it is God's work and gift that the Holy Spirit effects in us. However, it is poured out upon us along with other virtues in baptism, so that it accomplishes diverse good works as long as it is formed and adorned with divine love. However, where love is not present, then faith alone is unable to do good, meritorious works on its own, as St. Paul says in 1 Cor 13[:13], where he ascribes good works above all to love. ["*And now faith, hope, and love abide, these three; and the greatest of these is love.*"] For, as he says in Rom 13[:10], love is the highest and ultimate perfection of the law.

Article VII

Schwabach: *God has instituted the preaching office or spoken word (gospel) through the Holy Spirit for obtaining such faith. There is no other path to obtain faith apart from the spoken word.*

We also confess that children are saved by means of faith, as it is poured into them through the Holy Spirit in baptism (for without faith no one can be pleasing to God, as found in Heb 11[:6]). Nonetheless, it is necessary for the baptized to be instructed in the matters and articles of faith, and to proclaim to them these same things. This does take place through the preaching office, yet by means of inner illumination, without which the preaching office would have little power. On the basis of this it was decided that both preaching and infused faith are without exception necessary for the salvation of the souls of those persons who have reached adulthood.

Article VIII

Schwabach: *In addition to the spoken word, God has instituted external signs: baptism and Eucharist. God gives faith and the Holy Spirit to all who desire him also with these.*

We confess that there are not only two sacraments, baptism and Eucharist, as claimed in the article. Rather there are five others beneficial to Christians, through which God also gives faith and his Spirit to those who desire them. This is so clearly and exhaustively supported in holy scripture that requoting it here would take much too long.

Article IX

Schwabach: *Baptism consists of two parts, of water and the word. These are not mere water or pouring (as the blasphemers teach).*[21] *Rather together they are a holy, vital, powerful thing, as Paul says in Titus 3:5; Eph 5:26, and it should be extended to small children as well. [Matt 28:19; Mark 16:16]*

That the sacrament of holy baptism has been instituted by the Lord God to wash away all sin and to sanctify those who are baptized Paul clearly states in Titus 3[:5–6], "Through his mercy he has saved us, through the washing of the second birth and the renewal of the Holy Spirit, which he has poured out on us richly." Therefore, baptism cannot be considered a mere empty sign, as the Jewish sacraments were, because it sanctifies inwardly those whom it touches outwardly.

---

21. This refers to the Anabaptists' refusal to baptize children.

Article X

Schwabach: *The Eucharist also consists of two parts: bread and wine. The true body and blood of Christ are truly present in the bread and wine according to the word of Christ: "this is my body, this is my blood" [Matt 26:26] (as the other side admits). Christ's words foster faith in those who desire the sacrament and do not act contrary to that faith.*

We confess that in the sacrament of the Eucharist, the body and blood of Christ, while before the consecration bread and wine are present, after the consecration we no longer claim that bread and wine continue to be there, but rather merely their appearance. Instead, in each species the true body and blood of Christ is present, moreover, the whole Christ, undivided and complete. This is due to the power of the words that Christ himself has spoken and instituted. And while belief in this sacrament must already exist before it is received, it becomes apparent how through the divine love expressed in it, faith is increased and nourished. Thus, it is then also called a sacrament of unity, incarnation, and love.

Article XI

Schwabach: *Private confession should not be compelled by laws. Confession is, however, comforting, salutary, and beneficial for troubled or erring consciences through its absolution. It is necessary only to confess those sins that trouble, not to enumerate all sins.*

We do not accept that private confession should not be compelled by laws, just as little as baptism. Because an unbaptized person does not belong to the church, therefore the church does not yet have jurisdiction over them [pl. sic], as Paul teaches in 1 Cor 5[:9–13]. A baptized person, however, is now subject to holy church, [and] should thus also be disciplined by its gracious mother, and if necessary, directed by coercion. This is so, since confession has been commanded for all times from the beginning of the world, first of all in the natural law *confessio mentalis* (or interior confession) and in the time of the written law among the Jews *confessio caeremonialis* (or ceremonial confession) by divine commandment, which was, no doubt, more difficult than our confession. [Confession is therefore mandated by God,] since Christ has come not to undo the law but rather to affirm it [cf. Matt 5:17], and he himself has said to his apostles, "Those whose sins you forgive, they shall be forgiven." [John 20:23] In like manner in various other places confession has been proclaimed and set forth as a necessary practice. Further, John says in 1 John 2[:1:9], "If we confess our sin, God

[who] is faithful, forgives us our sin." This is what all the holy church fathers understood as sacramental confession.

Thus the church has sufficient and well-founded cause to require such a comforting, salutary, and beneficial thing of unwilling persons who otherwise refuse to recognize their own good. The whole Christian church has, then, done and decreed this by way of the chapter *Omnis utriusque de poeni*,[22] which every Christian is obligated to obey, since Christ has said publicly, "Whoever does not listen to the church, let him be to you a Gentile and a tax-collector." [Matt 18:17]

That, however, each person need confess only some of the sins of which he knows himself guilty and others not, as he pleases, that the Christian church does not allow him. In fact, Augustine calls such a confession hypocrisy rather than a true confession. For there are many people, especially in these times, who have a tattered and torn conscience, indeed who tread it underfoot, whose conscience is untroubled by broken vows and oaths as well as by other far grosser sins. Although absolution does take away all sins, as Luther confesses, confession must also include all the sins that are known to the penitent.

Article XII

Schwabach: *There is one holy Christian church on earth until the end of the ages. It consists of believers of Jesus Christ who hold to and preach its beliefs and practices and are persecuted for doing so. The church exists wherever the Gospel and sacrament are rightly observed. It is not bound to specific places, times, persons, or pompous rituals.*

Our Christian faith declares that there is and remains one holy Christian church on earth, until the end of the world, since we pray: "I believe in the universal holy church." And there is no doubt that this church consists of those who believe in Christ.

However, there is also one Christian authority in such a church, so that the church not exist in disorder. Paul shows this in Eph 4[:10], "that Christ, as he ascended into heaven, left behind him various persons, such as apostles, prophets, evangelists, pastors, and theologians for the purpose of perfecting of the saints, of building up the body of Christ, etc." And further

22. This rather jumbled reference is to Constitution 21 of the Fourth Lateran Council (1215), *Omnis utriusque sexus fidelis*, which enjoined annual confession on laypeople. See Joseph Alberigo, et al., eds, *Conciliorum Oecumenicorum Decreta*, 3rd edition (Bologna: Istituto per le scienze religiose, 1973), 245. It was incorporated into the Decretals of Gregory IX, book 5, title 38, under the chapter *De poenitentiis*. See Emil Friedberg, ed., *Corpus iuris canonici* (Leipzig: Tauchnitz, 1879–81), 2:887.

in 1 Thess 5[:12] he writes, "We implore you, brothers, respect those who are working among you and exercise authority in the Lord." Further, he admonishes the Hebrews at chapter 13[:17], "Be obedient to your teachers and submissive to them, for they keep watch as those who shall bear responsibility for your souls, etc." The assembly of such leaders and spiritual authorities, since it has authority in the churches to keep order and to instruct, are also often referred to as "the church," of which Christ also reminds us, saying in Matt 18[:17], "Tell it to the church." Therefore, the church is named and recognized as far more than solely all believers in Christ.

From this it is clearly evident that those persons, as Luther confesses in this article, who hold to, believe, and teach his laws, articles, and matters presented above, can neither be "the church" nor be called "the church," because they have withdrawn from and voluntarily strayed from the unity of the church and from obedience to its ordained leaders and spiritual authorities of the same jurisdiction and doctrine with these and many more heretical articles.

And whether or not they are being persecuted and martyred in the world on account of such mad erring and disobedience, they should know that the devil also has his martyrs.

However, that the Christian church should not be governed by laws and regulations is clearly against the Holy Spirit and Paul in Acts 15 and 16, where he commanded to keep the teaching and precept of the apostles and elders in Jerusalem that were decided in the meeting. Therefore, the ceremonies established and ordered by these leaders of the church mentioned above for the celebration of God's honor and for the attraction and increase of devotion of Christians can certainly not be considered as unnecessary opulence but rather as Christian adornment and a sign of Christian love and faith. Therefore, it can be also neither unsuitable nor unbeneficial to bind the ceremonies to particular places, times, persons, und gestures. As long as the church must exist on earth, during that time, it must exist and be maintained among persons and places as Paul teaches in 1 Cor 14[:40], "Everything among you should proceed in good order and decently."

Article XIII

Schwabach: *On the last day Jesus Christ will judge all humankind, redeeming believers and condemning unbelievers and the godless to hell.*

This article is in itself not to be disputed, if it is understood in such manner that those believers who have done good will be judged for eternal bliss, as stated in John 5[:29], "Those who have done good will rise again on the Last Day to resurrection of life, etc." Further, Christ himself says, "Not everyone who says to me, 'Lord, Lord,' enters the kingdom of heaven, but only the one who does the will of my father." [Matt 7:21]

Article XIV

Schwabach: *Until the Lord comes in judgment on the Last Day and abolishes all political power and lordship, we should remain obedient to the secular authorities. A Christian, if called to political office, may serve therein without danger to his salvation.*

Everything that is declared in this article concerning secular authority and governance should be understood in regard to religious authorities and governance as well. Religious authority must of necessity be maintained within the church, no less than secular authority must be maintained so that everything proceeds in good and decent order. For this reason pastors and teachers, etc. [are necessary], as is set forth sufficiently in Article XII above and stated by Paul.

Article XV

Schwabach: *Article XV condemns as doctrines of the devil priestly celibacy, abstinence from meat, and monasticism and its vows as works intended to gain salvation, whereas Christ alone is the only way.*

This article is entirely Wycliffian, full of untruth and calumniations. For no one is able to document or prove effectively that marriage is forbidden to anyone [by the Catholic Church]. If, however, priests voluntarily through vows abstain from marriage, then the Christian church has legitimate grounds for forcing them to observe their vows, as also happens similarly with monastic persons and should rightly be the case.

Moreover, that priests and monastics should live chastely has been seriously maintained and has been taught us from the time of the apostles until today, for the apostles abstained [from relations with] their wives in accordance with Christian teaching in Matt 19[:1–12]. Further, it has never been found that their disciples holding priestly office had wives, while we do know that the priests and Levites of the Old Testament did have to live holy and chastely and abstained from relations with their wives whenever they were to serve in their office, as found in Lev 6[:2] and attested in many other passages. And David was denied the priestly bread by Ahimelech until he had first abstained from women for three days. [1 Sam 21:1–7] How much more suitably then should Christian priests keep themselves always chaste, who now are bound to serve not the shadow but the truth, as daily they are obligated to distribute the true bread of heaven, the chaste body of Jesus Christ, to receive it themselves and to give it to others. For Paul, too, advises married persons to abstain from marital relations for a while, for the sake of prayer. [1 Cor 7:5]

Although eating meat is, in itself, not a sin, and even if eating meat as such were to be considered a sin, it is not forbidden by the church. Since, however, Christians on their own do not follow the apostolic teaching on fasting as taught by Paul in 2 Cor 6[:5] and 2 Cor 11 [:23–27], the church, like a solicitous loving mother, had legitimate cause to require such fasting and to order abstinence from meat for several days for the sake of taming our insolent bodies. Thus, no one might truthfully charge that he is forbidden to eat meat except in such a manner [during the stipulated days].

Since monastic vows are often extant, praised, and recommended, both in the Old and now in the New Testament, and since the apostles have also demonstrated and implemented by their investiture of many virgins, who then can say that such monastic vows—abstinence from women and eating meat—should be satanic teaching (as Luther says)? And he wishes to prove this misleadingly [by referring to] St. Paul in 1 Timothy 4. Whereas Paul himself recommended virginity, moreover consecrated Teclah in Jonio[23] along with many others as monastic virgins [cf. 1 Cor 7:25–38]. Thus, such vows and abstinence are good and secure footpaths in Christ [and are] the genuinely true way to grace and salvation.[24]

Article XVI

Schwabach: *The Mass must be abolished as an abomination, since it has been understood as a work for obtaining salvation for another person. The Eucharist should be distributed under both species, and should be given to everyone according to their faith and need.*

That the Mass, which up to this very day has been understood as being a sacrifice and good work and indeed is, should now be an abomination is Luther's malicious blasphemy, which he will never be able to prove, as many

23. This reference is apparently to "Thekla in Iconium" from the Acts of Paul and Thecla. See Dennis R. MacDonald, "Acts of Thekla," *Anchor Bible Dictionary* (1992) 6:443–44.

24. The German text is ambiguous: *und sein solche gluepdte und enthaltung guete uund gewise richtsteige in Christo, welche zuer gnaden und seligkayt der recht warhafftig weg ist.* Since the verb *ist* is singular, it could suggest grammatically that *Christ* alone is the way to salvation. However, the relative pronoun *welche* is plural and would thus seem to reference *"celibacy and abstinence."*

scholars have dared him to prove and [he] will also never be able to do so. For this reason, the holy Mass, which has been considered a sacrifice and good work for the living and the dead from the time of the apostles till now, as the writings of all holy church fathers attest, this Mass will continue to exist until Christ comes again, as Paul says, "*Mortem domini annunciabitis, donec veniet.*" [1 Cor 11:26][25]

Further, it is unnecessary to demand that the most holy body of Christ should be distributed under two species to every believer. Actually, such a thing would be the source of great loss of faith and a cause of heresy, as though Christ should not be wholly present in one species, since he is, after all, particularly wholly present in each species. For the sake of the autonomy, effectiveness, or spiritual fruit [of this truth] it is called in Latin *essentiae & efficaciae*. Because of this and other reasons as well, further because of deceit and disrespect, the church in two councils, those of Constance and Basel, has decided and mandated the distribution under one species, as had been done in the church long before then. With this practice nothing at all detrimental happens to lay persons, particularly because from this practice their grace and merit in Christian obedience is renewed and increased.

Article XVII

Schwabach: *Ceremonies that oppose God's word should be abolished. Others may be used freely or not, avoiding unnecessary offence or disturbance of the general peace.*

There is no doubt that there must be ceremonies and divine services in the church. However, which ceremonies are opposed to God's word, as Luther states, has not yet been revealed. Whenever some who have this characteristic are pointed out, then this matter should be discussed.

However, that everyone should [be able to] make up new ceremonies every day according to his fickleness, wantonness, and instability would be opposed to communal peace and would cause great offence. Paul, too, is against [such actions], for he says, "All things among you should be maintained decently and in order." [1 Cor 14:40][26] And with that everyone may rightfully let matters rest, etc. [!]

25. "You will proclaim the Lord's death until he comes."

26. The authors like this passage, using it—with different wording—in Articles XII and XIV.

10

Paul Bachmann

*Response to Luther's Open Letter
to Albert of Mainz*

—WILLIAM R. RUSSELL

INTRODUCTION

THE IMMEDIATE CONTEXT FOR this piece is the Diet of Augsburg (1530). That spring-summer, royals and prelates of the Holy Roman Empire gathered in the southern Bavarian city to evaluate the official theology and practice of the "Lutherans" (who preferred to be called, "Evangelicals"). Luther and his cohort wrote what was to become the founding theological document of Lutheranism, *The Augsburg Confession*. The document was edited into its final form by Philipp Melanchthon after the Saxon party had reached the city. The task fell to Philipp, because Luther was prohibited from attendance by the Edict of Worms (1521).

Although protected in his prince's castle at Coburg, Luther remained engaged in the proceedings. He sent a letter to the highest-ranking church official in Germany, Archbishop Albert of Mainz,[1] on July 6th, after the Augsburg Confession was presented but before the Roman Catholic theologians issued their official response. The reformer appealed for tolerance at the center of his letter:

---

1. Albert of Brandenburg.

Because we can have no real hope of unity in the faith, I beg your Grace, in all humility, to encourage the other side to allow for peace. Let them believe what they will and let us believe the blameless truth of our confession. It is obvious that nobody, including the pope and the emperor, should compel another to believe (indeed, this is not even possible). If God Almighty does not force anyone to faith, then how could a lowly creature have the temerity to force others to believe a certain way, let alone accept what they know is false-teaching? May God grant that your Grace, more than anything, would be a new Gamaliel and provide similar peaceful wisdom.[2]

Luther's reference to Albert "as a new Gamaliel" would not only flatter the archbishop, but it would also read the Bible (Acts 5:34–39) into the proceedings at Augsburg.

When [the Temple Elders] heard this, they were enraged and wanted to kill [the apostles]. But a Pharisee in the council named Gamaliel, a teacher of the law, respected by all the people, stood up and ordered the men to be put outside for a short time. Then he said to them, "Fellow Israelites, consider carefully what you propose to do to these men. . . . I tell you, keep away from these men and let them alone; because if this plan or this undertaking is of human origin, it will fail; but if it is of God, you will not be able to overthrow them—in that case you may even be found fighting against God!" (NRSV)

Abbot Paul Bachmann, O. Cist., aka Amnicola (1466?–1538), was tapped to pen this response on behalf of the Archbishop. Born in Chemnitz, Bachmann studied at the University of Leipzig in the early 1490s, where he lived with his Cistercian brothers at the Bernhard College. An able administrator, Bachmann assumed positions of increasing responsibility in his order—traveling as his abbot's representative to the mother house in Citeaux over a dozen times (the last in 1514). In 1522, he was consecrated abbot of the monastery at Altzelle an der Mulde, Saxony (100 kilometers from Wittenberg). In 1537, he was named vicar-general of the region.

Bachmann had been an early and consistent opponent of the Lutheran Reformation, and his polemics against Luther appeared in the context of other prominent Roman Catholic opponents of the reformer's work (e.g., Johannes Cochlaeus [who prefaces this piece], Hieronymus Emser, etc.). His attacks were pointed and often personal—in 1524 calling Luther a "wild

2. WA 30/2:400–401. The translation here is a revision of Roland Bainton, *Here I Stand* (New York: Penguin, 1995), 254.

slobbering pig," and shortly before he died, Bachmann wrote the anti-Lutheran diatribe, *Against the Adder-Tongued, Sweet-Talking, Blasphemy Mill.*[3]

As a dutiful servant of his order, Bachmann fought mightily against the Protestant movements in Saxony—writing barbed attacks on Luther and struggling successfully to keep the monastic lands attached to his abbey, from being appropriated by the Saxon prince.

Bachmann's basic argument here is twofold. First, he claims that Luther does not truly seek an honest discussion and assessment of his work by the church. His only interest is in his own new ideas. He will not listen to the church's evaluation. Obviously, holy mother church has condemned Luther's reform proposals already, and he refuses to submit. To underscore this, Bachmann repeatedly refers to "Luther," "Lutheran teaching," and "Lutheranism"—in this context, all polemical terms of derision.

Second, Bachmann links Luther to the violence and unpredictability of Thomas Müntzer and the "Peasants' War" (1525). The toleration of Luther's ideas would only encourage him and sow seeds of corruption and discontent. Lutheranism leads inexorably to violent rebellion—and the ruination of Christendom.

Bachmann entitled his sixteen-page response, "*Antwort auff Luthers Sendtbrieff, geschribenn gen Augspurg, an den Cardinal, Ertzbischoffen zuo Mentz Churfürsten [et]c.*" Published by the printer Alexander Weissenhorn of Augsburg in 1530, its limited press run has led to a paucity of extant copies. It opens with a Dedication to Abbot Conrad of Kaisersheim by Johannes Cochlaeus. Written in German, no other translations exist.

---

3. *Wider die Natterzungen, Honsprecher vnd Lestermeuler* . . . (Dresden: Stöckel, 1538).

TRANSLATION[4]

RESPONSE TO LUTHER'S OPEN LETTER ADDRESSED TO THE CARDINAL ARCHBISHOP OF MAINZ, ELECTOR, ETC. PUBLISHED IN AUGSBURG, 1530

Dedication and Preface of Johannes Cochlaeus

To THE HONORABLE FATHER-IN-GOD, Abbot Conrad of Kaisersheim by God's grace, my gracious master, etc. Grace and peace to you, from Christ our Lord.

Esteemed father, gracious master, I have recently received a booklet from an especially good friend of your Grace. In it he offers a response on behalf of my most gracious master, the Cardinal Archbishop of Mainz, Elector, etc., to Luther's open letter, which arrived recently here in Augsburg. Luther's venomous epistle deceptively applies the Second Psalm to our Imperial Majesty, the other Christian kings and princes, and even the holiness of the pope (along with the honor of the imperial crown). Indeed, its poisonous barbs and ferocious language could lead to the betrayal and selling-out of Germany.

Because I cannot help but see that this response flows from a free, Christian, and undauntedly courageous conscience, I want to help it see the light of day. It is an antidote to Luther's poison and the seeds of fear that he plants. With such a response, the poor, unsophisticated Christian people will not be deceived and misled by Luther's high sounding, dangerous world of words—words with which he attacks the old, true faith and would destroy it.

It is, therefore, my humble request, your Grace, that you would receive this response magnanimously and that you would carefully and seriously receive it with my highest recommendation.

Augsburg, September 6, 1530

Your Grace's dutiful servant, Johannes Cochlaeus, Dr. of Theology

Bachmann's Response to Luther's Open Letter

When damage or destruction befalls the commonwealth, it is everyone's duty, to the best of their ability, to step up and oppose that damage. Now that the commonwealth of the Christian church is being assaulted most

---

4. The translator extends a special note of gratitude to David Bagchi and Armin Siedlecki for their willingness to lend their skillful editorial eyes to the process of completing this translation.

189

severely and dangerously by Lutheran errors and heresies, and is beset with the most extreme danger of unbelief, therefore, in this case it is fitting that I too should play my part, just as much as the great theologians.

When the Samaritan entrusted the wounded man to the innkeeper, he said, "Look after him. Care for him." He did not say, "Make him well."[5] Similarly, God requires of each of us that we exercise the greatest possible diligence in our various offices and duties, and the matter will attain its ends as God wills it. And therefore, though I may achieve nothing useful, I can still attest to my zeal, of which David speaks (Ps 69[:9—"zeal for thine house hath eaten me up"]), and do my duty, and that earns me merit before God. Workers who are given impossible tasks still deserve to be paid for their efforts.[6] In the same way, God gives all of us our own works to perform, as David, Christ, and Paul, say.

For Luther, it is not enough for him that he has sown in the field of the Lord (the universal church) the weeds and thistles of all the old heresies condemned long ago. For now he strives as hard as he can to make the Imperial Diet of Augsburg amount to nothing or lapse into chaos, in order that his weeds may never be uprooted. For this reason he has written two books, one to all the clergy at Augsburg, sent from Wittenberg,[7] the other to the Cardinal Archbishop of Mainz, Elector etc., sent from "the wilderness."[8] These writings are so ill-formed (just like the error-strewn brain from which they flow) that one cannot tell if it is fish, flesh, or good red herring. At one moment, he would come to humbly petition us. The next moment, he threatens to fight. After that, he blasphemes and contradicts himself. He would confuse everything and lead a rebellion toward schism. It is clear what sort of spirit is upon him.

Luther offers his teaching with a simplistic confidence saying with Christ, "If I have spoken evil, give proof" [John 18:23] and "Whoever does what is true comes to the light" [John 3:21]. That is true, but it does not follow that everything that comes to the light is true. The heresy of Arius and of all the others came to light but were not the truth. Therefore they were destroyed and brought to nothing by the light. For "to come to light," properly speaking, is nothing other than to abide in the light and be judged by it. Therefore, lies, errors, and heresies come to light ("for nothing is so secret that it will not come to light," Luke 8 [:17]), but they cannot abide in

5. Marginal note: Luke 10[:35]; Mic 6[:8].

6. Bachmann uses an idiom, "*Der ein Morr weschet, ob der Mor nicht weyss wirt, ist dannocht der Bader seines lons wirdig.*" Literally, "Whoever washes a black man, and he does not become white, the washerman still deserves his pay."

7. WA 30/2:268–356.

8. WA 30/2:397–412.

the light but rather are censured and punished by the light. The same will happen to Luther's teachings, sooner or later. Arius's heresy was long-lived and caused much misery, but finally it was laid low (in accordance with Christ's promise that the gates of hell shall not prevail against the church [Matt 16:18]).

It does Luther no good, no matter how long he screams and demands that his errors be refuted, for he bangs on that his teaching is correct and may not be judged. But every street-peddler says her own pears are best! What heretic is there who has not praised his own teachings and extolled them as godly? Luther's teaching has been publicly judged and condemned quite enough, I imagine, for the 500 erroneous articles in his New Testament alone, to say nothing of the other errors that he has scattered around here and there in his writings and sermons. All these have been exposed by the theologian Emser, of blessed memory.

In addition, his teaching has been examined and declared to be heretical by the universities of Paris, Cologne, Louvain, etc. Further, his Imperial Majesty and even the magisterium at Rome found it wanting. Therefore, Luther falsely boasts that his doctrine has not been examined, and his demand for further refutations is a useless defense. Luther's teaching is so obviously proven to be against God and his bride, the church, that another disputation or hearing is not warranted and will only confuse the weak in faith even more.

As His Imperial Majesty, in the Edict of Worms, testifies, Luther has stitched and patched together all the ancient, condemned heresies. Therefore, another public forum with Luther would yield nothing more than a rejection, a contradiction, and an affront to the ancient councils of the church—a deviation from the faith and the denial of the Holy Spirit, who according to Christ's promise will remain with the church until the end of the world (John 14[:16]).

But say, sing, or write what you will, Luther (like all heretics) remains invincible. St. Augustine compared heretics to a water-logged piece of wood with which one tries to build a fire—it does not light, and only smoke and darkness arise from it. Often, it even puts the fire out. In the same way, we can dispute or debate with the heretic, if we want, interminably, but he will not give the light of truth, but only splutter and dribble the more, just like a water-logged piece of wood. He gives off the darkness and smoke of error and often, in those who are weak, puts out the fire of love and wisdom of which Christ speaks in Luke 12[:35] and John 12[:35-36, 46-50].

Error is not heresy, but error that will not be abandoned, that is heretical. As Augustine says, error in reason or in understanding is not absolute. The essence, true form and fulfillment of error and heresy, takes place in the will, wanting to hold on to a received error and not to let go of it, as the apostle Paul says of heretics.[9] Hence the saying, "It is human to sin and to err, but it is diabolic to persist in sin and error and not to abandon it."[10] The devil is always disputing with God, and although he would never win, he is forever screaming that God commits violence against him and condemned him unjustly, and so he rebels against God in pride. As the prophet says, "The pride of those who hate you rises up continually."[11] Blaspheming and maligning God and endeavoring to turn all creatures away from God's honor and service, Luther is always true to himself. Although the entire universal church disagrees with him, he openly claims he would accept no judge regarding his teaching, neither doctors, nor councils, nor the church, not even an angel, were he to come down from heaven. How is this unlike or different from the devil's pride? Paul had studied his gospel in the third heaven (as he confesses);[12] then he went up to Jerusalem and said before the apostles that he would not have labored and would not labor in vain; they recognized his teaching; and he received their blessing that he could freely preach, as it is written.[13] Luther accepts no such recognition, seeks no blessing or authorization, but trusts only his own head (contrary to scripture),[14] which he makes into the Holy Spirit. Puffing himself up in pride, he maligns not only the limbs and the head of the church but the universal church itself. As Luther puts it: In his pamphlet to the Bishop of Meissen, Luther inveighed against the church as an arch-whore, in which false bishops rule. He will have the scriptures alone as his authority. But how can a voiceless letter instruct or teach? The eunuch of Queen Candace said clearly to Philip that it would be impossible for him to understand the scriptures without an interpreter, and therefore, he asked Philip to climb into the chariot with him and to interpret or explain the prophet.[15] And Paul said to the Romans, "How will they believe the word of faith without a preacher, or how will they preach unless they are sent?"[16]

Luther, however, does not want to receive any messenger, even if it were an angel from heaven, and since the voiceless letter can neither discipline

9. Marginal note: Titus 3[:10–11].

10. "*Humanum fuit errare, diabolicum est per animositatem in errore manere*," Augustine, *Sermo* 164.14 (*PL* 38:901).

11. Bachmann quotes the Latin Vulgate of Ps 73:23 and then returns to German. Marginal note: Ps 73[:23, Vg.; 74:23, EVV].

12. Marginal note: 2 Cor 12[:2].

13. Marginal note: Gal 2[:1–2].

14. Marginal note: Prov 3[:5–7].

15. Marginal note: Acts 8[:31–34].

16. Marginal note: Rom 10[:14].

nor instruct, as we have heard, Luther escapes all judgment, relying only on his own brain, that is his Holy Spirit. O vanity of vanities, let Luther show a small congregation or gathering—even a single person—that has kept and believed all the articles he presents and teaches today, for he cannot do so.

The gospel, which promises the Holy Spirit to the church until the end of days (John 14), would be false, if the truth appeared only now through Luther, for the Holy Spirit is not without truth. But if the truth was hidden from the church except for Luther, then the Holy Spirit has not been in the church (as Christ had promised), or it contained falsehood, which is a blasphemous claim. Therefore, Luther's doctrine is nothing less than an affront to God and a figment of his own imagination. Indeed, the one who is king over all children of vanity (as it is written),[17] it is he who drives Luther, who shapes him according to his pleasure, in him Luther finds comfort and in him he trusts, with him he threatens and wants to frighten and defy the whole world. Why else does Luther say in his pamphlet to the clergy at Augsburg,[18] "The spirit of Müntzer is still alive,"[19] if not to find encouragement in his support and to pose him as a threat, but we are not frightened. Christ, the truth, has promised and assured us that the gates of hell will not prevail against the church;[20] on this rock we rely and are secure.

We have enough evidence for our faith, but Luther has presented no such testimony for his teaching, as we shall see. With us and for us are all of the holy fathers and the teachers of the church: Augustine, Ambrose, Jerome, Gregory, Bernhard [of Clairvaux], Bede, Leo I, Fulgentius,[21] and many others who were witnesses and martyrs, whom the church has deemed credible for a thousand years and has honored and acknowledged as instruments and vessels of the Holy Spirit.

I do not even speak of the witness of the holy martyrs and confessors, who have suffered great hardship, agony, and torment for the sake of faith. Our faith, which has endured through many heresies and persecutions, is more precious than gold in the fire, as it is written.[22] Therefore, we are not

17. Marginal note: Job 41[:25, Vg.; Job 41:34, EVV].

18. Bachmann refers to Luther's *Vermahnung an die Geistlichen, Versammelt auf dem Reichstag zu Augsburg* (WA 30/2:268–356; *LW* 34:3–63).

19. Thomas Müntzer (1489–1525) had been an early follower of Luther but broke with him in the early 1520s, over the use of force to establish the Reformation. Müntzer became a leader of the Peasants' War and was killed by royal forces at Mühlhausen, Thuringia. Bachmann claims here that Luther's reform proposal leads to the kind of violence and destruction fomented by Müntzer.

20. Marginal note: Matt 16[:18].

21. Bishop of Ruspe, North Africa (468–533).

22. Marginal note: Sir 51[:36, Vg.; 51:28, EVV]; Mal 3[:3].

afraid, even if the ship of Peter may shake and be tossed about by winds and waves, it stands firm. But truly, Luther lacks the resources, rations, and provisions and is worried not to accomplish what he set out to do,[23] for which he needs more humility, and he prays that the adversaries keep the peace and do not persecute him. If Luther possessed a little common sense, he should certainly recognize on his own how misleading is the spirit that is driving him. Twelve years ago, Luther said in the monastery of his order in Grimma, pounding his fist on the chair, "I want to sit on the throne and drive the Pope from Rome, and before two years have passed, no cap or tonsure will remain, and singing, bells, and organ-pipes in church will all be abolished." Twelve years have now passed, and Luther has been proved a liar, for still today there are caps and tonsures, in the churches we still sing, ring bells, and play the organ, etc. This is how the lying spirit led Luther by the nose and would mislead him still further.

Now the spirit is compelling Luther to ask supplicants to let each one do as they please. No one should be compelled to have faith. It is true, no one should be compelled to have faith, if he did not already have it. But anyone who spitefully casts away the faith and initiates a new error in order to tear apart and to split the church and to lead others away from God, that person should—and indeed must—be compelled, as both the Old and New Testaments attest: As Deut 13[:1–5] says: "If a prophet should appear among you, who boasts of a vision or revelation and leads you away from God along ways that you do not know and have not learned, that prophet or author of his own visions shall die," etc. Luke 9[:62]: "No one who puts a hand to the plow and looks back is fit for the kingdom of God." Here Christ requires the steadfastness of faith on pain of the loss of salvation. Also, Paul gave Hymenaeus and Alexander over to Satan for the sake of faith.[24] Thus, the church also has the authority to compel faith that has been set aside, as scourge and force (as Isaiah says) may bring about the understanding to reject error.[25]

Furthermore, Luther desires that both sides should put a stop to hostilities and cease persecuting one another. I will let the apostle Paul respond, as he spoke to the Corinthians: "What partnership is there between righteousness and lawlessness? Or what fellowship is there between light and darkness? What agreement does Christ have with Baal? Or what does a believer share with an unbeliever? What light does the temple of God

23. Marginal note: Luke 14[:7–11].
24. Marginal note: 1 Tim 1[:20].
25. Marginal note: Isa 28[:17–18].

share with idols? You are the temple of the living God,"[26] etc. And again in
1 Corinthians, "Do you not know that a little yeast leavens the whole batch
of dough? Remove the evil from within yourselves."[27] And in the eighteenth
chapter of the third book of Kings Elijah speaks to the people of Israel,
which was divided (as we Germans are now) and split into two parts: "How
long will you limp along in two parts. If the Lord is God, then follow him.
If Baal is God, then follow him."[28] So I say, if Luther's teaching is correct,
then why do we not accept it? If our teaching is correct, then why do we not
hold onto it faithfully? Christ is (with all due respect) no whoremonger. He
does not have two wives, as he himself testifies, "One is my dove, my perfect
one" [Song 6:9]. And in the creed we confess one holy, universal, apostolic
church—not two churches.

Now, let us pay attention to the nature and characteristics of the spirit
that drive Luther.[29] The spirit of Christ that reigns in the church is a spirit of
unity, and his city, his dwelling place in peace, Ps 75[:2–3, Vg.; 76:2–3, EVV],
but Luther's spirit is a spirit of division and schism. This is what he sought,
this is what he achieved, this is what he intends to maintain, or threaten to
erect one mountain on top of another, to instigate much grief and hardship,
as happened before in the peasants' uprising. Therefore, Luther says that the
spirit of Müntzer is still alive and now he expounds and interprets the words
of the Psalm—"Why do the nations conspire?" [Ps 2:1][30]—and applies them
to the current imperial diet. However it is easier to disdain than Luther can
say. All heretics have proclaimed that their teaching is from God and have
mocked and scorned their opposition, but the counsel of Gamaliel [Acts
5:34–39], which Luther invokes for protection and the freedom to spread
his teaching, is more against Luther than for him. Gamaliel speaks by the
inspiration of the Holy Spirit and about the teaching of the apostles, among
whom he was not counted, but Luther speaks from his own spirit and about
his own teaching. Therefore, his testimony is false, bearing witness only to
himself.[31] Luther said as much in his postil for St. Katherine's Day. His gospel does not warrant protection, as it protects itself. Why does he now seek
human help and support of others? If Gamaliel's counsel should apply, as it
did during the time of the apostles, why does Luther not hold to the wisdom
of the apostles? The apostles never asked that they remain undisturbed and

26. Marginal note: 2 Cor 6[:14–16].

27. Marginal note: 1 Cor 5[:6–7].

28. I.e., 1 Kgs 18:21.

29. Marginal note: 1 Cor 14[:33].

30. Quotation from the Latin Vulgate.

31. Marginal note: John 5[:30–31].

that their teaching not be opposed, as Luther does now, but they rejoiced that they were worthy to suffer for the sake of Christ. Luther claims that it is a sin against the Holy Spirit to attack the plain truth. Indeed, but there is more to it. Should we let Luther's teaching go out unhindered? I say no, Luther's teaching is not the plain truth. How is it proven that Luther's teaching is the plain truth? Because Luther's himself says so, or because Luther stretches, forces, and mangles the scriptures according to his own ideas and opinions? Such reasons would make any heretic's teaching the plain truth, for all of them proclaim their own teachings as the word of God and drag the scriptures by the hair, as Augustine says, "They have taken from the gospel, in order to wage war against the gospel." Thus, Luther abuses the scriptures and interprets them forcefully against their true meaning, in order to justify his own error and heresy. The true meaning of the scriptures shall not be sought outside the universal church, as the church has the spirit of her bridegroom Christ (John 14[:15–17]). Christ did not promise his spirit to particular people, although there have been many who had it, but to no one did Christ publicly promise it, save for the church, therefore, all who do not heed the church shall be like a heathen to you,[32] and whoever interprets the scripture differently than the church is a thief and a murderer. He comes, intending to steal, rob, kill, and slaughter. He does not come through the door. Rather, he breaks in and enters on the side (John 10[:1]). Now Luther speaks of the sin against the Holy Spirit. Before he wrote and taught that there was no sin by unbelief: faith alone can save and no sin can condemn, except unbelief. Why then does he now speak of the sin against the Holy Spirit? Of that he is indeed most guilty himself, like all arch-heretics, as he admits in his writings against Zwingli. Now Luther wants to include prayer with punishment and grace, but before he destroyed prayer along with all other good works and caused most people of his sect to abandon prayer altogether (as his church inspectors attest).[33]

Luther further says that the cardinal archbishop of Mainz did no small service to God, when he allowed his teaching to go out freely, for such teaching does no harm, keeps the peace, allows bishops to remain what they are, and asks that one leaves them everything and does not take anything from them. Indeed, it helps to keep all bishops, etc. However, the contradiction

---

32. Marginal note: Matt 18[:15–17].

33. Luther's participation in the Saxon Visitation of 1528 impressed him with the need to instruct pastors and laity in the Christian faith, and he noted in the preface to his *Small* Catechism (Wittenberg: Schirlentz, 1529) that many did not even know the Lord's Prayer. The catechism included a detailed exposition of this prayer. See Scott H. Hendrix, *Martin Luther: Visionary Reformer* (New Haven: Yale University Press, 2015), 197.

of these articles is true and far too obvious today. He once mocked them as false idols and carnival fools,[34] but now he almost honors and defends them. Oh, the stench of such shameful lies and the foxtail of the lame![35] He says his teaching does no harm, but the experience of the peasants' uprising says differently. This awkward, deceitful book is not worthy of a response, but for the sake of the simple and uninformed, who are deceived and mistake lies for the truth and darkness for light, I would quickly offer this response, but for those who understand, who carry the sword, and have the authority within the church, I have often greatly wondered why they have watched this man for so long and have tolerated various, public errors, through which the church has been torn apart, despite the foul insults directed at popes, emperors, kings, princes, and nobles in general or in particular.

Luther reviles the church of Rome as "the Scarlet Whore of Babylon."[36] He vilifies the pope as antichrist and a "Florentine fruit,"[37] etc. He calls the emperor a bag of maggots, confined to his sickbed by scabies. Luther scorns princes, as fools, tyrants, and slack-jawed monkeys. Bishops are to him false idols and carnival fools. Priests, monks, and nuns are temple-slaves, hypocrites, and unbearable burdens on society.

I do not know if the world has ever borne a person like him.

It is on account of such actions (for which one can find many examples in the scriptures) and for no other reason, that the sin of the world, its abundance of malice, yields error and offense, as witness to Christ Matt 18[:7], "Offense is inevitable." It is inevitable not as simply like recognizing without comment that it can be no other way, but rather like seeing someone running fast and far and saying, "It is inevitable that he will be tired." Therefore, the world is full of malice, on account of injustice, for error and offense are inevitable. But woe to the one who causes offense. God punishes sin with other sins, and the resulting sins are not only sins in themselves, but

---

34. These refer to rituals performed by bishops, who used oil in their consecrations and led worship in showy, ostentatious ways. WA 6:407, 19–25. See also Timothy J. Wengert, "The Priesthood of All Believers and Other Pious Myths." Institute of Liturgical Studies Occasional Paper 117. (Valparaiso, IN: Valparaiso University, 2006).

35. The foxtail was an attribute of fools and was especially associated with dishonesty and deception.

36. Martin Luther, *Von dem Papsttum zu Rom, wider den hochberühmten Romanisten zu Leipzig* (Wittenberg: Melchior Lotter the Younger, 1520). WA 6:281–324.

37. Two cousins of Florence's Medici family served as popes during the early years of the Reformation (Leo X [1513–21] and Clement VII [1523–34], separated by the short papacy of Adrian VI [1522–23]). With the *Fleur-de-Lys* as the symbol of Florence, this epithet intimates that the papacy not a sacred, spiritual institution, established by Christ. Rather, the papacy is a corrupt and human institution, controlled by the fabulously wealthy Medici.

also retribution and punishment for sins already committed, as the apostle says about heathens in the first chapter of Romans [Rom 1:28–31]. In Exod 4[:21], we read that God hardened Pharaoh's heart. That is, God's grace was withheld because of Pharaoh's past sins. Thus, Pharaoh fell into hardness and stubbornness of heart. Therefore, it is (as Peter says) horrible to fall into the hands of the living God, and the prophet Jeremiah:[38] "Know and see how evil and bitter it is that you (understand, through willful malice and deliberate sin) have abandoned your Lord God." There is no need to dispute about the evil of the world. We hear every day in everyone's laments what it is like. Therefore, I believe and freely confess that the Lutherans' error and heresy is a punishment and an affliction for the sin of the world (as I have already said) and anyone against whom God is angry shall fall prey to this heresy, but anyone who is pleasing to God shall escape, Eccl 7[:26]. The world is drawing toward its end and leans into its downfall. Every day it decreases in fear and love of God (as an old person loses strength), and sins and vices multiply like evil humors and moistures in a spent person. As Christ says about the end of the world in Matt 24[:5–12], evil will be overflowing and the love of many people will grow cold. Therefore, as inconceivable as it is for an old person to be renewed or reformed, it is even more inconceivable that now at the end of time the old faith be renewed or reformed or be continually restored. For the Christian truth has been revealed for all and has been preached clearly and openly by the apostles and their successors, as Christ says, "What you have heard, preach from the rooftops" (Matt 10[:27]). Christ has not warned us that nothing be withheld or remain hidden until the time of Luther, to heed the new ecclesiastics, evangelicals, [and] prophets who pull the holy gospel out from under the bench,[39] of which Luther haughtily and falsely boasts, but he has warned us about false prophets,[40] which is what we consider Luther. Therefore, I say and freely confess: should God ordain that the present imperial diet accept Luther's teaching and proclaim it as just and correct, I shall submit and yet turn away from it, for I do not know, nor do I dare to find salvation in another faith, but the one that I have learned in the church and have suckled at my mother's breasts.

For me, the holy fathers still live: Augustine, Ambrose, Jerome, Gregory, Bernard [of Clairvaux], Bede, Fulgentius, Leo, and others like them.

---

38. The reference to Peter may have in mind Acts 10:42 (but cf. Heb 10:31), and the reference to Jeremiah is to Jer 2:19.

39. "Under the bench" (*under den banck*) is a proverbial expression used to refer to something regarded as worthless. See Jakob and Wilhelm Grimm, *Deutsches Wörterbuch* (Leipzig: Hirzel, 1885), 1:1107.

40. Marginal note: Matt 7[:15] and 24[:11, 24].

To them I cling, their teaching I affirm, and in their faith I shall die. Luther says that they have, as human beings, erred and stumbled. I would rather err with the fathers named here and stumble with them, as the Lutherans speak of them, than to walk straight with Luther or confess his teaching. I maintain that Luther is certainly no god but the antichrist's true herald. May God give his grace and send his Holy Spirit into this assembly of the Holy Empire, so that all matters are carried out according to God's will. Amen. 1530.[41]

---

41. Bachmann (or the printer) sets this concluding prayer off from the text proper.

11

Johann Eck

Address at Regensburg

—DAVID RYAN STEVENSON

INTRODUCTION

LONG INTO THE DEBATES of the Reformation, in April 1541, the Holy Roman
Emperor Charles V convened the Diet of Regensburg (or Ratisbon, from the
French name of the city, Ratisbonne). Theologians Julius von Pflug, Johann
Eck, and Johannes Gropper represented the Catholic position against the
Protestants Philipp Melanchthon, Martin Bucer, and Johann Pistorius the
Elder.[1] The aim of the colloquy was to review a number of draft articles
called the Book of Regensburg that had been proposed the year before by
Bucer, Gropper, and the imperial secretary. The articles dealt with theologi-
cal issues and were intended as a starting point for discussion, with the goal
of finding compromise and resolution to the decades-long debate.

1. Vinzenz Pfnür, "Colloquies," in *OER* 1:375–83 ("Regensburg, 1541," 377–80). For
Eck's involvement in the theological controversies of 1530 and 1540/41, see Albrecht P.
Luttenberger, "Johann Eck und die Religionsgespräche," in *Johannes Eck (1486–1543)
im Streit der Jahrhunderte*, edited by Erwin Iserloh, RGST 127 (Münster: Aschendorff,
1988), 192–222. For a more recent treatment of the Diet of Regensburg and citations
of relevant literature, see: Saskia Schultheis, *Die Verhandlungen über das Abendmahl
und die übrigen Sakramente auf dem Religionsgespräch in Regensburg 1541* (Göttingen:
Vandenhoeck & Ruprecht, 2012); and on Eck more generally, see Jürgen Bärsch and
Konstantin Maier, eds., *Johannes Eck (1486–1543): Scholastiker—Humanist—Kontroverstheologe* (Regensburg: Pustet, 2014).

Johann Maier von Eck was no stranger to these disputes. Born November 13, 1486 in the village of Eck, he studied theology in Heidelberg, Tübingen, Cologne, and Freiburg before joining the faculty at the University of Ingolstadt.[2] He had already proven himself as a theologian, when Martin Luther issued his *Ninety-Five Theses* in 1517. At the behest of the bishop of Eichstätt, Eck wrote the *Obelisks*, an acerbic retort to the *Theses*, soon countered by Luther's *Asterisks*.[3] Eck soon encountered Luther directly at the Leipzig Disputation in 1519, where Eck achieved some level of infamy. Soon after, Pope Leo X appointed Eck to help draft the papal bull *Exsurge Domine* against Luther and even appointed him a special nuncio to publish it in Germany.[4] He later participated at the Diet of Augsburg in 1530 and wrote the main rebuttal to the Protestant princes' Augsburg Confession. By the time of the Diet of Regensburg, Eck was famous for his brash debating style and focus on the centrality of the sacraments, specifically the Eucharist.[5]

The *Address of the Theologian Johann Eck, given at the imperial assembly of Regensburg, with the bishops, speakers, and priests present at the Feast of the Lord's Supper* is a published version of the sermon that Eck gave at the colloquy, probably on April 15, 1541, on the Lord's Supper. The printing held in the Kessler Reformation Collection of the Pitts Theology Library (Candler School of Theology, Emory University) was published in Ingolstadt by Alexander Weissenhorn.[6] After a month of near agreement, Article 14 was the first major break between the two camps. The papal legate Gasparo Contarini had inserted language into the draft from Worms that emphasized the doctrine of transubstantiation, and the Protestants themselves were divided on the topic. Eck, who had long defended the Catholic position, spoke out specifically against Swiss reformer Huldrych Zwingli, who argued for a symbolic view of the Lord's Supper, a position rejected

2. Thomas W. Best, *Eccius Dedolatus: A Reformation Satire* (Lexington: University Press of Kentucky, 1971), 15–16.

3. Best, *Eccius Dedolatus*, 16.

4. Walter L. Moore, "Eck, Johann," in *OER* 2:17–19; Klaus Rischar, *Johann Eck auf dem Reichstag zu Augsburg 1530*, RGST 97 (Münster: Aschendorff, 1968), 4.

5. Rischar, *Johann Eck*, 132. Eck was so bold that a contemporary satire was written about him, where, punning of his name, his sharp "edges" are planed off like a piece of wood, cf. Best, *Eccius Dedolatus*, 21.

6. This pamphlet is the same as the one held by the Bayerische Staatsbibliothek, VD 16 E 402. It appears that other versions were printed at the same time in Antwerp, one by Johannes Steelsius and another by Marten Meranus. See Andrew Pettegree and Malcolm Walsby, eds., *Netherlandish Books: Books Published in the Low Countries and Dutch Books Published Abroad before 1601* (Leiden: Brill, 2011), 1:#11003, #11004, respectively.

by Luther.[7] After nine days of debate, the article was tabled. Eck became ill soon after and did not participate after Article 15. The colloquy soon fell apart and the Book of Regensburg was not adopted, with the Catholics being criticized for having been too agreeable on the controversial articles. In the two years between Regensburg and his death in 1543, Eck wrote two treatises, the *Apologia* in 1542 and *Replica* in 1543, defending his positions at the diet.

Despite the political fallout from the colloquy's failure, Eck's Latin address was published later that year in the form of a letter from Eck to the bishop of Bamberg. Here he argues from the traditional medieval consensus but anticipates the Protestant critiques. Staying away from Scholastic sources, he relies on biblical and patristic citations to support his claims, effectively seeking to nullify traditional Protestant objections.[8] He harks back to the heresies of antiquity and links them to the contemporary reform movements. Nevertheless, Eck concludes his speech with an acknowledgment that the Catholic Church requires some institutional reform, specifically regarding the hierarchy and clergy, and then he closes with an image of heaven attained through the participation in the Eucharist.

The translation of Eck's address displays Eck's characteristic method of argumentation—energetic rhetoric, strong appeals, and well-researched reasoning. Since the Diet of Regensburg failed in no small way due to Eck's obstinate refusal to compromise on sacramental principles—as evidenced by this address—it is important to examine it both for its theological and historical importance.[9]

A note on translation: The original publication of the *Address of Johann Eck* is either a transcript or notes of Eck's sermon at Regensburg. It contains marginal notes with biblical citations, references to patristic or medieval authors or topics, and headings (i.e., "Summary" or "Conclusion"). These have been set in the footnotes. Since his biblical citations follow the Vulgate rather than those behind modern English Bibles, all corrections, updates, or comments have been set in square brackets in the notes. For the sake of

---

7. Pfnür, "Colloquies," 377–80; *NCE*, s.v. "Zwinglianism." An English translation of Zwingli's liturgy for the Lord's Supper recently was issued by the Pitts Theology Library as: *The Implementation of the Lord's Supper / Huldrych Zwingli*, translated by Jim West (Atlanta: Pitts Theology Library, 2016).

8. Moore, "Eck, Johann," 18.

9. For a further examination of Eck's Eucharistic theology and controversies, cf. Erwin Iserloh, *Die Eucharistie in der Darstellung des Johannes Eck: Ein Beitrag zur vortridentinischen Kontroverstheologie über das Messopfer*, RGST 73–74 (Münster: Aschendorff, 1950).

clarity in English, the longer Latin sentences have been broken into smaller units.

TRANSLATION

Address of the theologian Johann Eck, given at the imperial assembly of Regensburg, with the bishops, speakers, and priests present at the Feast of the Lord's Supper. M. D. XXXXI. Eck greets the most reverend Bishop of Bamberg, Weigand.

I am sending you an address given to the clergy yesterday (since by the inconvenience of your health you were unable to be present). I know that more things should have been dealt with: I know how feet should be washed, but it was neither the time nor the plan to say harsher things to those present, whom the severity of my address would have made much more obstinate rather than bringing them back to better things. Farewell, most reverend bishop, from my lodgings at Regensburg.

In your name, sweet Jesus.

This is the bread that came down from heaven, John 6[:58].

The orators of this age, who discuss all worldly matters, are accustomed to charm the spirits of their listeners with their remarkable speaking ability and excuse the smallness of their talent with long circuitous words, because they are unequal to the task that they have prepared to undertake. But, most reverend bishops, venerable fathers and lords, it is not fitting for us Christians to seek out carefully the little flowers of speech and the artifices of a painted tongue. Rather, with all humility, gentleness of soul, and fear of the Lord, we do not shrink back from discussing the most profound and concealed mysteries of our faith. In the same way, Paul was not ashamed of the gospel:[10] however much these mysteries must be untangled, no words will suffice, nor can they suffice, when our intellect is unable to comprehend these mysteries. Accordingly, God is beyond all our comprehension,[11] above everything that is said or thought. As astonished Isaiah exclaimed, "Truly you are the hidden God";[12] as Saint Paul confesses, "Who alone dwells in your inaccessible light?"[13] Thus David, knowing that Moses never spoke

10. Marginal note: Rom 1[:16].

11. Marginal note: Ans[elm, probably his *Proslogion* or *Monologion*.]. Anselm of Canterbury (ca. 1033–1109) was bishop of Canterbury, a doctor of the church, and most widely known for his ontological proof of God, namely, "that beyond which nothing greater can be conceived." *NCE*, s.v. "Anselm of Canterbury, St."

12. Marginal note: Isa 45[:15].

13. Marginal note: 1 Tim 6[:16]; Exod 32; 2 Kgs 22 [Vg; 2 Sam 22:12, EVV].

with the Lord except in darkness, said in his time of trouble, "he has placed darkness around the edge of his hiding place"; the same is claimed in the Psalms: "Clouds and mist are his boundary, just as the darkness and the light are his."[14] On the profundity and incomprehensibility of these mysteries, Dionysius the Areopagite correctly said that theology is veiled in the mist of silence.[15] I understand silence, not only the one Plato dreamed about in the *Phaedo*,[16] but the one that John, aware of the mysteries, saw through revelation: "And when he had opened the seventh seal, there was a great silence."[17] Nevertheless, the angels are no longer silent but unendingly exclaim: "Holy, Holy, Holy, Lord God of hosts."[18] Therefore, if we are unable to understand the most profound mysteries, nevertheless let us attempt to do so in the words that we have, as a blind man might speak about the sun. As a result, the theologian should observe the divine silence of astonishment and wonder, yet on earth he never ceases to praise the Lord and proclaim his great deeds. In the presence of the most revered body of Christ, I proposed that this mystery must be stammered out. Holy and honored assembly, piously and kindly listen to my speech about the most venerable sacrament of the altar with calm ears. (It is not a speech I must give, but will, as I am able and as God has allowed me out of his mercy.) Aid me with prayers, I beg you, so that our speech may go quickly, and say from the deepest parts of your hearts: "Come, Holy Spirit."[19]

Come to me, about to speak of the victim sacrificed for salvation, who immediately offered himself as such a bounty, with so many fruits and such breadth of material that I do not at all fear that I will lack words for this argument. Rather, what holds me back is the doubt that I will be able to choose better things from that immense heap of mysteries, which will satisfy your souls more and affirm the goodness of God more strongly. For Paul, apostle

---

14. Marginal note: Ps 96[:2, Vg.; 97:2, EVV]; Ps 138[:12, Vg.; 139:12, EVV].

15. Marginal note: *De myst. Theol.* [Pseudo-Dionysius, *De mystica theologia*]. For an English translation, see *Dionysius the Areopagite on the Divine Names and The Mystical Theology*, translated by C. E. Rolt (Berwick, ME: Ibis, 2004), 191. Pseudo-Dionysius the Areopagite (ca. sixth century) was the Neoplatonist author of four treatises that exerted great influence on many Christian writers through the Reformation and beyond. *NCE*, s.v. "Pseudo-Dionysius."

16. Marginal note: Plato [*Phaedo*, cf. 60E.]. Cf. Plato, *Phaedo*, translated by Harold North Fowler (Cambridge, MA: Harvard University Press, 1965), 211.

17. Marginal note: Rev 8[:1].

18. Marginal note: Isa 6[:3].

19. This invocation is set on a new line and in larger font. The same is the case for "This is the bread that came down from heaven" (205).

of the Gentiles, prescribed this rule for us: "Do all things for the glory of God."[20] But let me resume and pursue the original theme of this address.

This is the bread that came down from heaven, John 6[:58]

It was especially beautiful when Cyril and the other holy fathers noted that Christ spoke about the eternal wisdom of God in the same speech as bread of different sorts and that Christ skillfully crosses from one topic to the other, where he aptly provides an understanding of the matter. For before teaching about the Eucharist, in an astonishing miracle, he fed 5,000 men on five barley loaves, leaving twelve baskets of fragments behind.[21] He equally satisfied those famished in body with regular bread; this is a great accomplishment and worthy of admiration. But it was greater when by this miracle he lifted their minds, so that they might taste the greatness and sublimity of Christ and understand the sacraments. And they did understand so they might soon profit. Because here is the true prophet who is about to go into the world, namely the prophet promised in Deuteronomy 18.[22] But when the crowd returned to him, Christ the savior showed them a taste of this mystery by a sort of general preamble, so that they might return better prepared to understand the following mysteries in their own way. "Work," he said, "for the bread that does not perish, but endures into eternal life, which the Son of Man will give to you."[23] Here is another food not of this world, which the Lord promised he would give. And so that it may bring about desire and longing in them, he promised that it would endure into eternal life, and lest they doubt his promise, he bore witness that this would happen by the authority of God. It is upon him, he said, that God the Father has set his seal [John 6:27]. Those things were more profound than could be understood by the rough crowd. But they were written out for us in full, so that by the manifest words of Christ, our faith in lasting mysteries might be strengthened. O seal most divine.[24] O inexplicable figure of speech, through which God the father set his seal on this bread, by fully pressing down his figure, not only a likeness, as is typical in other seals and reliefs, and as the servants of God were stamped, and as the foreheads of the ones groaning and grieving over the abominations,[25] but in joining his very own divine essence entirely to his son: so he may be *homousios* and consubstantial in

20. Marginal note: 1 Cor 10[:31].
21. Marginal note: John 6[:1–14]; the first bread.
22. Marginal note: Deut 18[:15].
23. Marginal note: John 6[:27].
24. Marginal note: Exclamation.
25. Marginal note: Rev 7[:3]; Ezek 9[:4].

contrast to the most faithless Arians, blasphemers of the Son of God, as blessed Hilary has liberally described in his book *On the Trinity* in detail.[26]

As we have said, the words of Christ were more profound and hidden. But, step by step, by his remarkable manner of instruction, we may still hear him carry the crowd to an understanding of the Eucharist. For who according to scripture blinded Pharaoh's heart,[27] who roused the hearts of the crowd, so that he might cast down heavenly bread, the bread of the desert, manna, so reverently stored in an urn in the Ark of the Covenant?[28] They say that Moses gave them the bread from heaven to eat. But they ought to have known the most perfect rule of Saint Paul,[29] namely, that all that happened to the ancestors happened in figure, because the law contained a shadow of future things.[30] For that reason, they ought to inquire after the hidden and concealed truth. But since they are ignorant, Christ immediately exposes the figure, dispels the shadow, and reveals the hidden truth, saying, "Moses did not give you bread from heaven, but my Father gives you true bread from heaven."[31] Note the word "truth." If someone were to say, "Why do you put the word 'shadow' before me?," [I say that] Moses's bread was figurative and a symbol, not true. It is said that the bread was given from heaven, because in the custom of the commoners, the sky is called "heaven." It was thus "made in heaven," that is, in the sky, by the ministry of angels. But the heavenly and true bread of the Trinity descends from heaven and gives life to the world, because it endures into eternal life. Indeed, those eating manna did not have eternal life, as David would say, "While food was in their mouths, the anger of God rose against him, and he killed the strongest among them."[32] With a similar weapon, our savior strikes against the Jews, saying, "Your fathers ate manna and died; he who eats this bread lives in eternity.[33] It is in this way, you Jews, leaving behind the metaphor, regard the truth. For I am the living bread, I am the bread of life: this is the bread, which came down from heaven."

26. Marginal note: Hilary [of Poitiers, *On the Trinity*, in *PL* 10:9–471]. Hilary of Poitiers (ca. 315–ca. 367) was bishop and doctor of the church, wrote the first major work on the Trinity in Latin, and was a major opponent of the Arians, a heretical group who denied the divinity of the Son. *NCE*, s.v. "Hilary of Poitiers, St."

27. Marginal note: Rom 9[:17].

28. Marginal note: Wis 16[:20–29]; the second bread.

29. Marginal note: 1 Cor 10[:11].

30. Marginal note: Heb 10[:1].

31. Marginal note: John 6[:32].

32. Marginal note: Ps 77[:30–31, Vg.; 78:30–31, EVV].

33. Marginal note: John 6[:49–51].

Therefore, I believe that the holy fathers correctly understood the words of Christ about the *supersubstantial* and *supercelestial* bread,[34] and about the bread of divine essence and deity. The enjoyment of this bread satisfies all holy ones, whom nothing else in the entire world can satisfy. For God alone is שׁדי, wholly sufficient[35]—it is close to our colloquial *Satt* [German, "filled"]—since he is truly the bread that gives life. He is the bread that all invited to the great supper of the gospel eat;[36] truly blessed are those who are called to the supper of the lamb.[37] No one should think that to speak of "bread" is not agreeable to the divine majesty. For Christ liberates us from this fear, when he promised his apostles, "For I confer on you, just as my father conferred on me, a kingdom, so that you may eat and drink at my table in my kingdom."[38] O most sacred banquet, where God himself is bread, which consoles, restores, tends, and satisfies the heart of humanity into eternity, as he promised through Hosea: "Now the Lord feeds them as if a lamb in a broad pasture."[39] David, however, had known this in spirit, hoping, when he said: "I will be satisfied when your glory appears."[40]

It would be helpful to put what has been said in order and context. Our savior began with ordinary, material bread, although of miraculous origin, and then he crossed into figurative bread, manna. However, he wanted the crowd to seek the truth in the figure. For that reason, ascending high into heaven, he guided their thoughts to the highest summit and peak, that is, to the bread of heaven. Because the Jews promised all the best things from heaven for themselves, namely, they themselves were pure, they were hoping for help, liberation, and victory from heaven. Moses fully expressed this in one verse: "The Lord will open for you his best storehouse, the heavens."[41] Indeed, after he ascended, the Lord digressed to another heavenly bread, namely of his own blessed body, the bread of the Eucharist, the bread of the

34. Marginal note: The third bread.

35. On the basis of Michael S. Berger's suggestion (private communication, October 31, 2018) the Hebrew resh in the printing held by the Kessler Collection should be emended to dalet, and so the reading would be Shaddai. "That would be close to Eck's references to 'satisfy'—most commentators view the word as 'she-dai'—'who is enough.'" This suggestion is confirmed by an examination of the LXX, which often renders שׁדי (*Shaddai*) as ὁ ἱκανός ("the sufficient one"). See Job 21:15; 31:2, etc. See also K. H. Rengstorf, "ἱκανός . . .," *TDNT* (1965) 3:294; Georg Steins, "שׁדי," *TDOT* (2004) 14:446.

36. Marginal note: Luke 14[:15–24].

37. Marginal note: Rev 19[:9].

38. Marginal note: Luke 22[:29–30]; Ps 109[:1, Vg.; 110:1, EVV].

39. Marginal note: Hos 4[:16].

40. Marginal note: Ps 16[:15, Vg.; 17:15, EVV].

41. Marginal note: Deut 28[:12].

altar (which, in addition, can reasonably be said to have descended from heaven through the communication of properties).[42] "And the bread," he said, "which I will give to you is my flesh for the life of the world."[43] This is the most rich and true promise: but he who promises that he is the way, the truth, and the life is indeed God, for it is impossible that God would prove false.[44] Therefore, no Catholic is allowed to doubt the truth of the body. They should believe most firmly, and not at all doubt, that the true body of Christ is really and truly present in the sacrament of the altar, as with the clearest and most unambiguous words he himself affirmed it, saying, when he took the bread, "This is my body."[45]

The Manichean dreamers died out, denying that the body of Christ the savior was true, but rather was no more than a phantom and ghost.[46] The Valentinians died out, denying that Christ's flesh was truly human,[47] but ethereal or heavenly, conveyed from heaven, for our Lord and Savior was conceived by the Holy Spirit, born of the virgin Mary, as a high flying eagle said. And the word became flesh:[48] for from the most blameless blood of blessed Mary, the blessed little body of the boy Jesus was formed, as John Damascene beautifully explains.[49] The old and new Capernaites[50] have died out, denying the truth of the body and blood of the Lord in the most holy sacrament of the altar with reckless daring, like the Wycliffists,[51]

42. Marginal note: The fourth bread.

43. Marginal note: John 14 [6:51].

44. Marginal note: Heb 6[:18].

45. Marginal note: Matt 26[:26].

46. Marginal note: Manicheans. Manichaeism was named after the prophet Mani (ca. 216–276) and was a dualist gnostic religion that focused on the duality between Good/Evil, separating the world of sin from the Light.

47. Marginal note: Valentinians. Valentinus (ca. second c.) was the leader of a schismatic, gnostic movement.

48. Marginal note: John 1[:14].

49. Marginal note: Damascene [John of Damascus]. He discusses the Valentinians in *On Heresies* 31 (see Saint John of Damascus, *Writings*, trans. Frederic H. Chase, Jr., The Fathers of the Church [Washington: Catholic University of America, 1958], 119). The quote here is similar to "the most chaste and pure blood" of Mary in *An Exact Exposition on the Orthodox Faith*, 3.2; Saint John of Damascus, *Writings*, 270.

50. Appears in the text as "*Capharnaitæ*," without any marginal note, referring to Jesus's audience.

51. John Wyclif (ca. 1330–1384) was an Oxford scholar and reformer who attacked the doctrine of transubstantiation in his *De eucharistia* (ca. 1380). He considered the Bible to have sole authority, and his theology of the Eucharist is closer to Luther's consubstantiation. *NCE*, s.v. "Wyclif, John."

Berengarians,[52] and Zwinglians,[53] barking blasphemies. How can this man give us his own flesh to eat? This teaching is difficult: who is able to hear it?[54]

For these and very many other errors that have sprung up around this sacrament have been rejected.[55] But following the faith of the holy, Roman and apostolic church, we believe that our Savior has manifested in fact what he promised us with these words: that the bread that was to be given would be his own body, that his body was born from the virgin Mary, suffered, crucified, and is truly present in this wonderful sacrament, with all his parts integrated. Thus he is certainly in the sacrament, completely so in all his parts, and the substance of the bread is changed into the body of Christ, while the remaining accidents of the bread miraculously persist. So God activates and preserves the bread's natural actions, as if the substance of the bread had remained present. Because although literally one customarily speaks of "the body of the Lord" by itself, under the species of the host alone, however, because Christ rose once from the dead to die no more, his body must be alive and have a soul. Blood is the seat of the soul, and what God has once assumed he can never put off. And thus the blessed soul of Christ's body, his most precious blood, and most praised divine nature are present through concomitance.[56] And so all these things are also in the chalice by

52. Marginal note: Berengarians. Berengar of Tours (ca. 1000–1088) believed that a conversion of the believer's sentiment occurs during the consecration of the bread and wine, not of the Eucharistic elements themselves. *NCE*, s.v. "Berengar of Tours."

53. Huldrych Zwingli (1484–1531) was a Swiss reformer known for his debates with Luther about the nature of the Lord's Supper. He posited the symbolic presence of Christ in the elements of the Eucharist. *NCE*, s.v.v. "Zwingli, Huldrych" and "Zwinglianism."

54. Marginal note: John 6[:60].

55. Marginal note: The faith of the Roman church concerning the Eucharist.

56. The doctrine of concomitance taught that, in the same way as in a natural, living body, flesh and blood are not separated, so Christ's flesh under the form of bread is never without its concomitant blood, nor without the grace which divine blood conveys. See James J. Megivern, *Concomitance and Communion. A Study in Eucharistic Doctrine and Practice*, Studia Friburgensia, n.s. 33 (Fribourg: n.p., 1963). It was used by Eck and other Catholic controversialists to counter Protestant demands for communion in both kinds. This doctrine, which had been confirmed by the Council of Constance, no doubt contributed to the growth in popularity of stories of bleeding hosts in the twelfth and thirteenth centuries. Eck employs such a story, taken from Alexander of Hales, explicitly to support the concomitance doctrine in other writings. See Johann Eck, *Enchiridion locorum communium adversus Lutherum et alios hostes ecclesiae*, ed. Pierre Fraenkel, CCath 34 (Münster: Aschendorff, 1979), 138; idem, *Homiliarum adversus Lutherum et caeteros haereticos de septem ecclesiae sacramentis tomus quartus* (Paris: Jérôme de Marnef and Guillaume Cavellat, 1575), fol. 98v. For the doctrine's official reception at the thirteenth session of the Council of Constance, 15 June 1415, see *Decrees of the Ecumenical Councils*, edited by Norman P. Tanner, 2 vols. (London and Washington, DC, 1990), 1:419.

the same principle, namely concomitance. This is the true and catholic faith of the Christian religion, in which it is taught that Christ completely fulfilled his promise. "The bread that I will give you is my flesh, for the life of the world" [John 6:51].

Let us reconsider Bede, so that we may draw out a more profound sense of our savior's words. For instance, let us fully examine his words, when he says: "The Lord gave this bread, when he handed over the mystery of the body and blood to his disciples, and when he handed himself over to God the father on the altar of the cross."[57] The venerable teacher here explains the double transfer: on the one hand, the sacrifice is not stained with blood and is in mysteries, namely, the one where Christ gave bread as his body. But on the other hand, the sacrifice is bloodied, when Christ offered his body to God as a victim on the cross for the redemption of the human race.

This is clearly understood from the Greek, when it reads thus: Καὶ ὁ ἄρτος δὲ ὄν ἐγὼ δώσω, ἡ σάρξ μοῦ ἐστὶν, ὦ ἐγὼ δώσω ὑπὲρ τῆς τοῦ κόσμου ζωῆς.[58] Twice he says, "I will give": "I will give," he says, "the bread," and "My flesh for the life of the world." Consequently, in the Greek Mass Basil and Chrysostom called the sacrifice of the Mass the "unbloody offering" to stir up the mind of the listener quickly to understand the other bloody offering as well.

And so let us admire the highest love of our Lord Jesus Christ towards us, when he was about to carry off his own blessed body to heaven, he left this—himself—behind for his beloved spouse, to use as a most precious treasure. Indeed, nothing more sacred or more precious could be left to us as such a symbol of his love and proof of his beatitude than his very own body, given on the cross for the salvation and redemption of the human race. Let us admire his love, when about to fix himself with nails onto the cross, he pours out blood streaming from the side of his breast to wash and purify our souls.

O ineffable love of Christ, O most ardent love of our Savior, O unheard of and stupendous kindness of the Lord, who feeds his servants with his own flesh and gives them drink from his blood. When there are so many indications of his love, who would despair of his mercy? By how much did Christ burn with love, Luke testifies, when he said to his disciples, "I have

---

57. Eck seems to refer to Bede's *Commentary on the Gospel of Luke*, in Beda Venerabilis, "In Lucae Evangelium Expositio," *Corpus Christianorum. Series Latina*, edited by David Hurst, OSB (Turnholti: Typographi Brepols, 1960), 102:377. The Venerable Bede (672/3–735) was an English monk, historian, theologian, and doctor of the church.

58. Marginal note: John 6[:51].

desired to eat this Passover with you."[59] What else does he wish with these words than that we—with burning affection at the time of Passover—should eat Christ as our Passover lamb, in memory and thanksgiving for his most bitter suffering and death. And so that it may be remembered forever, and never fade away, the Lord ordered this: "Do this in memory of me."[60] His minister set apart for the gospel ordered this: "For as often as you eat this bread and drink this cup, you proclaim the Lord's death, until he comes" [cf. 1 Cor 11:26]. Moreover, there is no doubt that on this day Christ desired to eat this Passover with us.[61] If he only were to see that we have the desire and (since it is especially important) the devotion! For that reason, the figurative roasted lamb was eaten by divine decree,[62] so we might learn to have the fire of devotion in the true lamb, and so that we might pleasantly and ardently take up such a stranger. But if we feel that our heart is so cold that it does not want to bring forth any spark of devotion, and if we feel that it is so hard, that it will not be subject to the hammers of fear and love (according to St. Bernard's teaching),[63] we should imitate Moses, who struck the rock twice with a stick, and a huge amount of water poured out. So the faithful should strike their dry and hard hearts with the stick that is the holy cross,[64] so that the waters, not of contradiction and unbelief but rather of most bountiful devotion, may flow out. For there is nothing that equally moves and excites devotion as frequent meditation on Christ's passion, as Bernard,[65] Ludolf the Carthusian,[66] and others liberally described in detail.

---

59. Marginal note: Luke 22[:15].

60. Marginal note: Luke 22[:19].

61. Marginal note: Luke 22[:15].

62. Marginal note: Exod 12[:8–11].

63. Marginal note: Bernard [of Clairvaux, *On Loving God* (PL, 182:972–99), 989]. For an English translation, see Bernard of Clairvaux, *On Loving God with an Analytical Commentary*, translated by Emero Stiegman (Kalamazoo, MI: Cistercian, 1995), 27–28]. Bernard of Clairvaux (1090–1153) was abbot, theologian, and doctor of the church.

64. Marginal note: Num 20[:8–11].

65. Marginal note: Bernard [of Clairvaux, cf. *On Loving God* (PL 182:972–99)].

66. Marginal note: Landulph. The Carthusian Ludolph of Saxony (ca. 1300–78) is best known for his *Vita Christi* which, as Eck's reference suggests, was less a biography than a meditation on the chief events of Jesus's life. His characteristic approach, of encouraging believers to imagine themselves part of the biblical scene, influenced Ignatius Loyola. See the entries on "Ludolf of Saxony" and "Ignatius Loyola, St" in the *Oxford Dictionary of the Christian Church*, edited by F. L. Cross and E. A. Livingstone, 3rd ed. (Oxford: Oxford University Press, 1997).

And so that we may finally bring our speech to a close,[67] let us add to all the previous things only this: our venerable sacrament, the bread of heaven and the sacrifice of the altar, was not only given as memorial, food, and treasure, but was also given as medicine and stimulant for our souls. Just as the church recognizes the virtues of the sacrament when it confesses that it washes away wickedness, purges sin, wipes away the wounds of our soul, comforts the mind, and anoints us abundantly with heavenly grace (in my desire to be brief I will not describe in detail how the medicine of every sin may be found in Christ's passion), in this way too our heavenly Samaritan[68] heals our wounded, corrupted, and depraved nature, and provides a saving antidote, which exceeds all poultices, ointments, pills, and whatever other sorts of medical mixtures there are. The Lord abundantly lavishes upon us all good things from the most precious treasury of the Eucharist, where he has hidden the riches of clemency, goodness, and mercy. This sacrament has the power to remove the bad and to confer the good. Since we have the most prompt remedy of the soul, so easily exposed to all, why do we not receive and embrace with our hands that which is shown to all? Let us worship the anchor of salvation and all goodness. We are the most ungrateful of all if we do not exceedingly give thanks to our Savior for the innumerable kindnesses and wondrous mysteries of this sacrament.

For this sacrament is the communion of all the faithful, the participation and symbol of all Christianity.[69] As a result, we—the many who partake of one bread and one chalice—are one bread and one body. For those about to go from this life into another, the viaticum is the most helpful comfort of the soul. Having received it, they may walk in the courage of that bread up to the mountain of God, Horeb.[70] Besides the viaticum, the sacrifice is offered daily in the Mass, for sins, for the health of the living and the cause of the dead, in the action of thanksgiving and praise to God living world without end. If I were to describe all these things in detail, it would become laborious and perhaps would be boring for you.

It remains,[71] most reverend and distinguished listeners, both reverend fathers and venerable priests, that we should pray as suppliants to God the most good and most great, to whom we, all loyal, fittingly receive that most worthy sacrament for the salvation of our souls. What is it then that will happen, when the Lord washes our feet, and we wash each other's feet? For

---

67. Marginal note: Summary.
68. Marginal note: Luke 10[:25–37].
69. Marginal note: 1 Cor 10[:17].
70. Marginal note: 1 Kgs 19[:8].
71. Marginal note: Conclusion.

we have already been washed, in that we have been baptized. Now we wash only the feet of their evil state, for it is on our feet that the clay of this world pollutes us. The bride in the Canticles was cautious and wise: "'I washed my feet,' she said, 'How could I pollute them?'"[72] A man walks on foot, he advances on foot; truly, our life, condition, conduct, and office are signified by our feet.

Therefore, let the most reverend bishops and prelates wash their feet,[73] lest they be fouled by the clay of ambition, avarice, and lust. Let them wash, lest they care more for earthly matters than heavenly things. Let them bear the care of the poor, and let them be attentive to the divine worship.

Let the canons wash their feet,[74] so that they may live honestly and in accordance with the rule of his name. Let them observe the daily liturgy of the hours, wear proper ecclesiastical attire, and not march around like soldiers.[75] Let them live elegantly no more from the inheritance of the crucifix and the benefits of the church and, having been admitted into Christ's army, let them no longer be soldiers for the devil.

Let the venerable priests wash their feet,[76] satisfying Christ's established wish, so that they may not scandalize the people in words, deed, and dress. Let them strive for integrity and especially avoid public inebriation and intemperance. For thus it will happen: when those who take up the bread of life in this life and constantly offer God the sacrifice of the altar are about to die, they will take up the sacrifice within the viaticum as the guardian of their longest pilgrimage. When they arrive at the kingdom of heaven, where Christ has prepared us many mansions in the house of his father,[77] he will surround them, make them lie down, and—crossing over—minister to them. And thus having been restored by the bread that came down from heaven, we will sing in the heavenly court with all the saints and elect to God and the lamb, with a hymn of praise forever. Let it be, let it be.

Printed in Ingolstadt by Alexander Weissenhorn.

72. Marginal note: Song 5[:3].
73. Marginal note: The bishops.
74. Marginal note: The canons.
75. Marginal note: The canons regular.
76. Marginal note: The priests.
77. Marginal note: Luke 11 [John 14:2].

Index of Topics

Absolution, 28, 30, 34, 180–81
Adoptionism, 128
Almsgiving, 25, 26, 32, 33, 38, 39, 40,
    122, 123, 124, 148, 177
Anabaptists, 13, 151, 179
Anointing, 119, 212
Apostles' Creed, 175
Athanasian Creed, 175
Augsburg Confession, 15, 170, 171,
    174, 186, 201
Augsburg, Diet of: *See* Diets
Authority, ecclesiastical, 12, 15, 19,
    22–30, 32, 42–43, 60, 61, 67–69,
    71, 75,78, 83–84, 85, 88, 90,
    94, 97, 117, 128, 142, 164, 172,
    181–83, 192, 194, 197, 205, 208
Authority, secular, 4, 6–7, 87, 127,
    164, 183

Baptism, 62–63, 95, 105, 119, 128,
    146, 150, 154–55, 176–80, 213
Basel, Council of: *See* Councils
Beghards, 87, 90, 92
Beguines, 87
Blasphemy, 63, 66, 68, 73, 109–10,
    119, 129, 138–39, 142, 166–68,
    174, 184, 193
Bohemians, 47, 51–60, 62, 67, 78, 92,
    112
Book of Regensburg, 200, 202

Canon law, 2, 32, 34, 42, 45, 48, 50,
    61–62
Carthage VI, Council of, 69

Celibacy/Matrimony, 95, 120, 128,
    154, 183–84
Ceremonies, religious, 162, 182, 185
Church Fathers, 15, 32, 48, 61, 70,
    135, 155, 176, 181, 185, 193,
    198–99, 203, 205, 207
Colloquies
    Colloquy of Marburg, 70
    Colloquy of Regensburg 14
Confession of sin, 23–26, 29–34,
    36, 39, 95, 118, 120, 148, 150,
    155–56, 180–81
Confirmation, 72, 95
Confutatio of the *Ausgburg Confession*,
    xiv, 11, 15, 170, 173–74
Constance, Council of Elibitanum
    (Elvira), Council of / Synod of:
    See Councils
Contrition, 24–26, 29–36, 38–39, 148,
    155–57
Councils
    Council of Basel 185
    Council of Constance, 23, 26, 36,
        51, 55, 60–62, 70, 80, 87–88, 92,
        97, 132–33, 161, 185, 209
    Council of Elibitanum / Synod of
        Eliberitanum (Elvira), 50
    Council of Nicaea, 61, 66, 68–71, 92
Council of Trent, 11, 15
Crusade, 33, 37–38

Diets
    Diet of Augsburg, xiv, 13, 169,
        171–74, 186, 190, 201
    Diet of Nuremberg, 12

215

Diets *(continued)*
  Diet of Regensburg, xiv, 200–202
  Diet of Speyer, 170
Donatists, 62

Ebionites, 128
Edict of Worms, 11, 155, 167, 170, 186, 191, 201
Elvira (Eliberitanum), Synod of, 50
Eucharist, 12–13, 42, 63, 72, 84–85, 87, 101, 120, 159, 162–63, 179–80, 184–85, 201–2, 205–13

Faith, 2, 5, 14–15, 42–43, 51–52, 72, 77, 79, 81, 94–96, 100, 103, 105, 107–10, 113–14, 119, 121, 123, 133, 144–50, 155–57, 164–65, 170–71, 178–82, 184–85, 187, 189, 191, 193–94, 196, 198–99, 203, 205, 209–10
Fasting, 25–26, 32, 98, 122, 124, 128, 148, 163, 184
Fear of God, 104, 119, 122, 143, 150, 154–56, 158
Feast Days, 63, 130, 132, 143, 157, 162–64
Final Judgment, 70, 78, 91, 103, 106–7, 113, 124, 139, 150, 183
Forgiveness, 26–27, 37, 146, 148, 150, 155

Gospel, 4, 76, 89–91, 93, 103, 105, 108–9, 111–12, 114, 127, 131, 133, 137, 145, 149–52, 155, 168, 178, 192–93, 195–96, 198, 203, 211
Grace, 21, 33, 36, 75, 105–6, 112, 120, 125, 129, 132, 145, 148, 151–52, 157–59, 177, 184–85, 187, 189, 196, 198–99, 209, 212

Heresy/Heretics, 4, 12–16, 18, 20–23, 29, 33, 36–37, 42–45, 48, 51, 53–57, 59–60, 62–63, 67, 69, 72, 75, 78, 80, 84, 87–88, 90–92, 94–97, 100, 105, 108, 112–13, 120–21, 123–24, 127–30, 132, 138, 141–42, 146, 149, 151, 154, 168, 171–72, 174, 176, 182, 185, 190–93, 195–96, 198, 202, 206
Holy Spirit, 61–62, 67, 70, 77, 80, 86, 92, 105–9, 111, 113–14, 119–20, 122–23, 125, 130, 133–35, 149, 151, 157, 160, 162, 167, 178–79, 182, 191–93, 195–96, 199, 204, 208
Hussites, 29, 54–57, 60, 66, 120–21

Indulgence/Indulgences, xiii, 3–4, 7, 11–12, 18–23, 25–28, 30–33, 35, 37–43, 75, 90, 148, 165, 173
Jews/Jewish, 54, 56, 65, 68, 94, 98, 108, 110, 113–14, 128, 134–35, 137, 147, 152–53, 162, 168, 179, 180, 206–7

Karsthans, 104, 109

Lateran IV, Council of, 181, 210
Leipzig Disputation, xiii, 5, 11–12, 16, 47, 50–55, 57–58, 61, 68–70, 72–73, 75, 78, 102, 201
Love, 26, 32, 38–42, 45, 51, 80, 86, 88–89, 96, 103, 106–7, 109–10, 113–14, 123–25, 145, 156, 160, 163, 178, 180, 182, 191, 198, 210–211
Lutheran/Lutheranism, xiv, 2, 4, 6–7, 12–13, 16–17, 53–54, 58, 60, 64–65, 69, 72–73, 86, 102, 106, 108, 111, 113–14, 121, 126, 164, 170–72, 175, 186–88, 190, 198–99

Manichean, 80, 208
Marburg, Colloquy of: *See* Colloquies
Mary, Blessed Virgin, 91, 118–19, 140, 176, 208–9
Merit of the Saints, 40–41, 143, 160, 164–66
Milvian Bridge, Battle of, 128
Monasticism/Monastic vows, 5–6, 10, 48, 54, 82, 87, 104, 183–84, 188
Monophysite/Monophysitism, 80, 128

Nicaea, Council of: *See* Councils

Nicene-Constantinopolitan Creed, 175
Nuremberg, Diet of: *See* Diets

Ordination, 72, 87, 95, 142, 173, 182
Original sin, 176–77

Papacy, 2, 15, 66, 83–87, 91, 94, 97, 103, 109, 111–12, 116–17, 145, 197
Peasants' War, 7–8, 11–12, 188, 193
Penance, 22, 24–37, 95, 110, 112, 120, 128, 133, 146, 148, 156, 159
Pikhart/Pikhartian, 120–21, 126, 128, 130, 132, 135–37
Poor Clares, 6
Prayer, 25, 51, 55, 58, 62–63, 77, 113, 122, 133, 135, 143, 148, 150, 157, 159–61, 163, 166, 174, 177, 184, 196, 199, 204
Priest/Priesthood, 8, 11, 13, 23, 25, 27–32, 34, 48, 50–52, 54, 56, 63–65, 73, 77, 81, 87, 97–100, 102, 104–5, 109, 112–13, 119–21, 126, 130–31, 136, 142, 150, 159–60, 175, 183, 197, 201, 203, 212–13
Print/Printing, 2–6, 8–10, 12–13, 16, 18–20, 22, 48–49, 60, 67, 78–79, 84–85, 101, 104, 115–16, 118, 135, 143, 171, 173, 188, 199, 201, 207, 213
Purgatory, 23, 31, 35, 41–42, 84, 155

Rebellion, 12, 102–3, 105–14, 166, 168, 174, 188, 190
Reconciliation 14, 36
Regensburg, Colloquy of: *See* Colloquys
Regensburg, Diet of: *See* Diets
Repentance, 25–28, 30–32, 34, 45, 53, 66, 136, 146–47, 149, 155–56, 161, 174

Sacraments, 12, 22–23, 25, 33, 44, 57, 72, 83–85, 87, 89, 94–97, 100, 117–20, 124–25, 142, 146, 148–49, 151, 153, 157–58, 162, 177, 179–81, 201–2, 204–5, 208–9, 212

Saints, 13, 23–24, 36, 48, 50, 56, 61, 68, 72, 87, 90, 118–20, 127, 129–37, 139–40, 143, 163–66, 181, 203, 206, 208, 213
Satan/devil, 26–27, 52, 56, 62, 78, 91–92, 95–97, 99, 106–7, 110–14, 116, 120–21, 123, 125–29, 132–35, 137–38, 143, 145, 149, 159, 167, 177, 182–83, 192, 194, 213
Saxon Visitation, 143–44, 146–66, 196
Schwabach Articles, 7, 169–85
Scripture, xiii, 2, 12, 21–25, 28, 30, 32, 35, 38–41, 43–45, 48, 50, 53–55, 67–71, 77, 79–80, 88, 94–96, 100, 103, 106–7, 111, 117, 119, 125, 127, 131–34, 144–47, 149, 151, 153, 158–59, 162, 164, 178–79, 192, 196–97, 206
Sin, 23, 25–32, 34–37, 39, 72, 90–91, 111, 114, 125, 132, 146–50, 155, 157–59, 161, 164, 176–81, 184, 192, 196–98, 208, 212
Speyer, Diet of: *See* Diets
St. Peter's Basilica, 13, 19

Tartars, 154, 161
Ten Commandments, 143, 152–55, 157
Torgau Articles, 170
Tradition, 32, 42, 59, 79–80, 103–4, 108, 118, 162–63, 171–72, 202
Transubstantiation, 23, 57, 87, 201, 208
Trent, Council of: *See* Councils
Turks, 56, 63, 147, 154, 161

Unity of the church, 59, 96, 105, 114, 119–20, 123, 125, 144, 180, 182, 187, 195
Utraquists, 87–88, 92, 97

Works, good, 26–27, 31–32, 35, 37–39, 41–42, 121–22, 124, 133, 143, 147–50, 152, 156–58, 164–66, 177–78, 196

Zwinglians, 209

Index of Modern Authors
(Post-1542)

Alberigo, Giuseppe (Joseph), 71, 181

Bagchi, David, 1, 4, 7, 9–11, 15, 47, 117–18, 189
Bainton, Roland, 187
Barker, P. S. D., 6
Bärsch, Jürgen, 200
Baumann, Eduard H. L., 2
Bautz, Traugott, 50
Becht, Michael, 2
Becker, Hans, 4
Berger, Michael S., 207
Best, Thomas W., 201
Borromeo, Agostino, 74
Brand, John, 59
Brecht, Martin, 47
Brockmann, Thomas, 8
Brooks, Peter Newman, 6, 8
Büschgens, Käthe, 116, 135

Chadwick, Henry, 59
Chase, Jr., Frederic H., 208
Chrisman, Miriam Usher, 6
Cross, F. L., 125, 211

Dipple, Geoffrey, 11, 116
Dykema, Peter, 11

Edwards, Jr., Mark U., 4–5, 9, 12
Enders, Ludwig, 74, 76

Fabisch, Peter, 20, 22, 49
Feenstra, Robert, 61

Flood, John L., 11
Fowler, Harold North, 204
Fraenkel, Pierre, 209
Frazel, Thomas D., 3
Friedberg, Emil, 50, 181
Friedensburg, W., 16
Frymire, John M., 8
Fudge, Thomas, 120

Ganss, Henry G., 82, 117
Giles, J. A., 54
Gilmont, Jean-François, 11
Grimm, Jakob, 4, 198
Grimm, Wilhelm, 4, 198

Hendel, Kurt K., 18, 82
Hendrix, Scott H., 5, 12, 19, 117, 196
Henze, Barbara, 17
Herte, Adolf, 142
Hilberg, Isidore, 68
Hinlicky, Paul R., 1
Hispanus, Petrus, 54
Horst, Ulrich, 2
Hurst, David, 29, 210

Immenkötter, Herbert, 11, 15
Iserloh, Erwin, 20, 22, 57–58, 200, 202

Janelle, Pierre, 71

Kapp, J. E., 22
Kaufmann, Thomas, 104
Keen, Ralph, 3, 5, 13, 141

Köhler, Walther, 22
Kolb, Robert, 1, 170
Kramer, Dewey Weiss, 3–4, 18, 169

Lagarde, Paul de, 58
Langosch, Karl, 67
Laube, Adolf, 74, 78, 170
Leff, Gordon, 87
Lehmann, Paul, 82
Lewis, Charlton A., 67
Livingstone, E. A., 125, 211
Loescher, V. E., 22
Lohrmann, Martin J., 102
Lurz, W., 37
Luttenberger, Albrecht P., 200

Mabillon, Jean, 62
MacDonald, Dennis R., 184
Maier, Konstantin, 200
Matheson, Peter, 4
Megivern, James J., 209
Moore, Walter L., 201–2
Morris, John Gottlieb, 172–73
Mudrak, Marc, 74–75

Nelson, Derek R., 1
Nestingen, James A., 170

Oberman, Heiko, 11

Peter, Benedikt, 11
Petschenig, Michael, 62
Pettegree, Andrew, 201
Pfnür, Vinzenz, 49, 170, 200, 202
Pleij, Hermann, 6

Reinhardt, Volker, 15
Rengstorf, K. H., 207
Rex, Richard, 15–16

Richardson, Ernest Cushing, 59
Rischar, Klaus, 201
Rolt, C. E., 204
Ruland, Carl, 82
Rummel, Erika, 3
Russell, William R., 170, 175, 186

Schlageter, Johannes, 117
Schmidt, Friedrich, 87, 92
Schultheis, Saskia, 200
Schweizer, Joseph, 142
Sheils, W. J., 11
Short, Charles, 67
Siedlecki, Armin, 74, 189
Smolinsky, Heribert, 1, 74, 116–18
Spahn, Martin, 13
Steins, Georg, 207
Stevenson, David Ryan, 200
Stiegman, Emero, 211
Stupperich, Robert, 57

Tanner, Norman P., 209
Thurnhofer, F. X., 50, 65

Vandiver, Elizabeth, 3
Volkmar, Christoph, 4, 74

Walsby, Malcolm, 201
Walther, Wilhelm, 1, 3
Wedewer, Hermann, 1
Weiß, Ulman, 9
Wengert, Timothy J., 119, 197
West, Jim, 202
Wicks, Jared, 1, 20
Wiedermann, Gotthelf, 8
Wiesner-Hanks, Merry, 6
Wildenhahn, Karl August, 172
Wood, Diana, 11
Woodford, Charlotte, 6

Index of Names

Acesius, 128
Adolf II, 4, 86
Adrian VI, 10, 15, 132–33, 136, 197
Aerius of Pontus, 128
Albert of Brandenburg, 186–87
Alfonso de Villa Sancta, 16
Alveldt, Augustin, xiii–xiv, 2, 4–5, 8,
    10, 74, 82–89, 92–95, 97, 116–20,
    122–23, 125, 128, 131–32
Ambrose, St., 24, 123, 193, 198
Anastasius I Dicorus, 128
Anselm of Canterbury, 35, 203
Apollinaris of Laodicea, 128
Aristotle, 76
Arius, 66, 68, 80, 92, 128, 130, 190–91
Augustine of Hippo, 23–25, 29,
    31–32, 36, 43, 50, 60, 62, 68, 75,
    77, 79–80, 123, 181, 191–93,
    196, 198

Bachmann, Paul, xiii–xiv, 4–5, 8, 10,
    117, 186–88, 190, 192–93, 199
Bardesanes, 80
Basil, 210
Basilides, 128
Bede, 54, 60, 193, 198, 210
Benno of Meissen, xiv, 116, 121,
    129–31, 133, 135–38
Berengar of Tours, 209
Bernard of Clairvaux, 50, 62, 198, 211
Bernardi, Johannes of Feldkirch, 88
Bijns, Anna, 6
Bodenstein von Karlstadt, Andreas,
    xiii, 12, 57, 70, 75, 151
Bonaventure, 76

Braun, Konrad, 14
Bucer, Martin, 14, 200
Bugenhagen, Johannes, 143
Bullinger, Heinrich, 14

Calvin, John, 14
Catharinus, Ambrosius, 147
Catherine of Aragon, 16
Cerinthus, 128
Charles V, 9, 12, 169, 200
Chesneau, Nicolas, 143
Chrysostom, John, 210
Clement VII, 197
Clement V, 61
Cochlaeus, Johannes, xiii, 3–5, 8–10,
    12–16, 67, 74, 141–44, 146–47,
    149, 151–52, 154, 156, 158, 161,
    163–64, 166, 168, 187–89
Conrad, Abbot of Kaisersheim,
    188–89
Constantine, 128
Contarini, Gasparo, 201
Cyprian, 62
Cyril of Alexandria, 205

Dietenberger, Johann, 1–2, 8
Diocletian, 127
Dolcino, Fra, 80, 128
Donatus, 128

Eck, Johann, xiii, 5, 8, 12, 14–15,
    17, 47–75, 102, 128, 142, 165,
    200–203, 209–10
Elgersma, Rupert, 172–74

Emser, Hieronymus, xiii, 4–6, 8, 10,
    12, 47–69, 73–77, 79, 102, 105,
    116–18, 142, 152, 187, 191
Erasmus, Desiderius, ix, 2, 6, 48, 58
Eucherius of Lyons, 58
Eusebius, 71
Eutyches, 128

Fabri, Johann, 10, 12
Faustus of Mileve, 80
Felbaum, Sebastian, 8
Felix, 128
Fisher, John, 13, 15–16
Fulgentius, 193, 198

Gennadius of Constantinople, 59
George, Duke of Saxony, xiii–xiv, 4, 6,
    13, 16, 47, 73–74, 102, 142, 167
Gottgabs, Elizabeth, 7
Gregory the Great, 24, 28–29, 60, 123,
    138, 193, 198
Gregory VII, 136
Gregory IX, 181
Gropper, Johannes, 14, 200
Grumbach, Argula von, 4

Hasenberg, Johann or Jan Horák, 142
Henricus Brunonis de Piro, 61
Henry IV, 136
Henricus Henrici de Piro, 61
Henry VIII, 6, 13, 16
Hilary of Poitiers, 206
Horace, 51, 53
Hus, Jan, 14, 23, 29, 36, 47, 56, 60, 68,
    75, 78, 80, 84, 87–88, 90–92, 97,
    129–30, 132
Illyricus, Thomas, 2
Innocent III, 37
Innocent VI, 42

Jacob of Mies / Jacobellus, 97, 132
Jerome, 24, 42, 50, 58–61, 80, 97, 123,
    150, 193, 198
Jerome of Prague, 61, 97, 132
Joachim I, Elector of Brandenburg,
    171, 173
John of Damascus, 208
John XXII, 132

Jovinian, 128
Julian the Apostate, 128
Julianus, 128
Julius I, 69

Lampetius / Lampecius, 80
Landsberg, Martin, 48–49
Lang, Johannes, 75, 78
Leo I, 193, 198
Leo X, 5, 19, 63, 151, 197, 201
Lombard, Peter, 22–23
Lonicer, Johannes, 83, 88
Lucian of Samosata, 52
Ludolph of Saxony, 211

Marcion, 128
Mary, Queen of Scots, 93
Maxentius, 128
Melanchthon, Philipp, 13–14, 23, 52,
    57, 69, 75, 78–79, 170–71, 186,
    200
Mensing, Johannes, 172–73
Moibanus, Ambrose, 14
Mongo, Peter, 128
More, Thomas, 2, 6, 13, 16
Morhart, Ulrich, 143
Mosellanus, Peter, 75, 78
Muhammad, 128
Müntzer, Thomas, 151, 188, 193, 195
Murner, Thomas, 2–3
Musculus, Wolfgang, 14
Nestorius, 128

Oecolampadius, Johannes, 57, 149
Origen, 59
Osiander, Andreas, 14

Pelagius, 80
Peter of Spain, 53
Pflug, Julius von, 200
Pico della Mirandola, Giovanni, 59
Pighius, Albertus, 14
Pirckheimer, Caritas, 6
Pirckheimer, Willibald, 75, 78
Pistorius, Johann the Elder (Johann
    Pistorius the Elder), 200
Plato, 204

Podiebrad, Georg von (also,
    Poděbrad, Jiři z), 97
Powell, Edward, 16
Pseudo-Dionysius the Areopagite, 204

Radini Tedeschi, Tomasso, 76, 78–79
Redorffer, Wolfgang, 172–73
Rem, Bernhard, 6
Rem, Katharina, 6
Rem, Veronika, 6
Reuchlin, Johannes, 48
Rokycana, Jan, 132
Rufinus, Tyrannius, 59

Schatzgeyer, Kaspar, 2
Schleinitz, Ernst von, 142
Schleinitz, Johann von, 50
Schmidt, Conrad, 50, 87, 90
Schumann, Valentin, 153
Socrates, 53
Stöckel, Wolfgang, 84, 101
Sylvius, Petrus, 12

Terence, 54
Tetzel, Johann, xiii, 3–5, 7, 18–25, 34,
    37, 44–45, 63, 173
Thomas Aquinas, 22–23, 42, 76, 119,
    132

Trajan Decius, 127

Urban IV, 42
Urban VI, 94

van Esch, Jan, 121
Vigilantius, 80
Voes, Henri, 121

Weigand of Redwitz, 203
Weissenhorn, Alexander, 188, 201,
    213
William I, Margrave of Meissen,
    137–38
Wimpina, Konrad, xiii, 5, 7, 9, 20, 44,
    169, 171–73
Witzel, Georg, 14, 16–17
Wulffer, Wolfgang, xiii–xiv, 4–5, 10,
    102–5, 108–10, 113–14
Wycliffe, John, 23, 29, 36, 61, 80, 84,
    87, 90, 92, 97, 124, 129, 130, 132,
    161

Zack, Johann, 75
Zwingli, Huldrych, 149, 151, 170, 196,
    201–2, 209

Scripture Index

Genesis

1–2	154
4:7	112
4:8	121
4:8, 19	125
4:12, 23	106
4:25–26	121
4:26	121
5:8, 22–23	121
9:22–27	125
10	55
10:8–10	125
10:9	56
14:8	126
14:18–20	98
16:12	58
19:24	126
23	130
37:19	57
50:25	130

Exodus

3:5	99
4:21	198
4:40	122
7:1	99
7:1–2	99
12:8–11	211
13:19	130
18:24	71
20	122
20:2	153
20:2–17, 23–26	98
21:17	71
22:20	124
22:28	71
23:32	126
24:18	98
28:17–20	100
32	203
34:13–15	124

Leviticus

6:2	183
8	99
18	154
18:6–18	152

Numbers

1:45–46	127
13–14	121
16:1–35	126
20:8–11	211
25:5, 7–8, 11–13	121, 124

Deuteronomy

	137
4:2	149, 154
13:1–5	194
13:3	57
18:15	205
18:18	99
24:6	64
25:1–2	28
25:9–10	99

Deuteronomy *(continued)*

28:12	207
32:39	155
32:49	28

Joshua

2	121
7:24–25	137

Judges

21	126

Ruth

4:1–17	99

1 Samuel

2:6	110
2:6–7	155
10:3–4	122
21:1–7	183

2 Samuel

22:12	203
24	29

1 Kings

9	122
12:2	126
15:1–14	126
16:31–32	126
18	136
18:21	195
18:40	124
19:8	212
19:10, 14	126

2 Kings

4:38	122
8	127
16	127
19:3	119

22:3–6	122
23:16–18	130
23:17–18	136

1 Chronicles

24	122

2 Chronicles

11:20–22	126
15:16	126
19	122
21–23	127

Job

21:15	207
41	125
41:34	193

Psalm

2	189
2:1	195
7:15–16	108
10:12–15	113
14:1	138, 164
17:15	207
18:41	161
26:5	125
34:9	134
36:1–4	119
38:3	155
53	177
62:12	158
69:9	190
73:22	93
74:23	192
75:11	56
76:2–3	195
78:30–31	206
78:41	134
80:13	67
82:6	133
89:30–34	29
91	50
91:3	52
97:2	204

99:6	98
106:16	134
106:17	126
109:7	157, 159
110:1	207
110:4	98
111:10	156
119	163
125:3–5	114
139:12	204
150:1	134

Proverbs

1:17	98
2:13–14	125
3:5–7	192
4:16	125
16:9	177
16:27–28	118
25:23	129
26:5	139
28:26	163

Ecclesiastes

1:14	156
5:2–3	92
7:20	158
7:26	198
8:11	91
10:20	60

Song of Songs

5:2	166
5:3	213
6:9	195

Isaiah

	122
1:16–20	112
6:3	204
7	127
14:13–14	126
28:17–18	194
29:13	159
34:9	71

45:15	203
48:22	107
64:6	158
66:2	156
66:24	114

Jeremiah

	122, 134
2:19	198
6:29	107
16:16–17	73
49:16	69

Ezekiel

	122, 134
9:4	205
18:21	28
22:18–22	107
33:14–16	28
33:15–16	109

Daniel

	134
7:21	56
11:21–32	127

Hosea

	134
4:16	207

Joel

2	106
2:1–11	106

Amos

5	106
5:18–20	106

Micah

6:8	190

Habakkuk

2:4	146

Zephaniah

1:2–18	106

Zechariah

	134

Malachi

2:2	63
3:3	193

II Esdras

	134

Wisdom of Solomon

7:14	39
16:20–29	206
2: 24	125

Ecclesiasticus/Sirach

	134
2:17	177
13:23	58
15:11–20	112
16	125
27:25–26	108
43:20–21	129
44	134
44–50	131
49:15	136
51:28	193

Baruch

3:5–8	109

Matthew

	151
1:21	113

3:8	25
3:10	158
4:2	99
4:4	95
5:15	106
5:17	124, 180
5:20	151
5:45	99
6:3	63
7:6	73
7:7	160
7:15	107, 168, 198
7:19	158
7:21	183
7:22	112
8:12	114
9	113
9:1–8	25
10:1–4	122
10:27	198
11:5	156
11:13	60
11:15	108
12:24	137
12:45	148
13:24–25	127
13:24–30	124
13:29–30	124
14:25–29	138
15:8	159
16:18	123, 191, 193
16:18–19	123
16:19	27
17:2	99
17:3–4	99
18:7	197
18:15–17	72, 196
18:17	45, 181, 182
19:1–12	183
19:4–9	95
20:8	166
20:26	72
22:23	127
24:4–5, 23–24	112
24:5–12	198
24:11, 24	198
24:11, 24–26	127
25:32	113

26:26	180, 208
28	175
28:19	179
28:19–20	122

Mark

	151
2:1–12	25
3:29	120
7:6	151
7:24–30	95
9:41	166
9:48	114
10:29–30	136
11:24	160
16:16	179

Luke

	138, 151
5:18–26	25
7:37–51	25
8:17	190
9:62	194
10:1	122
10:7	166
10:17	27
10:25–37	212
10:35	190
11:8	160
11:41	40
12:35	191
13:2–4	95
13:26	112
13:28	114
14:7–11	194
14:15–24	207
16:16	60
16:22, 27–28	140
18:1–8	160
18:9–14	150
22:15	211
22:19	211
22:29–30	207
22:31–32	123
23:34	89
24	146

24:29	95

John

	138
1	175
1:1	99
1:12	110
1:14	208
3:3	95
3:8	108
3:15	178
3:18	107
3:19	107
3:21	190
4:21	135
5:29	158, 182
5:30–31	195
6:1–14	205
6:27	205
6:32	206
6:49–51	206
6:51	208, 210
6:53–58	95
6:58	203, 205
6:60	209
7:16	108
8:1–11	25
8:2	135
8:7	111
8:44	125
10:1	196
10:1–18	96
10:11, 14, 16	94
10:8–12	123
10:34	133
12:3–6	138
12:35–36, 46–50	191
13:27	135
14	193
14:2	213
14:15–17	196
14:16	191
15:16	95
15:18–20	123
16:2–3	107
16:2–4	123
16:13–15	122

18:23	180
20:17	52
20:23	180
21:15–17	94, 96, 100
21:15ff.	123
21:17	66

Acts

1:1	131
1:8	95
1:13–26	125
2:41	122
2:41–47	122
2:46	135
3:1	135
4:4	122
4:4, 32–37	122
5	138
5:1–10	124, 136
5:34–39	187, 195
6:2–6	125
8:14	68
8:31–34	192
9:15	86
10	68
10:4	177
10:34	111
10:42	198
11:28–30	123
15	182
15:13–21	68
16	182
20:28–31	127
21:17	125
21:26	135
23:8	127

Romans

1	123
1:16	203
1:17	95, 146
1:28–31	198
1:32	55
2:2–16	113
2:4–5	111
2:6–8	158

2:11	111
3:10	164
3:20	155
5	177
7:23	177
8:1	177
8:23	119
8:27	63
8:28	164
8:33–39	106
9–11	109
9:3–5	109
9:16—10:4	108
9:17	206
10:2–3	113
10:10	178
10:14	192
10:15	135
11:4	114
11:26–28	114
11:34	60
12:4–5	120, 135
12:19	135, 137
13:10	178
14	162
15:4	134

1 Corinthians

2:14	120, 133
3:16–17	135
3:8	166
3:8, 14	158
4:4–5	111
4:5	139
5:6–7	195
5:9–13	180
6:15–20	130
6:19	134
7:5	184
7:25–38	184
10:4	123
10:6, 11	134
10:8	33
10	162
10:11	206
10:17	212
10:31	205

11:1	107
11:19	124
11:26	185, 211
12:3–6	112
12:12–13	120, 133
12:12–26	111
13:1–8, 13	113
13:13	178
14	108
14:33	195
14:40	182, 185
16:1	123

2 Corinthians

2:11	107
2:14–16	106
2:14–17	112
3:5	177
3:13	99
6:5	184
6:14–16	195
6:15	107
8:1–4	123
11:13–15	127
11:15	107
11:23–27	184
12:2	192
12:2–4	111
13:3	93

Galatians

1:8	112
2:1–2	192
2:10	123
2:11–13	71
3–5	162
5:3	154
5:13–15	114
5:6	178
6:7–8	111

Ephesians

4:4	133
4:4–6, 15–16	120
4:4ff.	123
4:8	134
4:10	181
4:16	111
5:15–17	85–86
5:23–30	120
5:26	179

Colossians

1:10	158
1:17–18	121
2	162
2:16–17	162
2:17	153

1 Thessalonians

5:12	182

1 Timothy

1:20	194
2:5	165
4	184
5:1	72
5:8	39, 40
5:13	130
5:20	124
6	72
6:16	203

2 Timothy

2:14—4:18	124

Titus

3:5	179
3:5–6	179
3:10	124
3:10–11	192

Hebrews

3:2, 5	99
3:5–6	100
6:18	208
7	98
7–9	65

9:7, 24   100
10:1   206
10:31   198
10:38   146
11:6   179
12:6–7   112
13:11–16   121
13:17   182

James

1:6   161
1:9   111
2:10   111
2:17, 26   156
2:18   109
3:11   59
5:14–15   95

1 Peter

2:9   105
3:13–14   85
5:8   56

2 Peter

1:20–21   108

1 John

1:8   111
1:9   180
2:1ff.   127
2:4   178
2:18–19   135
3:15   106

Revelation

                 134
1:5   100
2:9   125
3:20   177
7:3   205
8:1   204
12   127
13   119
13:1   142
13:8   121
19:9   207